THINKING skills

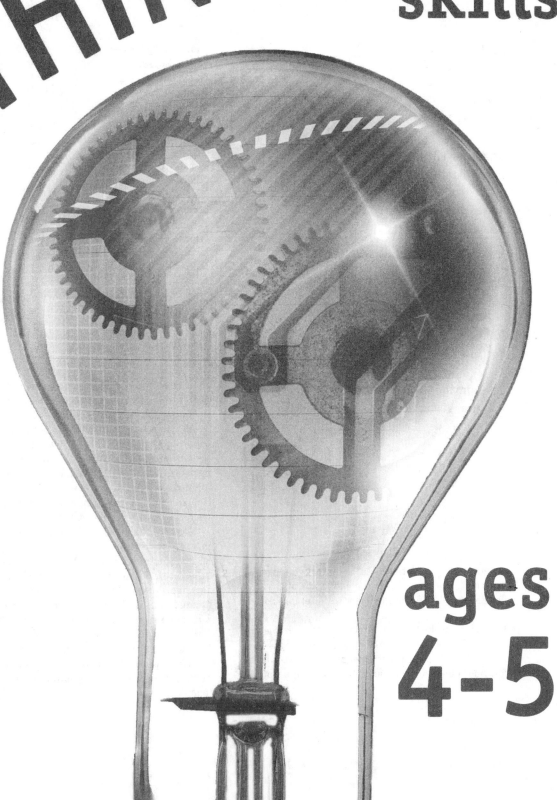

ages 4-5

CREDITS

Author
Georgie Beasley

Editor
Christine Harvey

Assistant Editor
Dulcie Booth

Series Designers
Rachael Hammond
Joy Monkhouse

Designer
Rachael Hammond

Illustrations
Martin Aston

Cover image
© Digital Vision and © Dynamic Graphics

Published by Scholastic Ltd,
Villiers House,
Clarendon Avenue,
Leamington Spa,
Warwickshire CV32 5PR

www.scholastic.co.uk

Text © 2004 Georgie Beasley
© 2004 Scholastic Ltd

Designed using Adobe Indesign

Printed by Bell & Bain Ltd, Glasgow

4 5 6 7 8 9 0   6 7 8 9 0 1 2 3

British Library Cataloguing-in-Publication Data
A catalogue record for this book is available from the
British Library.

ISBN 0-439-98338-X

Material from The National Curriculum © Crown
copyright. Reproduced with the permission of the
Controller of HMSO and the Queen's Printer for Scotland.

Material from the National Literacy Strategy *Framework
for Teaching* and the National Numeracy Strategy
Framework for Teaching Mathematics © Crown copyright.
Reproduced under the terms or HMSO Guidance Note 8.

CONTENTS

INTRODUCTION

Thinking Skills is a series of books which outlines detailed lesson plans for developing children's thinking and helping them to develop key skills of learning. The series gives ideas on how to incorporate the teaching of thinking skills into current curriculum teaching by making changes to the way activities are presented and, in particular, matching tasks to the different ways that children learn.

There are five thinking skills identified in the National Curriculum 2000 document:
◉ information-processing skills
◉ reasoning skills
◉ enquiry skills
◉ creative thinking skills
◉ evaluation skills.

Teachers are probably most familiar with information-processing skills and are used to planning activities to develop these skills in mathematical development activities. Similarly, evaluation skills are usually developed well in gymnastics, dance and music activities, when children are encouraged to evaluate the quality of their own and other's performances and to consider ways to make any improvements. The aim of this series of books is to find contexts in all subjects in which to develop all types of thinking skills.

ABOUT THIS BOOK

This book covers the six areas of learning outlined in the *Curriculum Guidance for the Foundation Stage* and the National Literacy and Numeracy Strategy objectives, where appropriate.

The activities in this book follow the early learning goals and show clearly how to adapt familiar activities to make sure that suitable emphasis is given to developing children's thinking. Sometimes specific questions are outlined which encourage the children to identify why a particular activity is being done.

All activities in this book are practical and organised within the contexts of the early years classroom. Therefore, role-play, dressing up, sand, water and the use of the outside environment are used frequently as a context within which to get the children thinking. Very often the same activity can be organised in a different way to allow the children to organise their own thoughts and work. This will encourage thinking rather than over-directing knowledge. Too often children are told how to go about doing an activity rather then giving them the opportunity to decide for themselves what they are learning and why, thus developing their creativity. The activities in this book promote learning through play as a preferred style of learning which is wholly appropriate for children of this age.

QUESTIONING

Asking questions of very young children is not easy, as they are hindered by their own ideas. They do not consider that they may give the wrong answer and this openness in responding allows the teacher to judge their thought processes more closely and to build on these with subsequent questions. We all think in a different way and the first thing to remember about asking questions is that children of this age are most definitely not thinking the same things, or in the same way, as the teacher. Sometimes closed questions are required to start to push the thinking in the right direction. Open-ended questions can then be used effectively to probe children's understanding, and to help the teacher find out what the children are thinking and also what they already know.

There are different kinds of questions that can be asked to encourage and actively develop children's thinking. The skill of questioning isn't always getting the question right but being able to respond to the children's answers with another suitable question. This way the teacher is not giving the children a right or wrong answer but using questioning to direct their thinking to the correct answer. This will enable the children to think their way to the correct answer by themselves and iron out any misconceptions that they may have. There are suggestions to get teachers started on this process and these can be used as prompts to help you direct the children's thinking towards the required answer for the purpose of the activity.

THE ORGANISATION OF THE BOOK

There are six chapters in this book. The first five focus on developing each of the five types of thinking. The last chapter includes two thinking-skills projects – 'The cinema' and 'Sing a Song of Sixpence'. These projects are intended to develop all the thinking skills in a themed cross-curricular way. Teachers may wish to save these projects to the last half-term, but in order to complete the project children will be required to work over a longer period of time than is required for the other activities in the book.

Each chapter begins with a short explanation of the thinking skill being focused on and is followed by two sections of activities – to introduce then extend skills – each section covering most if not all of the curriculum subjects. Each section has a quick-reference grid for teachers to see what the activities contain and quickly evaluate which fit easily into their own schemes of work.

The first section introduces the relevant thinking skill in short activities. These contain a learning objective specific to the activity and related to the early learning goals or the Literacy or Numeracy Strategies. A 'Thinking objective' outlines the

particular thinking skill that the children will be developing in the activity. This is expanded under 'Thinking skills', which detail how the activity will bring out the thinking skills in line with the learning objective. A useful resource list is provided along with a detailed explanation of how to conduct the activity. These detailed activities have been designed to encourage and develop the children's thinking skills through practical investigation and enquiry. They are structured to encourage the children to ask why that particular activity is being carried out. Particular emphasis is placed on 'how' the children will learn – the way the learning is organised and the involvement of the children in this process – rather than the 'what'. Suggestions for questions to spark discussion and encourage the children to pose questions for investigation themselves are a focus of the activities.

The second section contains extended activities which, in addition to those sections outlined above, also contain a differentiation section with suggestions for how lower attaining children can be supported and the thinking of higher attaining children can be extended. The 'Where next' section gives ideas on how teachers can consolidate, practise, reintroduce or extend the particular activity and thinking skill. There is assessment advice on how to gauge the children's success in thinking through a problem or planning an investigation. 'Learning outcomes' relate to the 'Thinking objectives', expanding on them to describe what the children have achieved and can now do as a result of the lesson.

INFORMATION-PROCESSING SKILLS

INTRODUCTION

Information processing for younger children is about waking up the mind. Young children learn best when exploring the world around them from first hand, by using their senses. Making them aware of the range of things they can learn from their surroundings helps develop the important skills of observation, noticing what is going on around them and making sense of all the things that they meet. They will learn about different things from what they see, hear, touch, smell and taste. By developing these multi-sensory skills, the children will start to question what they are experiencing and to think beyond the literal and face value of experiences.

Information processing is about the children being able to collect, sort, sequence and analyse a range of information to support learning across all the areas of learning which are measured through the stepping stones and early learning goals. By learning to process information in different ways, the children will begin to make sense of the world in which they live. The process is more than just the children presenting data in different forms. It is also about them deciding whether the information is useful for a particular purpose. Organising information in certain ways can support memory development and help to make links and relationships between different bits of information.

The activities in this chapter are practical and based in play situations. This will allow the children to direct their own learning to a certain extent. They will learn to collect information in many forms from facts and knowledge, to shape, colour, texture, size, numbers and quantities. The starting point of much learning can be collections of a wide range of objects. By applying the information-processing skills outlined below, the children will make sense of everything they come into contact with. They will begin to look more closely and rather than just seeing things, they will start to notice things about them in terms of their shape, size, relationship with similar and different objects, the way they are built and the way they move.

The activities require the teacher to stand back and let the children organise some of the learning themselves, and to let children explain what they are doing so that their thinking can be assessed. The teacher can then move things forward by asking relevant and open questions to shift the direction of the work or consolidate the children's ideas.

The following skills all form a part of information processing:
- sequencing
- pattern and relationship
- sorting and classifying
- matching
- locating and collecting
- comparing and measuring
- analysing.

INTRODUCING INFORMATION-PROCESSING SKILLS

Area of learning and ELG, NLS or NNS objective	Activity title	Thinking objective	Activity	Page
Personal, social and emotional development ELG: To form good relationships with peers	What shall we play?	To sort and classify games	Sorting games using criteria such as those to play with one friend, lots of friends and on their own	9
Communication, language and literacy ELG: To read a range of familiar and common words NLS objective: To recognise printed and handwritten words in a variety of settings	What is it telling us?	To locate and analyse signs	Locating labels and signs and analysing what they say	9
Communication, language and literacy ELG: To retell narratives in the correct sequence NLS objective: To use knowledge of familiar texts to re-enact or retell to others	What comes next?	To sequence a story	Acting out and retelling a familiar story	10
Communication, language and literacy ELG: To use a pencil and hold it effectively to form recognisable letters NLS objective: To understand how letters are formed	Coloured writing	To analyse and sequence	Learning how to write the letters of the alphabet	10
Mathematical development ELG: To talk about simple patterns NNS objective: To talk about, recognise and recreate simple patterns	Symmetry	To locate and collect	Finding things that are symmetrical	11
Mathematical development ELG: To find one more or one less than a number from 1 to 10 NNS objective: To find one more or one less than a number from 1 to 10	Pairs	To compare and match	Comparing everyday objects and cubes to make pairs	12
Knowledge and understanding of the world ELG: To observe, find out about and identify features in the place they live and the natural world	Where is it?	To match features to photographs	Finding features in the locality on photographs	12
Knowledge and understanding of the world ELG: To look closely at similarities and differences	Toys	To sort toys	Sorting toys using observable criteria	13
Knowledge and understanding of the world ELG: To find out about past and present events	Bathtime	To compare and sequence	Sequencing the activity of bathing and comparing equipment and facilities used to bathe in the past and today	14
Physical development ELG: To move with confidence, imagination and in safety	Skipping	To analyse and sequence	Learning a new skill and and the way that movements are put together to be able to skip	15
Physical development ELG: To show awareness of space, of themselves and of others	Finding space	To analyse and measure	Analysing how much space is around them and measuring by estimating	16
Creative development ELG: To recognise and explore how sounds can be changed	The long and the short of it	To match sounds	Matching sounds to how instruments are played	16
Creative development ELG: To sing simple songs from memory	Facial expressions	To understand pattern and relationship	Learning a new song, using patterns to remember what comes next	17

WHAT SHALL WE PLAY?

AREA OF LEARNING: PERSONAL, SOCIAL AND EMOTIONAL DEVELOPMENT. ELG: TO FORM GOOD RELATIONSHIPS WITH PEERS.

LEARNING OBJECTIVE
To identify which games they play on their own and with friends.

THINKING OBJECTIVE
To sort and classify games.

THINKING SKILLS
The children will consider different games shown in photographs and explain how each game is played. They will consider different ways to sort their photographs, coming up with criteria by which to sort, and will then classify their photographs according to the sorting criteria.

WHAT YOU NEED
Photographs of the children at play, enough for each pair of children in your group to have one, and a few extra ones to talk about as a class group; three hoops; labels on which to write sorting criteria.

WHAT TO DO
Before you intend to do the activity, take photographs of the range of games and activities the children take part in during playtime. At the beginning of the lesson, hold up one of the photographs and ask the children to describe what is happening in the picture. Ask, *Where is the picture taken? What are the children in it doing?* Talk about the game that is taking place and the people involved in it. Then do the same with another photograph.

Organise the children into pairs and give each pair a photograph to talk about for a few minutes. Ask them to think about what is happening in the picture. Focus their discussions by asking some questions, such as *What game is being played? Whereabouts on the playground is it being played? How many children are involved in the game? Is anyone playing on their own? Are children playing in pairs or in groups?* Then invite each pair to say what game is being played and how many children are involved in the game in their photographs.

Organise the children into a circle and put three hoops in the centre. Focus the children's attention on the hoops and ask them to think of ways that they could sort the different games they have looked at in their photographs. Ask them, *Do any games use equipment, like a ball, and need more space? How many games involve a lot of children or only one*

person? How many games take up little room because the players will be sitting still? When you have agreed on what the sorting criteria should be, label the hoops accordingly. These could be, 'Play on our own', 'Play with one friend' and 'Play with lots of friends'. Using the two photographs you discussed at the beginning in a class group, decide together which hoop to place them in to meet the sorting criterion. Once the children understand what to do, invite each pair to decide in which set to put their photograph.

When they have finished, invite some children to say which activity or game they like playing best and why. Which is the children's favourite game? Why do they like to play in groups or in pairs the most? Spend a few moments talking about how they can encourage others to join in with group games.

WHAT IS IT TELLING US?

AREA OF LEARNING: COMMUNICATION, LANGUAGE AND LITERACY. ELG: TO READ A RANGE OF FAMILIAR AND COMMON WORDS. NLS OBJECTIVE: TO RECOGNISE PRINTED AND HANDWRITTEN WORDS IN A VARIETY OF SETTINGS.

LEARNING OBJECTIVE
To read signs found in the local environment.

THINKING OBJECTIVE
To locate and analyse signs.

THINKING SKILLS
The children will look at words on signs found in the locality, read them and analyse what each tells them. They will collect more words on signs and analyse these in the same way.

WHAT YOU NEED
Photographs of words on signs in the immediate environment (include words such as *entrance*, *exit*, *post office*, *telephone*, *bus stop*, road signs, shop names and some that give instructions, such as *no entry*, *no smoking*, *fire escape* and *first aid*).

WHAT TO DO
Show the children the photographs of words you have collected in the immediate locality. Look at each one together and ask the children to say what the sign says. Ask, *What does this word say? How do you know? Is there something that helps you work out what it says?* (For example, the sign may include a picture or symbol, which helps the children work out what the word says.) *Are there any pictures?*

Analyse each word and discuss with the children what it is telling us to do. Model this for the first few if the children need it, so that they get the idea of what to say. For example, *Entrance* means it is where we can go inside. Look some of the words up in a dictionary with higher attaining children and read together the definition for each one.

Take the class for a walk around the school, or into the local environment, and collect more names for the children to read. Challenge them to find the words you have already discussed. Record the new words that the children find and use them to make large labels to hang around the classroom when you return.

WHAT COMES NEXT?

AREA OF LEARNING: COMMUNICATION, LANGUAGE AND LITERACY. ELG: TO RETELL NARRATIVES IN THE CORRECT SEQUENCE. NLS OBJECTIVE: TO USE KNOWLEDGE OF FAMILIAR TEXTS TO RE-ENACT OR RETELL TO OTHERS, RECOUNTING THE MAIN POINTS IN THE CORRECT SEQUENCE.

LEARNING OBJECTIVE
To learn to retell and act out a favourite story.

THINKING OBJECTIVE
To sequence a story.

THINKING SKILLS
The children will choose picture cards to retell a story in the correct sequence. They will select the next card in the story sequence and act this out.

WHAT YOU NEED
A copy of the children's favourite story; picture cards showing the stages of favourite stories for both the class and group activity; props for the class role-play activity; a role-play area where the children can act out the story; puppets for the group activity.

WHAT TO DO
Read the children's favourite story, stopping in places and prompting them to say what happens next. When you have finished, choose children to be the characters in the story and explain that you are going to act out the story together.

Show the children the picture cards that retell the story. Ask the children to say which one shows the beginning of the story. Ask, *Which characters are at the start of the story? What do they say? What do they do?* Invite the children you have chosen as characters to act out this part of the story, using any props they need. For example, if the story is 'The Gingerbread Man', for the first picture card a child will need to be the cook and someone else the gingerbread man, and they will need props to act out making gingerbread men.

Ask the children which character joins the story next. What do they say and do? Get the children to act out this part before showing them the picture cards and asking them to choose the relevant one. Repeat this process until the actors have retold the whole story and the picture cards are displayed in the correct order to show the sequence of the story.

Organise the children into groups to act out their own story from a set of cards. Ask an additional adult to quickly help the children to organise the picture cards into the correct order before allowing the children to follow these to act their story out independently. Another group can act out a different story using puppets. The picture cards should help them to act out the story in the correct order and help them not to forget any important parts.

COLOURED WRITIN[G]

AREA OF LEARNING: COMMUNICA[TION,] LANGUAGE AND LITERACY. ELG: TO USE A PENCIL AND HOLD IT EFFECTIVELY TO FORM RECOGNISABLE LETTERS, MOST OF WHICH ARE CORRECTLY FORMED. NLS OBJECTIVE: TO UNDERSTAND HOW LETTERS ARE FORMED.

LEARNING OBJECTIVE
To learn how to form letters correctly.

THINKING OBJECTIVE
To analyse how letters are formed and to sequence the letter formation.

THINKING SKILLS
The children will be analysing how a selection of letters are formed and that a series of letters can be formed by following the same formation sequence. Because they are thinking about how to form letters for themselves, it will help them remember the correct formation the next time they write.

WHAT YOU NEED
A flip chart or board; A4 sheets (one for each child); coloured crayons, paint and brushes, felt-tipped pens or coloured chalks; a sand pit.

WHAT TO DO
Look with the class at the letter *i* and decide how to form this together. Ask, *Do you start at the top or the*

bottom of the letter? Decide together how to write this letter and describe the correct formation, top to bottom, as you form the letter on the flip chart. Set this to a familiar tune if you wish, such as 'Here We Go Round the Mulberry Bush', singing:

> *Top to bottom makes an i*
> *Makes an i*
> *Makes an i,*
> *Top to bottom makes an i –*
> *Put the dot on top.*

Look together at the other letters in the following letter chain over the next few weeks, covering one letter at a time: i, b, h, j, k, m, n, p, r, and t. Make up a directional rhyme for these to the same tune. This will help the children remember the analysis ming the letters. For example, scribe how to make *b* you start at the top and go down to the bottom before returning half-way up and going round to the right. Pick a feature, which will help the children go in the right direction, such as towards the window or towards the door. You could sing:

> *Top to bottom*
> *Go half-way up*
> *Then go round*
> *To join it up,*
> *Make a b for all to see –*
> *Watch me write a b.*

Repeat this for the other letters, but this time invite the children to say how the letter is formed. When the children have learned all the letters in the chain, ask them to say what is the same about the formation. If they need help ask them questions, such as *Do all the letters start at the top? Where do they finish? How many can you write without taking your pencil off the paper? For how many do you need to take your pencil off to finish?*

Show the children how to make coloured letters by going over and over the same letter using different coloured crayons. Let the children enjoy the design you have made and decorate the rest of the paper with the letter you have chosen. Depending on the children's needs, ask them to make coloured writing by tracing over a letter correctly in different colours and decorating their page.

Other letter strings, writing patterns or numbers can be supplemented if they are more relevant to the children's stage of learning. The colours can be added in paint, felt-tipped pens or chalk on a blackboard. Set the activity up as an independent task by adding letters to the writing table, painting easel or chalk board, or ask the children to draw letters in the sand.

SYMMETRY

AREA OF LEARNING: MATHEMATICAL DEVELOPMENT. ELG: TO TALK ABOUT SIMPLE PATTERNS. NNS OBJECTIVE: TO TALK ABOUT, RECOGNISE AND RECREATE SIMPLE PATTERNS.

LEARNING OBJECTIVE
To learn which shapes are symmetrical.

THINKING OBJECTIVE
To locate and collect.

THINKING SKILLS
The children will think about what symmetrical means and use this as criterion for locating and collecting a range of shapes and objects from their immediate environment which are symmetrical, or which have a symmetrical pattern.

WHAT YOU NEED
Display board and paper to cover it; table or display surface; shapes or objects that are symmetrical or have symmetrical designs; boxes to create different levels in the display; a piece of plain fabric; symmetrical objects or shapes located around the classroom where the children will be able to find them; a mirror; a camera; paper; paint and brushes.

WHAT TO DO
Before the lesson, cover the display board with paper and arrange a table or similar surface in front to create a display surface.

Gather the children together and look at a small collection of objects from the classroom that are symmetrical in their shape. For example, a pair of scissors, a bulldog clip, a pair of trousers and a flower vase. Describe each one to the children, focusing on the outline shape of each item in turn. In your description, model talking about how the item is the same on both sides. Test this out with a mirror and show the children how the object looks whole even though they can only see half of it. Open and close the scissors, pointing out to the children how one side mirrors the other exactly when they are open and closed. Fold the trousers so the legs fit exactly one on top of each other to show how both sides are the same. Explain that these items are all symmetrical, because one side is a mirror image of the other.

Tell the children that you want them to look around the classroom and find one thing that is symmetrical or has a symmetrical pattern. Let the children roam for about three minutes, making sure they return to the carpet when they have found one object. Ask them to say how they know their object is symmetrical. Ask, *Which items are symmetrical? How do you know? How can we show that this shape, or object, is symmetrical? Can we fold it in half? Can we test it with a mirror?*

Show the children your boxes. Ask them to say whether they are symmetrical. Agree with them that they are. Place them at intervals along the display surface and cover with a piece of plain fabric to create a stepped display area. Invite the children to place the objects they have found on the display surface.

Go outside with the children and collect or photograph things in nature that have symmetrical patterns and shapes, for example leaves, flowers, feathers, or take photographs of these. Go further afield with the children and photograph other things in the locality that are symmetrical, such as gates, fences, windows, streetlights and traffic lights. Add these to the display. Ask the children to draw and paint pictures of symmetrical objects and patterns to add to the display.

PAIRS

AREA OF LEARNING: MATHEMATICAL DEVELOPMENT. ELG: TO FIND ONE MORE OR ONE LESS THAN A NUMBER FROM 1 TO 10. NNS OBJECTIVE: TO FIND ONE MORE OR ONE LESS THAN A NUMBER FROM 1 TO 10.

LEARNING OBJECTIVE
To learn that even numbers have pairs of ones.

THINKING OBJECTIVE
To compare and match.

THINKING SKILLS
The children will compare objects and match them one-to-one to make pairs or even numbers. They will think about how they match everyday objects first of all, before moving on to the more abstract task of pairing up cubes.

WHAT YOU NEED
Pairs of items, for example slippers, gloves, trousers, scissors, glasses; a number of cubes that can be sorted into pairs; a tablecloth; four each of cups, saucers, plates, knives, forks, egg cups and either play or hard-boiled eggs.

WHAT TO DO
Talk to the children about what a pair is. Explain that a pair is two of something, made of one and one more. Show them some of the things in your collection, such as the trousers or the gloves, and talk about why they are called a pair.

Spread the tablecloth in the middle of the carpet and ask the children to take it in turns to lay places for four people. Tell them to start with the plates, then to match the cups and saucers, knives and forks, eggs and eggcups together before putting them in their place on the tablecloth. Explain that they are matching the things that go together to make pairs.

Show the children one cube and ask them what they need to do to make a pair. Get out two more cubes and ask the children to organise all three into pairs. What do they notice? Can they make pairs? What do they need to do? Ask them to add one more cube to make another pair. Ask them to tell you how many pairs they have made and count them by counting in twos.

Continue with this activity until the children have reached their counting level. Let lower attaining children count their twos in ones, but expect higher attaining children to start to count in twos. You could extend the activity by getting the children to identify odd and even numbers.

Reinforce the children's understanding of pairs by setting up independent activities for the children to match pairs of shoes, wellingtons, gloves, socks and slippers. Make some more obvious, such as shoes, gloves and slippers; and some less obvious, such as the same coloured sock and wellington boot, which can only be matched by colour, pattern or size.

WHERE IS IT?

AREA OF LEARNING: KNOWLEDGE AND UNDERSTANDING OF THE WORLD. ELG: TO OBSERVE, FIND OUT ABOUT AND IDENTIFY FEATURES IN THE PLACE THEY LIVE AND THE NATURAL WORLD.

LEARNING OBJECTIVE
To find out about the features in the immediate locality.

THINKING OBJECTIVE
To match features to photographs.

THINKING SKILLS
The children will look carefully at photographs of their immediate locality. They will consider the clues in the photographs and use them to locate where the feature is that is shown. Because there will be more than one of the same feature known to the children in some of the photographs, they will need to identify and use the clues around the features to help match the photographs to the location.

WHAT YOU NEED
A set of photographs of features in the locality that the children will be familiar with and will be able to recognise, such as telephone and post boxes, house and shop doors, traffic lights, parks, churches, road signs (the same name taken at two different locations) and other notable buildings; a large map or plan of the locality to which the photographs refer.

WHAT TO DO
Show the children a photograph from your collection which shows a building, such as the local church, mosque or library. Ensure that it will be obvious to the children what and where the building is. Talk about how the children know this is a building and location they know. Ask, *How do you know it is not a different place?* This type of question will encourage them to look at the things in the photograph that they can identify, perhaps features in the background that have given them additional clues.

Show them a photograph of the same building and location, but of a much smaller part or feature, for example the church door. This will encourage the children to look at the finer details when matching the features later.

Repeat this with a second photograph so that the children are comfortable with the identification process. Them move on to photographs which show features in the locality of which there will be more than one, such as a postbox or telephone box. Can the children identify whereabouts in their local area the feature is? Talk about how they know this. Help them identify background details if they don't automatically look for these.

When you have shown the children all the photographs in your collection, go for a walk in the local area, matching the photographs to the original features and making sure that the children were correct.

On return to the classroom, with higher attaining children, place the photographs onto a large map or plan of the area where the features are found.

TOYS

AREA OF LEARNING: KNOWLEDGE AND UNDERSTANDING OF THE WORLD. ELG: TO LOOK CLOSELY AT SIMILARITIES AND DIFFERENCES.

LEARNING OBJECTIVE
To learn to notice features that are the same and different about a collection of objects.

THINKING OBJECTIVE
To sort toys.

THINKING SKILLS
The children will be sorting by observable differences in this activity. They will look carefully at the similarities and differences between various toys, and will sort these into sets and subsets according to what they can see, feel and hear. This will include considering how the toys work and move, as well as the materials from which they are made.

WHAT YOU NEED
A collection of toys, including a number of soft toys, puppets, wheeled mechanical and non-mechanical toys; set rings; labels; a flip chart or board.

WHAT TO DO
Let the children play with the toys you have collected together before you start. Ask a few of them to say which is their favourite toy and why. Ask, *Is it because it moves by itself? Is it because it is soft and cuddly, or because it makes a lovely sound when squeezed?* Choose two toys that are very different, such as a soft toy and a toy lorry, and show them to the children. Then name all the things that are different about the toys together.

Focus the children on the materials that the toys are made from, and encourage them to use words that describe the features of the toys when considering the differences. For example, *This is a soft toy and can be squeezed; This one has wheels and moves when it is pushed.*

Then choose two toys that have something in common. For example, two soft toys, two mechanical toys or two wheeled toys. List all the things that are the same about them on the flip chart. Include the materials the toys are made from and any features that are the same, such as the number of wheels they have or the way they move.

Show the children two wheeled toys, one that works when pushed and the other that works by a wind-up mechanism. Explain that these toys are different because they are made to move in different ways, yet they are the same because they both have wheels.

Ask the children to sort all the toys with wheels into one set inside a set ring. Look at all of these in turn and then label them with the similarity *They all have wheels.* Next, get the children to separate them into wheeled toys that move when pushed and those that are mechanical, placing them inside the same set ring but separated by a line. Tell the children that they have divided the original set into two subsets. Point out that they are all wheeled toys inside the set ring, but those on one side are different from those on the other.

Let the children repeat the activity with the soft toys, but this time ask them to separate them into subsets according to whether they are puppets or not, or whether they are teddies who make a noise or don't, depending on what you have in your collection.

BATHTIME

AREA OF LEARNING: KNOWLEDGE AND UNDERSTANDING OF THE WORLD. ELG: TO FIND OUT ABOUT PAST AND PRESENT EVENTS IN THEIR OWN LIVES, AND IN THOSE OF THEIR FAMILIES AND OTHER PEOPLE THEY KNOW.

LEARNING OBJECTIVE
To find out that bathtime was a different experience in the past compared with today.

THINKING OBJECTIVE
To compare and sequence.

THINKING SKILLS
Over two lessons, the children will consider what their personal bathtime is like and will sequence the activity carefully. In the following lesson they will think about how people used to have a bath before bathrooms were commonplace in homes. They will compare the features and equipment used during bathtime, and the facilities available to people in the past. They will finish by considering what effect the differences had in how often people in the past and today bathe.

WHAT YOU NEED
A picture of a modern bathroom; a collection of modern bathing equipment, such as toys, bubble bath, flannels, sponges, towels and other bathtime resources that the children may be familiar with; a collection of bathing equipment used in the past, such as a bar of soap, a tin bath, flannels, brushes; a water pump if possible; a flip chart or board.

WHAT TO DO
Look at the picture of a modern bathroom and talk with the children about what is there. Do the children have a bathroom like this? Ask any children who have a bath in their bathroom to talk about it, to describe what it is made of and how they fill it with water. Some children may want to talk about showers. Move on to talk about the children's bathtime for a moment, recalling how many times they have a bath or shower each week (be sensitive to all the children in your group during this discussion). Show the children the different toys, flannels, sponges, towels and bubble baths you have in your collection. Compare these with the things that the children use during their bathtimes.

Question the children further if necessary so that you can list or draw pictures of their bathtime sequence on the flip chart. Remind them to think about how they fill the bath with their parents or carers, any bubble bath they add, the things they use to get clean and the toys they may play with. Set up an independent task in the water tray, acting out the sequence you have recorded by bathing dolls.

The next day, explain to the children that they are going to learn what bathtime was like in the past, when people did not have bathrooms in their houses. Perhaps there is a grandparent who remembers this and can come in to talk to the children. Show the children the tin bath and talk about what it is made from. Ask, *Where are the taps? How did people fill it with water?* Explain that there were no hot taps and the cold water was got from pumps which were sometimes in the house and sometimes outside in the garden or street. If you have a pump available show this to the children, demonstrating how to pump the handle to draw the water, otherwise explain how it worked.

Ask the children where they think people used to take a bath if there were no bathrooms. Focus their thinking by asking questions, such as *Would they go outside? Would it be warm enough?*

Fill the tin bath with water. Ask the children what they think people used to get clean with. Show them the bar of soap and pass it round for them to handle and smell. Invite one or two children to try to make bubbles with the soap in the water. Are they successful? Look together at the flannels and talk about how these and the soap were the only things people used for getting clean. Ask the children which they think is more fun, their modern bathtime or bathtime in the past.

Look back at the modern bathtime sequence on the flip chart and alongside this draw the sequence for bathtime in the past. Ask the children to compare the difference in bathing between the two times, such as where people have/had a bath, how they fill/filled the bath with water and the things they use/used to get clean.

Ask the children, *What happened to bath toys in the past? Did people play with toys in the bath? Why not? How often did people have a bath in the past? Why do you think they did not bathe as often as today?*

Set up an independent role-play activity for the children to recreate bathtime in the past. Let them try to make bubbles with the soap.

SKIPPING

AREA OF LEARNING: PHYSICAL DEVELOPMENT. ELG: TO MOVE WITH CONFIDENCE, IMAGINATION AND IN SAFETY.

LEARNING OBJECTIVE
To learn to skip around with confidence.

THINKING OBJECTIVE
To analyse and sequence.

THINKING SKILLS
The children will watch someone skipping and analyse the way that the movement is carried out. Using questions will help to focus the children's attention on the way the feet swap over before hopping on a different foot each time. They will then think about this sequence when trying out this new skill for themselves.

WHAT YOU NEED
A large space.

WHAT TO DO
Start the lesson with a general moving about activity, where the children move in different ways around the space. You could use your usual game or warm-up activity for this. Otherwise, let the children play Traffic Lights, as this is a good game through which to develop the children's imagination and get them moving confidently before you begin, whilst at the same time controlling the activity itself. Most teachers will know this game, but on the prompt *green*, the children should move fairly quickly until the next instruction is given. *Amber* means move more slowly, while *red* means stop and balance.

Explain to the children that today they are going to learn how to skip. Show them what you mean by skipping or, if any children start to skip immediately, ask them to demonstrate to the rest of the class instead, as this will help keep them attentive during the next part of the lesson.

Ask the children to watch carefully during the skipping demonstration, encouraging them to focus on the movement by asking questions, such as *What happens first? What next? Do you need to hop on both feet? Do you need to stay on one foot or use both? How often do you need to stay on one foot before hopping onto the next? How many times do you hop on each foot?* Carry out the demonstration again, and this time talk through the precise sequence of skipping. Point out what happens first, next and so on. Make sure the children understand that once the sequence is complete (that is, when a hop on one foot and then on the other has been done), the whole thing is repeated over again. It's as simple as that!

Allow the children to start practising the new skill, starting at a slow pace before building it up into a faster and more confident movement. Challenge the children to move all around the available space.

This activity can be adapted for teaching any new skill, including getting out different pieces of apparatus, throwing a ball, catching, and so on.

FINDING SPACE

AREA OF LEARNING: PHYSICAL DEVELOPMENT. ELG: TO SHOW AWARENESS OF SPACE, OF THEMSELVES AND OF OTHERS.

LEARNING OBJECTIVE
To learn to identify space around them and the different ways they can travel into it.

THINKING OBJECTIVE
To analyse and measure.

THINKING SKILLS
The children will be analysing how much space they have around them and how to travel from one point to another. They will need to measure, by estimating, the space available to them, the direction of the movements that this space allows and the types of movement they can, therefore, use. They will learn to think about where they are travelling for themselves, considering both their own and others' safety.

WHAT YOU NEED
Non-slip, flat, carpet squares; hoops; a large space.

WHAT TO DO
Give the children a carpet square each and ask them to find a space on the floor on which to place it. Warm the class up by asking the children to move in different ways around the carpet squares. Encourage them to hop, skip, run, walk and jump to add variety to their movements. Ask, *Did anyone manage to move around the space without touching the squares? Who moved in an interesting way by making a curved travel?*

Play a game where the children move between and around the carpet squares on the floor to a tambourine shake. When the sound stops they should all stand on a square. After the first go ask, *How did you use the space to find an empty square? Did you continue to use all the space or did you move directly to a particular square in a straight line?* Let the children play again, but this time challenge the children to move in a curved line only. As they move, ask, *Can you see a square? How far away is it? How can you move to it in a curved line? Could you move in a zig-zag pathway?*

Place hoops between the carpet squares so that the children can move around by either stepping inside a hoop or onto a square with small steps. They can either build a sequence of hoop, then square, then hoop, or move randomly from one piece of apparatus to another, depending on how far their legs will stretch. Let them explore the moves they can make for themselves. Allow them to jump onto the carpets if they are definitely non-slip, however, it is

not advisable to let them jump into the hoops in case they catch the edge and slip over. When the children have explored moving from hoops to squares for about two minutes, stop them and talk about whether they had to use long steps or short steps to move from one to the other. Repeat the activity, but this time introduce a rule that they can only have one person stepping inside a hoop or onto a square at a time. This will make them analyse the availability of the space around them. Move the hoops and carpet squares further away from each other so that the children have to make longer steps, and repeat the activity.

Finally, move the squares and hoops so that they are at different, random distances from each other. This will require the children to think about the distances between the hoops and the squares. They will need to measure or estimate the distance in comparison to their movements, and analyse whether they need a long or short step and the availability of the space around them.

Finish by removing the apparatus and asking the children to look for a space and to move into it. Ask, *Can you see a space? How far away is it? Is it close enough to jump into? Will you have to move in a straight line to get there? Would it make the pathway to the space longer if you followed a curved or a zig-zagged route?*

THE LONG AND THE SHORT OF IT

AREA OF LEARNING: CREATIVE DEVELOPMENT. ELG: TO RECOGNISE AND EXPLORE HOW SOUNDS CAN BE CHANGED.

LEARNING OBJECTIVE
To learn that sounds can be made in different ways according to the way instruments are played.

THINKING OBJECTIVE
To match sounds.

THINKING SKILLS
After familiarising themselves with a variety of instruments, the children will think about which

instrument is being played and how a particular sound is being made, matching the instrument to a set that they have. They will need to explore different ways of playing the instruments to match the sound they need to copy. This activity can be extended to develop the children's ability to recognise and match sound patterns.

WHAT YOU NEED

Tambourines, maracas, triangles and cymbals (enough for each child in your group and yourself to have one of each of the instruments); rubber and wire beaters; nail brushes; a screen.

WHAT TO DO

Show the children your collection of instruments and let them explore the sound that each makes for a few minutes. If appropriate, tell the children what the names of the instruments are. Set up the screen so that you have one set of instruments on your side and the children have an identical set on theirs. It is important that the children identify the instrument from the sound alone, so if possible do not let them see the instrument you are playing. Show them only if they cannot identify the sound being made. Pick up one of the instruments and play it. Ask the children, *what instrument is making this sound? What sort of sound is it? Is it loud or quiet? Does it last a long time or a short time?* Ask the children to take it in turns to find the matching instrument and to play the matching sound. Once they have grasped the idea, play the instruments in different ways to challenge the children. Ask them, *How have I changed the sound of this instrument? Is the sound longer, shorter, louder, quieter, faster or slower?* When the children have successfully identified each matching instrument and sound at least twice, move on to the second part of the activity.

Give each child a tambourine, maraca, triangle and cymbal and let them explore the different sounds they can make with these with the different beaters and nailbrushes. After a few minutes, sit each child in turn in front of their instruments on one side of the screen and sit at the other side. Play one of the instruments in a particular way. For example, shake the tambourine. Challenge each child to find the matching instrument from its set and to play it in the same way. Continue by playing the instruments in different ways for the children to match and copy.

FACIAL EXPRESSIONS

AREA OF LEARNING: CREATIVE DEVELOPMENT. ELG: TO SING SIMPLE SONGS FROM MEMORY.

LEARNING OBJECTIVE

To learn a new song.

THINKING OBJECTIVE

To understand pattern and relationship.

THINKING SKILLS

The children will listen to a song and learn the first verse before considering how the second and third verses are almost the same. They will look at how the pattern and relationship between the words in the verses help them to remember what comes next when singing the song from memory. They will use this knowledge to think of their own verses.

WHAT YOU NEED

A copy of the song 'Make a Face', words and melody by George Dewey, located in *Tinderbox, 66 songs for children,* chosen by Sylvia Barratt and Sheena Hodge with instrumental parts by Leonora Davies (A & C Black).

WHAT TO DO

Sing the whole song through together first. Then teach the children the chorus, followed by the tune of the verse, learning it one line at a time. Continue to sing the first verse through together until you are sure the children know it fairly well.

Sing the second verse through to the children and ask them, *Can you identify a pattern? What do you notice about the words? How many words are different from those in the first verse?* Sing the second verse through again, this time together. The children should find this easy if they can see the pattern and relationship between the two verses clearly.

Learn the third verse together before adding the children's own word ideas, such as *smiley, funny* or *surprising.* Ask them if they can think of any other words which fit the tune. This song can be extended by singing about different ways of moving, such as *skip, hop, jump around* and so on; by making different types of sounds; by adding different actions, such as clapping your hands, stamping your feet, nodding your head, making the sounds, movements and actions as happy as you can.

EXTENDING INFORMATION-PROCESSING SKILLS

Area of learning and ELG, NLS or NNS objective	Activity title	Thinking objective	Activity	Page
Personal, social and emotional development ELG: To select and use activities and resources independently	Self-initiated play	To locate and analyse	Choosing an activity during self-initiated play	19
Communication, language and literacy ELG: To extend their vocabulary, exploring the meanings and sounds of new words NLS objective: To make collections of words linked to particular topics	Vegetable soup	To collect words	Looking at different vegetables and identifying key words to describe these	20
Communication, language and literacy ELG: To show an understanding of the elements of stories NLS objective: To locate names of key characters	Who's who?	To locate and collect	Identifying nursery rhyme and story characters in stories they already know and in a story that is read to them	21
Communication, language and literacy ELG: To use their phonic knowledge to write simple words and make plausible attempts at complex words NLS objective: To identify initial and final phonemes in CVC words.	Sounds like	To sequence and match sounds	Spelling words by listening	22
Mathematical development ELG: To use language to describe shape. NNS objective: To being to name solids and flat shapes	Robots	To match shapes	Making robots from different shapes and matching pictures of shapes to those they have used in their models	23
Mathematical development ELG: To use language to compare two numbers NNS objective: To use language to compare two numbers	Musical numbers	To use pattern and relationship	Playing a game to learn the position of numbers on a number line	24
Knowledge and understanding of the world ELG: To talk about those features they like and dislike	Take a snap	To sort photographs	Sorting photographs of areas and objects in the local environment into sets they like and dislike	25
Knowledge and understanding of the world ELG: To identify the uses of everyday technology	Signals	To analyse information	Identifying signals in the world around them that give out messages	26
Knowledge and understanding of the world ELG: To find out about some features of living things	Caterpillars only crawl	To sort creatures	Noting the similarities and differences in the way that creatures move	27
Physical development ELG: To move with control and coordination	I can do...	To collect information	Finding out what kind of physical activities they can do	28
Physical development ELG: To handle tools and materials safely and with increasing control	Put it together	To analyse	Analysing how objects have been joined	30
Creative development ELG: To explore colour, shape and form in two dimensions	Marching people	To locate and match people	Finding individual people in a painting	31
Creative development ELG: To use their imagination in role-play	The shoemaker's workshop	To locate and collect	Identifying what resources to include in the role-play area in order to set up an area to match a story	32

SELF-INITIATED PLAY

AREA OF LEARNING: PERSONAL, SOCIAL AND EMOTIONAL DEVELOPMENT. ELG: TO SELECT AND USE ACTIVITIES AND RESOURCES INDEPENDENTLY.

LEARNING OBJECTIVE
To choose an activity independently during self-initiated play.

THINKING OBJECTIVE
To locate and analyse.

THINKING SKILLS
The children will decide for themselves which activity they would like to take part in in the activity areas around the classroom. They will need to be able to locate the correct activity on a board and analyse the information there to see if there is any space for them to join in with particular activities.

WHAT YOU NEED
A display board (in a space large enough for the children to see and at a height where they can reach it) with Velcro squares attached; laminated label cards, backed with Velcro, representing the types of activities which can be undertaken by the children (see 'What to do'; depending on the ability of your class you may wish to add pictures of the activities, too); laminated name labels, backed with Velcro, for each child in the class.

WHAT TO DO
Set up an interactive choice board with labels of the activities from which the children can choose already attached. For example, you may include a label of the role-play area, sand, water, small world toys and the playground. Make sure the number of Velcro squares next to each activity corresponds to the number of children usually allowed in each of the different activity areas. For example, four squares next to where you have displayed the labels for the water, sand and role-play activities, two squares by the chalkboard or programmable robot labels.

Put out the labels of the activities that you plan to follow that day for adult-focused activities and self-initiated play. Randomly place the name cards to one side of the board where the children can reach them independently.

Gather the children around the board and call out the groups that will be working with adults on focused tasks first. Ask the children in these groups to find their names and to put them on one of the empty Velcro squares next to the label of the focused task they will be doing. They can then move to the appropriate area in the classroom.

Focus the other children on the remaining activity areas on the board and invite them to decide which activity they would like to do. A few at a time, invite them to find their names and to place them on an empty square next to the activity they want to do. When all the children have selected an activity, go to your focused group.

Once all the children have their activities underway, monitor that when they have completed an activity they return to the board to move their name to a different one. Remind them that they can only choose an activity if there is an empty space available to stick their name against. When the focused activity is finished, adults should return the names of their current group so that the children can choose their next activity themselves. Adults should remove the names of their next group from the self-initiated tasks to make space before adding them to the focused activity they want them to do. To begin with, an additional adult will need to supervise this process to reinforce the routine and make sure that the children return to the board before swapping activities.

At the end of the session, the children should be encouraged to return their names to the original place to leave the board empty for the next part of the day.

DIFFERENTIATION
Supervise less able children, pointing out where the empty spaces are for each activity. Help them locate their name and direct them towards the activity they want to do. Higher attaining children should be allowed to do this independently or to help those who are having difficulty.

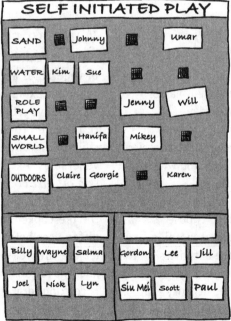

WHERE NEXT

Plan self-initiated play activities at the start of every day so that the children are busy as soon as they come into school. Choosing an activity and placing their name next to their chosen activity will become part of the daily routine.

Plan activities for a week with the children. Can they think of additional ideas, which require extra Velcro squares to be added to the board?

Set up similar boards when organising other choice activities, for example which fruit the children want to order for snack time, whether they want milk or juice, which flavour of lollipop they want for a special treat.

ASSESSMENT

Note the children who carry out the activity independently and who are able to locate the spaces on the board. Note those who still need help to locate the activities and/or analyse where the spaces are.

LEARNING OUTCOMES

The children will learn to locate information in the form of activities that are available for them to join in with, and to analyse whether there is a space available for them to do the activity.

FURTHER PERSONAL, SOCIAL AND EMOTIONAL DEVELOPMENT CHALLENGES

Self-registration

Set up a board for the children to place their names on to indicate that they are present that day. Separate this board into three columns – *sandwich*, *dinner* or *going home* – for the children to analyse and locate what they are having for lunch and which column to put their name in.

Playtime

Set up a similar board for the children to choose which activity they wish to take part in at morning, lunchtime or afternoon play. Put up the activities planned for the day on the board before asking the children to place their name next to the activity that they want to take part in at each playtime.

VEGETABLE SOUP

AREA OF LEARNING: COMMUNICATION, LANGUAGE AND LITERACY. ELG: TO EXTEND THEIR VOCABULARY, EXPLORING THE MEANINGS AND SOUNDS OF NEW WORDS. NLS OBJECTIVE: TO MAKE COLLECTIONS OF WORDS LINKED TO PARTICULAR TOPICS.

LEARNING OBJECTIVE

To identify the key word for a collection of words.

THINKING OBJECTIVE

To collect words.

THINKING SKILLS

The children will look at different types of vegetables, developing new vocabulary to name and describe what they are like. They will identify the key word for this group of foods. They will use picture dictionaries to collect words, thus developing this skill and understanding.

WHAT YOU NEED

A collection of vegetables, some raw and some pre-cooked; blender; dish; microwave; disposable cups and spoons; a flip chart or board; picture dictionaries (check to make sure the words you are collecting are in the dictionaries, and if not make one of your own using pictures and labels).

WHAT TO DO

Show the children your collection of vegetables and name each one together. Explain that collectively they are all called vegetables. Pass them around and ask the children to describe how they feel. Then ask the children to suggest what they think people do with vegetables. Ask, *How are they cooked? Do you take the skin off first or can you leave it on?*

Ask if anyone has ever had vegetable soup. Pass the pre-cooked vegetables around and note the differences between these and the raw ones. Then let the children watch as you use the blender and microwave to make vegetable soup. While the soup is cooking, draw pictures and write the names of the vegetables you have used in the soup on the flip chart. The children can use picture dictionaries to help them locate the words they need. Add the names of other vegetables that the children have thought of to the collection. Together identify that the key word for this collection of words is *vegetable*.

Enjoy the vegetable soup afterwards, making sure it is not too hot, so the children can hold the cups and drink it without burning their tongues.

DIFFERENTIATION

Work with lower attaining children to help them

locate the pictures in the dictionaries. Point out the words and write these for them if they are unable to copy them. More able children should use simple word dictionaries to locate words related to preparing and cooking the vegetables.

Where next

Children use the key word to search a CD-ROM to locate information on it. Look together at picture dictionaries that classify words by type rather than alphabetical order. Ask different groups to collect as many words as they can for different topics.

Assessment

Which children use dictionaries independently and each other's ideas to collect words that are linked in some way? Note the ones who understand that the collection of words have the key word *vegetable* to help classify them.

Learning outcomes

The children will learn to collect and begin to classify words according to whether they are linked to particular topics.

Further communication, language and literacy challenges

Collecting

Set up displays of objects that all belong to the same type or topic, for example seaside toys, fruit, crockery, pet equipment, paper, and so on. The list is endless. For each collection, get the children to name each item and the key word that classifies them.

Name as many as you can

Tell the children a key word and they think of as many items as they can which belong to that group. Collect all the words that the children think of.

Who's who?

AREA OF LEARNING: COMMUNICATION, LANGUAGE AND LITERACY. ELG: TO SHOW AN UNDERSTANDING OF THE ELEMENTS OF STORIES, SUCH AS CHARACTERS. NLS OBJECTIVE: TO LOCATE NAMES OF KEY CHARACTERS.

Learning objective

To recall characters from a range of familiar stories.

Thinking objective

To locate and collect story characters.

Thinking skills

The children will recall some of the stories they are familiar with and which characters are present in them. They will use this knowledge to locate the characters that appear in one particular story read to them during the lesson. These characters will be collected and recorded for them to count up later.

What you need

A copy of *A Wolf at the Door!* by Nick Ward (Scholastic); a flip chart or board.

What to do

Talk to the children briefly about their favourite nursery rhymes and stories. Ask, *Which characters do you like best? Which story or rhyme are they in?* Collect the names of some of the characters the children mention and write these as a list on the left-hand side of the flip chart.

Read the first three pages of *A Wolf at the Door!* to the children. Then show them the picture on page 4 of the character who has come to the door. Ask the children to say who they think the character is. Give them a clue, if appropriate, by telling them that it is someone from one of their favourite stories (if it is). Write the name of this character on the right-hand side of the flip chart.

Continue reading the story and each time the door is answered, show the children the picture and ask them to identify the character(s) each time. Continue to record the name of the character(s) on the right-hand side of the flip chart. Talk about the clues in the pictures that help the children to name the character(s).

When you have finished the story, count up all the characters you have collected together.

Differentiation

Read a favourite story to lower attaining children and together collect the names of all the characters in it. Higher attaining children should be challenged to collect as many different types of characters as they can, such as bears and wolves from other stories they have read.

Where next

Read traditional stories to the children which include popular characters. Collect the names of those characters which are the children's favourites.

ASSESSMENT

Note the children who understand the notion of 'character' and collect these from the story.

LEARNING OUTCOMES

Most children will learn to locate and collect a range of story and nursery rhyme characters, both during the lesson and from their prior experience of stories. They will begin to understand how characters are important in a story, adding interest and sense.

FURTHER COMMUNICATION, LANGUAGE AND LITERACY CHALLENGES

Bear characters

Challenge the children to look at the storybooks in your classroom library and to collect all the titles that have a particular type of character in their stories, such as a bear, wolf, princess or giant. Ask the children to locate the parts of the story in which these characters appear.

Nursery rhyme magic

Play a tape of favourite nursery rhymes and ask the children to collect all the animals that they hear referred to by drawing pictures of them. Which animal appears more often than any other?

SOUNDS LIKE

AREA OF LEARNING: COMMUNICATION, LANGUAGE AND LITERACY. ELG: TO USE THEIR PHONIC KNOWLEDGE TO WRITE SIMPLE REGULAR WORDS AND MAKE PHONETICALLY PLAUSIBLE ATTEMPTS AT MORE COMPLEX WORDS. NLS OBJECTIVE: TO IDENTIFY INITIAL AND FINAL PHONEMES IN CVC WORDS.

LEARNING OBJECTIVE

To learn to spell simple CVC words.

THINKING OBJECTIVES

To sequence sounds and match sounds to letters.

THINKING SKILLS

This activity sets the teaching of spelling within a real context, rather than trying to teach spelling in isolation. The children will learn to listen to the sequence of sounds in CVC words in the correct order, before matching the sounds to letters. By concentrating on words that you know, the children will understand the presence of sequences of sounds within simple words which will help them develop a strategy to spell them.

WHAT YOU NEED

A magnetic board; magnetic letters (several of the same consonants and vowels); a flip chart or board.

WHAT TO DO

Sit the children around the magnetic board. Show them the letters you have and together recall the names of those letters that the children already know. Separate them into vowels and consonants on the board.

Explain to the children that together you are going to write a simple story called 'Little Bear's day at the farm'. Start the children off by thinking of a beginning to the story, such as *One day Little Bear went to the farm with his mum*. Write this down on the flip chart, perhaps drawing a simple illustration to add immediate interest.

Ask the children to continue the story by saying which animals Little Bear saw there. Write the children's ideas down, starting each sentence with *He saw a...*, or *He saw some...* When you come to write in the animal names, ask the children to spell the words themselves. Use the magnetic letters on the magnetic board and break the words down, identifying the first sound of the word, then the middle sound and finally the last sound. Good words that you could use are *hen, dog, pig, cow, lamb, duck, bull* and *cat*.

As you progress through the different animal names, draw the children's attention to the fact that the first letter each time comes from the group of consonants, the second from the group of vowels and the last sound from the consonants again.

DIFFERENTIATION

Less able children should concentrate on the consonant sounds only, identifying the initial and final phonemes. Challenge higher attaining children to spell words with consonant clusters, such as *frog*, and long vowel phonemes, such as *goat, sheep, horse, goose* and *geese*.

WHERE NEXT

Let the children use the magnetic letters on the board to spell other CVC words. Ask them to choose a consonant, a vowel and another consonant, and then to sound the words they have made, breaking down the words into their sound sequences.

ASSESSMENT

Check the children who successfully identify the phoneme and match it to the correct grapheme. Note those who can match the short and long vowel phonemes to the correct grapheme and use this knowledge to sequence their spellings correctly.

LEARNING OUTCOMES

Most children will be able to match the initial phoneme to its grapheme. Some children will also be able to match the correct vowel and final sound to the graphemes and sequence the letters to spell the words correctly.

FURTHER COMMUNICATION, LANGUAGE AND LITERACY CHALLENGES

Consonant or vowel

Give the children simple CVC words and ask them to highlight the consonants in yellow and the vowels in blue. What do they notice about the sequence of the letters? Do all the words start with a consonant and have vowels in the middle? Explain that these are Consonant-Vowel-Consonant words.

Where am I?

Ask the children to find CVC words in a reading book. Ask them to identify the sequence of the consonants and the vowels. Together, read the words they have found as adult and child, or in a group or as a class.

ROBOTS

AREA OF LEARNING: MATHEMATICAL DEVELOPMENT. ELG: TO USE LANGUAGE TO DESCRIBE SHAPE. NNS OBJECTIVE: TO BEGIN TO NAME SOLIDS SUCH AS A CUBE, CONE, SPHERE AND FLAT SHAPES SUCH AS A CIRCLE, TRIANGLE, SQUARE AND RECTANGLE.

LEARNING OBJECTIVE

To learn the names of 2-D shapes: a square, rectangle, circle and triangle; and 3-D shapes: a cube, cuboid, cylinder and sphere.

THINKING OBJECTIVE

To match shapes.

THINKING SKILLS

The children will look carefully at the shapes used by a character in a story book to make robots with before finding matching shapes to make robots of their own. Afterwards, they will label the shapes they have used by matching a picture of each shape to the corresponding ones in their models.

WHAT YOU NEED

A copy of *Harry and the Robots* by Ian Whybrow (Gullane Children's Books); recycled materials that include boxes and containers matching the shape of those used in the story to make the robots; glue sticks; sticky tape; paint; paper pieces; scissors; a digital camera; stickers of 2-D shapes.

WHAT TO DO

Read the book *Harry and the Robots* to the children. Focus on the robots that Harry made in the story and talk about the shapes he used to make each one and those he used to decorate them with.

Show the children your collection of boxes and other materials and together find the shapes that match those used in the story to make the robots. In groups, challenge the children to make matching robots, or to make their own robots using the same shapes. Use glue or sticky tape to join the boxes together. Some children may want to draw pictures of robots instead by drawing around the shapes. Let them decorate their robots with stickers of 2-D shapes when they have finished.

Make individual worksheets for the children to complete. Take photographs of the finished robots and mount them in the middle of a sheet of paper. Draw pictures of a square, rectangle, circle and triangle down one side of the paper, and pictures of a cube, cuboid, cylinder and sphere down the other side of the paper. Ask the children to match the shapes by drawing a line from the shapes they used in their models to the 2-D and 3-D shapes at the side of the paper.

DIFFERENTIATION

Choose a robot for lower attaining children to copy and help them find the matching boxes they will need. Higher attaining children should be encouraged to match the faces of 3-D shapes to their corresponding 2-D equivalent.

WHERE NEXT

Make buildings with the children using blocks. Photograph the buildings and get the children to match the blocks they have used to corresponding shapes you have drawn on the board.

ASSESSMENT

Note any children who begin to match the faces of the 3-D shapes to 2-D ones. Who notices, for example, that the cylinder has two circles on its ends, or that a cube is made up of squares?

LEARNING OUTCOMES

Most children will identify 2-D and 3-D shapes by matching. Some will learn that 3-D shapes are made up of several 2-D shapes.

FURTHER MATHEMATICAL DEVELOPMENT CHALLENGES

Matching robots

Photocopy the pictures of the robots on the inside front cover of the book and ask the children to match the ones that are the same. Ask, *How many different kinds of robots are there? How many of each of the robots can you find?* Ask the children to draw small pictures of their own robot using black pencil lines only. Alternatively, use a program such as Paint on the computer to make coloured robots for the children to match and compile the different types onto sheets.

Robot shapes

Ask the children to draw a robot, using actual shapes to draw round. Then explain that they should swap drawings with a partner to 'make' each other's robots by matching the correct shapes on top of the drawings.

MUSICAL NUMBERS

AREA OF LEARNING: MATHEMATICAL DEVELOPMENT. ELG: TO USE LANGUAGE SUCH AS *MORE* OR *LESS* TO COMPARE TWO NUMBERS. NNS OBJECTIVE: TO USE LANGUAGE SUCH AS *MORE* OR *LESS* TO COMPARE TWO NUMBERS.

LEARNING OBJECTIVE

To learn the order of numbers on a number line, including whether they are one more or less than any given number.

THINKING OBJECTIVE

To use pattern and relationship with numbers.

THINKING SKILLS

The children will build on their knowledge of numerals and counting to learn where numbers come on a number line. They will think about their pattern and relationship with other numbers on the number line. They will need to consider each number's position, which numbers are next to, after and before it and whether it is more or less than any given number.

WHAT YOU NEED

A tape recorder or CD player with a suitable extract of music for the children to dance to; a matching number of numerals to the number of children in your group, choosing numbers that you want the children to learn (large carpet squares with the numbers on are suitable); a large number of cubes that will fit onto the children's fingers.

WHAT TO DO

Give the children the numbers and ask them to arrange them in a number line in the correct order on the floor. Look at each of the numbers first and identify each one to make sure that the children know what the numbers are.

Tell the children they are going to play a game. Explain that it is a bit like Musical Chairs, that you want them to dance around the numbers to music, but that when the music stops you want them to put their foot on the number that they are standing next to.

Have a practice run. Start the music and reinforce the way you want the children to dance around the numbers first. Then stop the music and when the children have placed their foot on a number, ask questions, such as *Who is standing on the number 10? Who is standing on the number 4?* Ask a few more questions, depending on the numbers in your range. Give the children who get the answer right a cube to hold, or to place on the end of their finger.

Play the music again. This time extend the questioning by asking, *Who is standing on a number that comes next to 10? Next to 3? Next to 20?* Again, give a cube to those children who are right. Monitor the cubes to make sure every child has received a cube at this point to keep them involved and motivated.

Continue with the game, introducing more challenging questions depending on the ability of the children, such as *Who is standing on a number which is one more than 10? One less than 8? On a number*

between 3 and 7? On a number after 3 and before 12?
The game finishes when one child has a cube on the end of each finger and becomes the winner.

DIFFERENTIATION
Work on numbers below 5 or 10 with lower attaining children. Concentrate on them learning which numbers are next to each other, which come between two numbers, and so on, to reinforce their skills of looking for pattern and relationship between two numbers. Extend the activity for more able children by using only odd or even numbers. Talk about the pattern and relationship between the even numbers and the odd numbers.

WHERE NEXT
Work with numbers organised in a square and talk to the children about numbers that are below, above or that surround a given number.

ASSESSMENT
Note the children who begin to think about the pattern and relationship of a number line to help them sort numbers in the correct order. Make particular note of those who identify the numbers that are more or less than any given number.

LEARNING OUTCOMES
Most children will start to look at pattern and relationship between numbers to help them remember the order and size of a number in relation to those next to it.

FURTHER MATHEMATICAL DEVELOPMENT CHALLENGES
Sorting the post
Organise envelopes with house numbers on and the name of an imaginary street, such as *12 Victoria Street*. Have one envelope for each child. Show the children a picture of your imaginary street of houses, or make this with your small world toys. Number the houses either 1–10, 11–20, or organise them with even numbers on one side of the street and odd numbers on the other. Ask the children to look at the numbers on their envelopes and decide which order the postman will deliver the letters in. Challenge the children to put the letters in the correct order for the postman.

Where does it go?
Make a number line with some numbers missing. Give the children a set of numbers and ask them to find the missing ones and put them in the correct place. Question them until they can say why the number goes where it does, including in their reason a reference to its position and relationship with the numbers around it.

TAKE A SNAP

AREA OF LEARNING: KNOWLEDGE AND UNDERSTANDING OF THE WORLD. ELG: TO TALK ABOUT THOSE FEATURES THEY LIKE AND DISLIKE.

LEARNING OBJECTIVE
To look for things in the local environment that they like and dislike.

THINKING OBJECTIVE
To sort photographs.

THINKING SKILLS
The children will sort a collection of photographs of areas and objects in the local environment into two groups, and this will help them decide those things that they like and those that they don't like. After completing the sorting activity they will need to talk about their choices, giving reasons for their classification.

WHAT YOU NEED
Photographs of places in the local environment that you know the children will like, and things that they will not (see 'What to do').

WHAT TO DO
Before the activity, go for a walk around the local area and take photographs of things that the children will like. Include pretty gardens, seats for sitting on, mown grass, trees in blossom or with autumnal coloured leaves, litter-free areas and quiet spots. Take photographs, too, of things you think the children will not like, including litter-strewn ground, or any other offensive deposits, noisy areas and untidy aspects.

In the classroom, show the children your collection of photographs and talk about what they can see. Talk about the things that the children like, for example the flowers, trees, tidy streets, pond and other natural and pretty objects. The children will decide for themselves what they like. Talk about the things that the children do not like and why.

Sort the photographs into two piles – things the children like and those that they do not like. Then ask the children to talk about why they like some of the things shown in the photographs and not others. Do they like things that are neat and tidy, pretty and well looked after? What about those things that are untidy, dirty and not looked after very well? Are there any photographs of places that they think some people would like that they did not? Do they think that everyone would not like the places that are untidy?

DIFFERENTIATION

Develop inference skills with more able children and talk about whether the area may be noisy, smelly, quiet or busy. Concentrate on two areas with less able children and help them note the differences between the two places. Ask them to say which one they would like to visit most and why.

WHERE NEXT

Look at posters that encourage people to use litterbins or to take their litter home. Ask the children to choose a photograph to display with the poster that they think would make the message clearer.

ASSESSMENT

Listen to the children's discussions and note the children who use the sorting activity to help them decide what they like and do not like.

LEARNING OUTCOMES

Most children will put the photographs into two sets according to likes and dislikes.

FURTHER KNOWLEDGE AND UNDERSTANDING OF THE WORLD CHALLENGES

At the end of the day

Take a photograph of the classroom at the end of the day and again when it has been tidied and cleaned. Look at the two photographs and ask the children to say what they like and dislike. Do they like it best after it has been cleaned? Make a list of rules for looking after the classroom.

SIGNALS

AREA OF LEARNING: KNOWLEDGE AND UNDERSTANDING OF THE WORLD. ELG: TO IDENTIFY THE USES OF EVERYDAY TECHNOLOGY.

LEARNING OBJECTIVE
To learn that information is all around us.

THINKING OBJECTIVE
To analyse information.

THINKING SKILLS
The children will listen to and look at a range of everyday devices that use technology and identify the message that these devices give. They will develop their observation skills, and begin to notice and analyse the meaning of sounds and visual signals in the world around them.

WHAT YOU NEED
A collection of pictures, or a video, containing warning signals, such as flashing warning lights on police cars, ambulances or fire engines, pedestrian crossing lights, a train level crossing or a lighthouse; a collection of recordings of sounds, such as a telephone ringing, a police siren, an alarm clock ringing, a door bell.

WHAT TO DO
Watch the video of, or show the children your collection of, signs and signals and identify what each one is with them. Ask them to say what each one is telling them to do. Encourage their suggestions by asking questions, such as *What is the instruction the signal is giving us? How should we behave when we see that signal?* Start with familiar things, such as pedestrian crossing signals, police car, ambulance and fire engine flashing lights, before moving onto those which the children may not be able to recognise, such as a lighthouse.

Repeat the activity with your recordings of sounds that give signals.

DIFFERENTIATION
Separate the signals into two different activities for lower attaining children. Start with the video or pictures and move onto the sounds only if, and when, they are ready. This will mean that they use their visual memory or learning first and their aural next. Higher attaining children can be challenged to find additional signals in the world around them, perhaps as a homework project.

WHERE NEXT
Take the children into the locality and record drawings and make notes of sounds of things that give messages.

ASSESSMENT
Note the children who can identify the signals and those who can analyse the message each one is giving.

LEARNING OUTCOMES
Most children will be able to understand that there are signals in the local environment and what they mean. They will start to pay more attention to what they see and hear as a result.

FURTHER KNOWLEDGE AND UNDERSTANDING OF THE WORLD CHALLENGES

Carrier bags
Show the children a collection of different carrier bags. Ask them to identify the colours, symbols and writing on each, and challenge them to identify the shop that each one comes from.
Road signs
Look together at photographs of different road signs and symbols, such as parking or toilet facilities. Encourage the children to try and identify what each one means. Ask, *What is it telling you to do? Where is it telling you to go?*

CATERPILLARS ONLY
CRAWL

AREA OF LEARNING: KNOWLEDGE AND UNDERSTANDING OF THE WORLD. ELG: TO FIND OUT ABOUT, AND IDENTIFY, SOME FEATURES OF LIVING THINGS.

LEARNING OBJECTIVE
To identify the way different creatures move.

THINKING OBJECTIVE
To sort creatures.

THINKING SKILLS
The children will first think about the way that caterpillars move and will then move on to think about the way other creatures move. Through a series of sorting activities they will begin to note the similarities and differences in the way that creatures move. They will also begin to realise that those creatures who walk or crawl have legs, those that fly have wings, those that swim have fins and those that slither have no legs at all.

WHAT YOU NEED
A piece of music for the children to move to ('Carnival of the animals' by Saint-Saëns has several suitable extracts); a large space for the children to move in; large labels with a type of animal movement written on them, such as *crawl, fly, swim, slither*; paper and drawing and painting materials.

WHAT TO DO
Play the children an extract from the music and invite them to move like a caterpillar. Link the activity to creative development by letting the children move freely. Stop the children and talk about how the caterpillar moves. Ask, *Does it crawl? Does it fly? What does the caterpillar have which means it has to crawl?* Let the children move around the room again, taking on board the discussion and seeing if they can improve their caterpillar movements. Talk about how some caterpillars make looping movements and why.

Collect the children's suggestions for other creatures and get them to move like these animals. Make sure you choose creatures that move in different ways, such as flying, running, slithering. Each time, talk with the children about the feature that the creature has to allow it to move in this way. For example, birds and butterflies have wings and fish have fins.

Invite the children to choose an animal that they have practised being during the activity and to move in that way. Explain that when the music stops all the animals that move in the same way should stand together in a small set. Play the music and let the children move around, noting who is making what movements. When the music stops, quickly make sure that the children have sorted themselves into the correct groups. Ask them, *Do you all crawl in this group? Do you all fly over here?*

Play the music again, and this time hold up one of your labels with a movement on when the music stops. Explain that all the animals that move in this way have to sit out of the game. Continue until you have a winning group.

Play the game as many times as you want. On return to the classroom, organise the children into groups and invite each group to draw and paint pictures of creatures that move in the same way.

DIFFERENTIATION

Encourage higher attaining children to think about creatures who move in more than one way, such as a ladybird or beetle. Allow them to choose which group to join during the activity. For lower attaining children, choose which animal they should be for them, and if necessary, tell them how they should move. Support them in finding the correct set.

WHERE NEXT

Ask the children to make models of different creatures and display these together with the pictures that they created in the main activity. Get the children to help you sort the display so that the pictures and models of animals are sorted according to the way they move.

ASSESSMENT

Note the children who can sort themselves into the correct set with no support. Note any higher attaining child's ability to select more than one set if appropriate.

LEARNING OUTCOMES

Most children will be able to identify how different creatures move sufficiently to be able to recreate their movements. They should also be able to join in the activity independently and find the correct set for the way their animal moves.

FURTHER KNOWLEDGE AND UNDERSTANDING OF THE WORLD CHALLENGES

Sort it

Use models, toys and pictures with the children for them to sort animals and creatures according to the way they move into different sorting rings. Decide together where to put those creatures that move in two different ways (ensuring that you explain to any children that need it why some creatures move in two different ways). Show the children how to overlap the sorting rings so that the creatures can be standing in two rings at the same time.

I CAN DO...

AREA OF LEARNING: PHYSICAL DEVELOPMENT. ELG: TO MOVE WITH CONTROL AND COORDINATION.

LEARNING OBJECTIVE

To learn that we can all do things with our bodies.

THINKING OBJECTIVE

To collect information.

THINKING SKILLS

The children will think about all the things they can do physically and build this into a 'wall of achievement' by collecting information to record over time. They will learn that although they can do something, they can always improve this skill over time and that there is a way to measure this achievement. Some children will begin to write their own targets and by continuing to collect information they will evaluate for themselves how well they are doing in reaching these.

WHAT YOU NEED

A large piece of paper with pictures of empty brick shapes in a wall drawn onto it; an A4-sized version for the children to use as a recording sheet (enough for each child in the class); felt-tipped pens; a stopwatch; a range of apparatus (depending on the children's ideas); a large space.

WHAT TO DO

Carry out a physical development lesson in which the children take part in a range of activities which require them to run, hop, skip, jump, climb, and so on. After the lesson, sit the children in a circle and talk about all the things they can do. Model this first if you wish so that you encourage them to think of the things that they can do physically, through moving. Talk about the things they accomplished in the lesson before, then move onto thinking about some of the other things they can do with their legs and feet. For example, riding a bike or scooter, throwing, catching, and kicking large, medium and small balls. Follow your usual routine for circle time, so if you use a toy to pass round to signal each child's turn to speak, do so. When the children have thought about their ideas, refine them further. For example, if a child's suggestion was *I can run*, ask them to say how fast or far they can run. This will make the children think of the detail of their achievements.

Get out your large piece of paper with the picture of a brick wall on it and explain to the children that you are going to make a record of some of their achievements when they use their legs and feet. Tell them that you are going to create a display which will celebrate what they can do. Choose one of the children's suggestions and inside one of the bricks draw a picture to show what they can do. Write underneath how fast or far they managed to run. Repeat this until you have recorded a few of the children's suggestions. Stop when you think the children understand what you are doing or become restless.

Give the children their own copy of the brick wall and invite them to think of at least three things that they can do physically and to draw them into three of the bricks. Encourage the children to add to their sheets over the next few weeks as they learn to do more things. Respond to their exclamations in lessons when they say, for example, *Look what I can do!*

Organise some of the things the children have drawn in their bricks to be set up so that they can practise and improve their skills over a few weeks. Either the children or an adult should write simple sentences under each picture in their bricks, explaining what they can do. This will enable them to compare whether they are improving at a particular skill.

DIFFERENTIATION

Concentrate on one type of skill with higher attaining children and ask them to record how they are improving this skill on their sheet. Let lower attaining children record the things they can do rather than how well they do it.

WHERE NEXT

Invite the children to collect information about what they can do with their hands, for example threading, lacing, painting, writing and cutting out. They can extend their records by stating in detail how they use the skill. For example, if they say they can cut out, ask them to say whether they can cut

around a picture, or follow a line to cut out a picture accurately.

ASSESSMENT

Use the recording sheets as a record of assessment to see if the children have learned to do more things, or whether they have improved at a particular skill. Monitor the sheets and use the information to pick out the skills that particular individuals or groups of children need to improve next, and identify this in your planning for the following week.

LEARNING OUTCOMES

The children will learn to collect information about all the things they can do and use the information to note the improvements they make in each skill area. The activity can be individualised depending on the skill you want the children to concentrate on in any particular week or term.

FURTHER PHYSICAL DEVELOPMENT CHALLENGES

Skittles

Set up a game of skittles for the children to play. Give each child a sheet to record how many skittles they knock down on their first, second and subsequent attempts. Is the number of skittles they knock down getting bigger with each go? Ask, *Does this mean your skill is improving?* Record the information the children have collected on a block graph if you wish, with the number of skittles on the vertical axis and the number of turns (first, second, third, and so on) on the horizontal axis. Talk to the children about whether the blocks or towers get taller as the number of turns increases. Ask, *What does that tell us about the information we have collected?*

Target

Set up targets for the children to aim for, for example running fast over a measured distance, finding out how far they can kick a ball, or whether they can hit the large, medium or small circle with a tennis ball on a target made up of concentric circles. Collect information about their progress every time they practise the skill on a class recording sheet. Add dates and ask the children to write how far, fast or what sized target they hit, each time they improve.

PUT IT TOGETHER

AREA OF LEARNING: PHYSICAL DEVELOPMENT. ELG: TO HANDLE TOOLS AND MATERIALS SAFELY AND WITH INCREASING CONTROL.

LEARNING OBJECTIVE
To manipulate garden wire into shapes and sculptures.

THINKING OBJECTIVE
To analyse.

THINKING SKILLS
The children will look at things that are made from wire and analyse how they have been joined. They will use this information to make wire sculptures of their own.

WHAT YOU NEED
Several wire coat-hangers; plastic-covered garden wire, some lengths of which have been made into sculptures; snips to cut the wire if scissors are not strong enough.

WHAT TO DO
Split the children into small groups and give each group a wire coat-hanger to look at carefully. Ask, *How is it made? Is it made from one or two pieces of wire? How do you know? Can you see how the hook is joined to the frame? How has this been done?* Show the children how the two ends of the wire have been twisted around each other to make the structure. Undo one of the coat hangers and stretch out the wire as straight as you can manage to show them. Look at the other articles you have made from graden wire and draw the children's attention to how the pieces of wire are twisted around each other to hold the pieces together.

Show the class a length of garden wire and invite someone to make it into a circle. Ask the rest of the children to suggest how they can join the two ends together to make the circle so that it won't come apart. Help the children to make the wire into a circle and invite other children to make several more circles in the same way. Move on to ask the children if they can think of a way to join several circles together. Provide them with support if they can not think of how to do this, by showing them how to wind another length of wire around the two circles to make a sculpture.

Give the children lengths of plastic-coated wire to make sculptures with. Let them experiment with different ways of joining the wire to make their creations.

DIFFERENTIATION
Help lower attaining children as they work, cutting, shaping and joining the wire and talking about how they are bending it into shape and joining it by twisting the ends and parts together. This analysis will help them think about how they are joining wire to make their sculptures. Higher attaining children should be challenged to work together to make a larger group sculpture from longer lengths of wire. Analyse together how they are bending, twisting and joining the wire to make it stable.

WHERE NEXT
Put out laces and boards and invite the children to use the laces to join two boards together. If you do not have laces and boards, use shoelaces and make boards from cardboard with holes punched in at intervals around the edge. Analyse with the children how to join them together by threading the laces through the holes of two boards and pulling the two tightly together.

Show the children how to sew paper shapes onto cardboard or fabric using needles and string or wool. Analyse with the children how they have joined these to the card.

ASSESSMENT
As the children work, talk to them about what they are doing. Assess whether they are analysing carefully how they are twisting, bending and joining the wire to make their sculptures. Note those who can describe how they have made the finished objects.

LEARNING OUTCOMES
Most children will be able to say how they made their sculptures by analysing the way they manipulated the wire into the different shapes.

FURTHER PHYSICAL DEVELOPMENT CHALLENGES
Books and leaflets
Give the children paper, hole punches, staples, glue and treasury tags and let them analyse how to join the materials to make books, cards, envelopes and leaflets. Invite them to discuss their ideas before making their article.

Do it up
Get the children to analyse how different items of clothing are done up, letting them experiment with zips, buttons, hooks, press-studs, laces, buckles and Velcro. Let them practise how to do this by dressing dolls.

MARCHING PEOPLE

AREA OF LEARNING: CREATIVE DEVELOPMENT. ELG: TO EXPLORE COLOUR, SHAPE AND FORM IN TWO DIMENSIONS.

LEARNING OBJECTIVE
To observe what some artists paint, focusing on colour and shape.

THINKING OBJECTIVE
To locate and match people.

THINKING SKILLS
The children will look carefully at a painting and match cut-outs of people to the corresponding people in the picture. They will do this by thinking about and matching the colour, shape, size and position of each person.

WHAT YOU NEED
A print of a painting by LS Lowry, laminated, that shows a number of people walking about; a photocopy of the painting; people cut out from a photocopy of the painting; red, blue and green water-based pens.

WHAT TO DO
Look at the laminated painting print by Lowry together and talk about the people and buildings in it. Ask, *What colour are they? How many people can you see? Are they all wearing the same kind of clothes? Does anyone look different?* Identify the people that look alike and the ones that look different. On your photocopy of the painting, underline the ones that look alike with a red pen and those that look different with a blue pen.

Look together at one of the people you have cut out from the photocopy of the painting. Talk about the person. Ask, *What does this person look like? How tall is he? Which way is he facing? Is he wearing a hat? Is he standing still or walking?* Ask the children to look for the person in the painting and when they have found him, draw a ring round him with a green pen. Then select another cut-out person and repeat the task.

Organise the children into groups and get one group at a time to find other people in the larger painting. The other groups can be involved in their self-initiated play activities. Set up the painting and individual people as an interactive display for the children to find other cut-out people in the painting at any time.

DIFFERENTIATION
Photocopy and cut out some people in the painting and turn them to look the other way to challenge the higher attaining children. Give those children who need more support additional clues, such as a smaller area in which to look when locating the people, or a particularly distinctive person.

WHERE NEXT
Give the children a copy of a similar painting and ask them in pairs to choose a person to copy for their partner to locate.

Use a computer to move people around in an image to a different place. Print off the two pictures and ask the children to locate and match the same people or objects.

ASSESSMENT
Note those children who locate and match the people easily because they are using skills of observation independently.

LEARNING OUTCOMES
Most children will be able to locate the people in the painting because of their ability to match the colour, shape, size and position of the people.

FURTHER CREATIVE DEVELOPMENT CHALLENGES
Where is it?
Take a photograph of the view outside the classroom. Make two enlarged copies. From one, cut out some features and ask the children to locate these in the other photograph and where they are in the actual environment.

Find the square
Find a black-and-white line drawing that is not too complicated. Make two photocopies. Divide them into squares, cutting one up and leaving the other whole. Display the cut-up squares by the side of the whole picture and challenge the children to locate and match the squares to the picture. Turn some of the squares at an angle to challenge higher attaining children.

THE SHOEMAKER'S WORKSHOP

AREA OF LEARNING: CREATIVE DEVELOPMENT. ELG: TO USE THEIR IMAGINATION IN ROLE-PLAY.

LEARNING OBJECTIVE

To act out the story of The Elves and the Shoemaker.

THINKING OBJECTIVE

To locate and collect resources.

THINKING SKILLS

The children will think about the story of The Elves and the Shoemaker before deciding for themselves the resources they will need in setting up a role-play area to match the story. They will locate and collect the things they need and organise these in the way they want to create their own role-play area.

WHAT YOU NEED

A copy of the story 'The Elves and the Shoemaker'; a range of resources for the children to locate, including play tools, fabric, laces, old shoes with different fasteners, notepads and pens, a telephone, a tool bench.

WHAT TO DO

Read the story 'The Elves and the Shoemaker' to the children and talk about the kind of workshop the shoemaker worked in. Explain to the children that you want to set up the role-play area to look like the shoemaker's workshop. On a large sheet of paper, draw the rooms that the shoemaker would have in his house. Ask the children to suggest what the shoemaker would have in each room. Ask, *What will he have in his workshop? What furniture will there be? What tools? What materials? How will he record what his customers want? Does he sell shoes? What does he need for this?* Draw small pictures of the things the children suggest in other rooms, for example the kitchen, sitting room and bedroom.

When the children have gone home, set up the role-play area as the children have suggested and place additional items for them to find the next day around the classroom. When they come in the next day, talk about the areas that you have made. In groups (one or two groups for each area), send the children off to find the other resources that they will need to act out the role of the shoemaker in their alloted rooms Refer to the drawings of the children's suggestions made the day before. Make sure that they are clear about the things they will be looking for. When the areas are set up with the children's resources in them, sit together and talk about the things that the children have found. Ask, *Are there any resources we still need? Where can we get them? How will you play in the role-play area? Will you act out the story? Will you make up a different story?* Over the next few days, ask an additional adult to play alongside the children, using the things they have located and collected. Allow the children to add to the resources during the week.

DIFFERENTIATION

Look at pictures of the story with lower attaining children and locate the things that the artist has drawn into the shoemaker's home. The children could use this information as a basis for their own collection of resources. Ask higher attaining children to imagine a different situation for the shoemaker and his wife, and to locate and collect resources for their own scenario.

WHERE NEXT

Repeat the activity with other favourite stories and rhymes. This could include nursery rhymes and poems.

ASSESSMENT

Note the children who use their knowledge of the story to identify, locate and collect the resources they need.

LEARNING OUTCOMES

Most children will have a good understanding of the things they need to act out in the story and will find these independently. Make sure that they are available in the classroom or at home.

FURTHER CREATIVE DEVELOPMENT CHALLENGES

Resourcing

Set up other activities where the children can identify and locate their own resources, for example a painting or collage picture. Invite them to make a list and to tick off each item as they collect it.

Recipes

Set up a cooking activity with the children. Read the recipe together and collect all the ingredients. Ask the children to collect any other things that they think they will need. While the recipe is cooking, make a list of all the equipment and ingredients that were used.

Reasoning skills

Introduction

Reasoning skills enable children to make considered decisions and to give reasons for those decisions. Asking children to explain what they are thinking or to talk through how they reached a particular conclusion will develop their reasoning skills. Four- and five-year-old children are usually just beginning to make links between different pieces of information and using this information to solve problems. This requires them to make judgements and interpret evidence, and to start to use deduction skills to work out who carried out a particular action, and how something happened or why. Very young children find it very difficult to infer something that might happen and why, so this skill requires teachers to direct children towards the inference process. The activities in this chapter enable this to happen. For example, in the activity 'Look out mouse' the children are led towards looking at pictures to infer who might appear next in a story.

One strategy for developing the children's emerging reasoning skills is concept or mind mapping. This is already used by many teachers to establish children's current knowledge and understanding of a concept or new process before planning work matched at a suitable level for groups and individuals. A simplified version of this strategy is used in some activities in this chapter, which asks the children to match pairs of words and give reasons for their choices, thus developing their ability to begin to link cause and effect. The activity 'Word links' shows how the start of concept mapping can be used to develop the children's reasoning skills in many areas of learning.

As well as concept mapping, children will need to develop their reasoning skills using other strategies. In reading, children will be developing their reasoning skills when they are trying to find a solution for a character in a story, by looking at pictures to try to predict the ending of a story or by explaining why something happened the way it did. Solving problems and explaining strategies are natural parts of mathematical development and are used to find answers to a particular problem. Throughout, the children should be asked to give reasons and express their opinions, thus developing their critical thinking skills beyond what they sense, to thinking about what they feel.

The following skills all form a part of the reasoning process:
⊙ explaining
⊙ forming opinions
⊙ making judgements
⊙ making decisions
⊙ interpreting
⊙ inferring
⊙ deducing
⊙ giving reasons.

INTRODUCING REASONING SKILLS

Area of learning and ELG, NLS or NNS objective	Activity title	Thinking objective	Activity	Page
Personal, social and emotional development ELG: To manage their own personal hygiene	Washing hands	To make judgements	Identifying the need to wash their hands after certain activities	35
Communication, language and literacy ELG: To use talk to organise and clarify thinking NLS objective: To use a variety of cues when reading	Toad's button	To deduce	Deducing from descriptions which is a character's button, by eliminating descriptions of buttons that don't fit	35
Communication, language and literacy ELG: To link sounds to letters, naming and sounding letters of the alphabet NLS objective: Developing knowledge of grapheme/phoneme correspondences	Word links	To give reasons	Making links between words with the same phonemes and graphemes	36
Communication, language and literacy ELG: To use talk to sequence events NLS objective: To learn new words from shared experiences	Planting bulbs	To give reasons and form opinions	Explaining how, where and why when planting bulbs around the school	37
Mathematical development ELG: To use developing mathematical ideas to solve problems NNS objective: To use everyday words to describe shape, size and position	Missing piece	To deduce	Deducing which piece of a jigsaw puzzle fits where	37
Mathematical development ELG: To relate subtraction to 'taking away' NNS objective: To relate subtraction to 'taking away'	Ten pin bowling	To deduce and interpret	Calculating how many skittles are left standing by counting the number that have been knocked down	38
Knowledge and understanding of the world ELG: To build and construct, selecting appropriate resources and adapting their work	A chair for a bear	To make judgements	Making a chair for one of the Three Bears from 'Goldilocks and the Three Bears'	39
Knowledge and understanding of the world ELG: To know about their own cultures and beliefs and those of others	Pancake day	To form opinions	Learning about the reason behind Pancake Day, linking it to religious beliefs	39
Knowledge and understanding of the world ELG: To find out about past events in their lives and in those of their families	Photographic memory	To interpret photographs	Gaining information about the past from photographs	40
Physical development ELG: To show awareness of space, themselves and others	Pirate adventure	To explain	Deciding where there is enough room to move to on a ship made of PE apparatus in a game	40
Physical development ELG: To handle tools with increasing control	Colouring	To make decisions	Choosing the thickness of brushes and pens to colour a picture	41
Creative development ELG: To recognise repeated sounds and match movements to music	Line dancing	To interpret music	Making up a line-dance sequence, interpreting the music to do so	42
Creative development ELG: To explore colour, shape and space in two dimensions	Pattern links	To give reasons	Linking patterns that have something in common	42

Washing hands

AREA OF LEARNING: PERSONAL, SOCIAL AND EMOTIONAL DEVELOPMENT. ELG: TO MANAGE THEIR OWN PERSONAL HYGIENE.

LEARNING OBJECTIVE
To learn how to care for personal needs.

THINKING OBJECTIVE
To make judgements.

THINKING SKILLS
This activity will help the children identify for themselves when they need to wash their hands. They will need to think for themselves and make judgements about when their hands need washing after certain activities. This is essential if they are to attain the early learning goal of managing their own personal hygiene.

WHAT YOU NEED
A large piece of paper; bowls of warm water; soap; towels (enough for each child to be able to wash their hands during the day); a flip chart or board; Blu-Tack; small squares of paper labels; 'well done' stickers.

WHAT TO DO
Gather the children together and talk about the times they need to wash their hands at home and at school. Make a list of the activities they suggest by drawing pictures and adding labels down the left-hand side of a flip chart. Discuss the process of washing hands with the class and reinforce the importance of using warm water and soap. As you talk about this, ask someone to volunteer to show the rest of the children how to wash hands properly. Give the volunteer the bowl of warm water, the soap and a towel. Explain why they need to dry their hands properly afterwards.

Make a chart out of the page on which you created the drawings of hand-washing activities earlier. Draw lines between each picture to make rows, and place this chart somewhere visible and within easy reaching access for the children.

The next day, show the children the chart you have made from the pictures. Explain how you want the children to add their name to the chart each time they wash their hands after one of the activities on it. Make sure that you plan certain activities that are on the chart, after which the children will be expected to wash their hands.

When the children have finished an activity that is on the chart, encourage them to wash their hands. Invite them to write their names on a label and attach this with Blu-Tack onto the chart, next to the picture of the activity in which they have just taken part.

At the end of the morning or afternoon session, talk about the number of times the children have washed their hands. Ask, *When did you wash your hands? Why did you need to do this after that particular activity? Did anyone forget to wash their hands? Who remembered to wash their hands without being reminded? Did any activities mean you had to wash your hands more than once during them, as well as afterwards?*

At the end of the day, work out with the children how many times they have washed their hands during the day. Get the children to look at the chart and ask, *Which picture has the most/least names next to it?* Ask the children also to make decisions about which activity caused them to wash their hands the most/the least. Give those children who remembered to wash their hands a sticker to say well done.

The next day, clear the chart of the children's names and, after drawing the children's attention to it, let them remember to wash their hands for themselves after activities. Keep the chart going until you are sure that the children are remembering to wash their hands when they need to.

Toad's button

AREA OF LEARNING: COMMUNICATION, LANGUAGE AND LITERACY. ELG: TO USE TALK TO ORGANISE AND CLARIFY THINKING. NLS OBJECTIVE: TO USE A VARIETY OF CUES WHEN READING.

LEARNING OBJECTIVE
To listen to a story and begin to understand the meaning of words.

THINKING OBJECTIVE
To deduce.

THINKING SKILLS
The children will eventually deduce which button belongs to a character in a book by eliminating those that do not fit the book's description, using one criterion at a time, until only one button is left.

THINKING SKILLS: AGES 4–5

WHAT YOU NEED

A copy of 'A Lost Button' from *Frog and Toad are Friends* by Arnold Lobel (Methuen young books); a collection of buttons in a range of colours, size, shape and thickness, with two and four holes, made from different materials, transparent and opaque, including one that is white, round, thick, big, with four holes, like Toad's missing button in the story.

WHAT TO DO

Read the story 'A Lost Button' to the children and talk with them about the characters and what happened in the story. Ask questions to prompt this discussion, such as, *How did the story start and finish? What happened in the middle? Can you name some of the characters?*

Talk about Toad's missing button. Ask, *What was it like? What colour was it? What shape, size and thickness? How many holes did it have?* Show the children your collection of buttons and ask them which one they think belongs to Toad. Let a few children choose the button they think is Toad's, asking them to give reasons for their choice

Read the first part of the story again, up to the point where Toad says that the button can't be his because his button is white not black. Ask the children to find all the white buttons, putting the others to one side. Read the next part of the story until you get to the point where Toad says that his button had four holes not two. Ask the children to find all the white buttons that have four holes, putting the others to one side. Continue like this until the children have deduced which button belongs to Toad. Ask, *How do you know that you have found Toad's button?*

WORD LINKS

AREA OF LEARNING: COMMUNICATION, LANGUAGE AND LITERACY. ELG: TO LINK SOUNDS TO LETTERS, NAMING AND SOUNDING THE LETTERS OF THE ALPHABET. NLS OBJECTIVE: DEVELOPING KNOWLEDGE OF GRAPHEME/PHONEME CORRESPONDENCES.

LEARNING OBJECTIVE

To learn to link phonemes and graphemes.

THINKING OBJECTIVE

To give reasons.

THINKING SKILLS

The children will look closely at different words, matched to their individual learning level, and think about the phonemes and graphemes contained in each one. They will link two words with the same phonemes or graphemes, and will need to give reasons for their linking of the two words.

WHAT YOU NEED

A set of words matched to the different learning needs of the children in your class (they can be based on a current reading text, new vocabulary linked to a current topic, high frequency words, or those containing particular patterns you want the children to learn); a large sheet of paper and writing materials; paper and writing equipment for the children to work in both groups and pairs; small sets of words for the children to use in pairs.

WHAT TO DO

As a class, look at the set of words you have collected and read these together. Ask the children if there are any that they do not know. Then choose one of the words, look at it carefully together and think about the phonemes and graphemes in the word. Ask the children, *Which letter makes the first sound? Which letter makes the second sound and which the last sound?* Then ask the children to find another word from the set that will link to the first word in some way. When the children have chosen a word, ask them to read it and to give their reasons why they have chosen this one. For example, ask *Does it start with the same sound, such as* cat *and* come? *Does it finish with the same sound, such as* sat *and* hit? *Does it start and finish with the same sound, such as* church *and* chaffinch? *Does it rhyme with the first word? Does it have the same letter string? Does it have the same vowel sound in the middle?* Use the terms *phonemes* and *graphemes* if the children are ready for this. Let the children think of these prompts to find another pair of words.

Work with the children in groups on sets of words matched to their individual and group needs. This time write down the two words the children have chosen on a large piece of paper and link them together with an arrow, writing over the top of the arrow the children's reasons for linking the words together. If the children cope well with this, challenge them to find one more word to link with the pair they have chosen for the same or a different reason.

Let the children work in pairs on a small set of words to develop this thinking. Encourage them to give further reasons for choices. If they are unable to write down their reasons, let them draw a line to link the words, highlighting the parts of the words that are the same. This will help them to explain the reasons to you orally.

PLANTING BULBS

AREA OF LEARNING: COMMUNICATION, LANGUAGE AND LITERACY. ELG: TO USE TALK TO SEQUENCE EVENTS. NLS OBJECTIVE: TO LEARN NEW WORDS FROM SHARED EXPERIENCES.

LEARNING OBJECTIVE
To describe what they did when planting bulbs, using the correct vocabulary.

THINKING OBJECTIVES
To give reasons and form opinions.

THINKING SKILLS
The children will think about suitable places to plant bulbs around the school. They will need to give reasons about their choices of planting areas and why they have formed the opinions they have.

WHAT YOU NEED
Bulbs; trowels; grassy or garden areas around the school; pictures of the flowers that will grow from the bulbs you are planting; a flip chart or board; a digital camera.

WHAT TO DO
Show the children the bulbs. Ask if anyone knows what these are and what they might grow into. Either agree with them and show them a picture of the flower the bulbs will become, or show them a picture and explain that a flower will grow from the bulb above the ground once it has been planted. Tell the children that they are going to plant the bulbs around the school. Explain that the flowers will only grow in the springtime, after Christmas, so they will have to be patient and make sure that they do not trample the area where they plant the bulbs. Talk about the colours the children are likely to see when the bulbs grow, to keep their interest in the activity at this point.

All together, or in small groups, go for a walk outside and talk about good places to plant the bulbs. Encourage the children to give reasons for their choices by asking questions, such as *Why do you want to plant the bulbs there?* Get them to consider their opinions of good areas to plant in by asking,

Will the bulbs be safe from roaming feet? Will the flowers be seen there once they grow? On return to the classroom, take a vote on where to plant the bulbs. You may decide to grow them in different places and then you can evaluate which ones have been the most successful and why.

In smaller groups, or as a whole class, go outside and plant the bulbs. Ask an adult to prepare holes in the ground in advance for the children to place their bulbs into. Ask the children which way up they think they should plant the bulbs. When they have finished planting and covering the bulbs, go inside and recall the sequence of the activity, perhaps writing this down for later reference or to accompany any photographs you may have taken of the occasion. Encourage the children to use the correct vocabulary and terms, such as *bulb, trowel, plant, root, soil,* modelling this vocabulary for them if they need more support.

MISSING PIECE

AREA OF LEARNING: MATHEMATICAL DEVELOPMENT. ELG: TO USE DEVELOPING MATHEMATICAL IDEAS TO SOLVE PRACTICAL PROBLEMS. NNS OBJECTIVE: TO USE EVERYDAY WORDS TO DESCRIBE SHAPE, SIZE AND POSITION.

LEARNING OBJECTIVE
To learn to look carefully at the whole to find missing parts.

THINKING OBJECTIVE
To deduce.

THINKING SKILLS
The children will learn to look carefully at different missing pieces in jigsaw puzzles and by using the clues around the missing piece, such as details of the picture, deduce which piece of jigsaw fits into which empty space. This skill can be transferred to their reading and spelling activities.

WHAT YOU NEED
A large floor jigsaw puzzle with which the children are not familiar; about six jigsaw puzzles at different levels of difficulty to match the ability groups of the children in your class.

WHAT TO DO
Ask an additional adult or some older children to fit together six jigsaw puzzles on separate tables prior to the activity. Remove several pieces from each jigsaw and place them on the tables, with the jigsaws to which they belong. Fit together the large floor puzzle, leaving out about four pieces.

Bring the children into the classroom and sit them around the floor jigsaw. Get them to talk about what they can see. Ask, *What is the jigsaw about?* Show the children a picture of the complete jigsaw if you have one and talk about the things that are in it – the people if there are any, the colours and detail.

Draw the children's attention to one of the spaces. Ask someone to say what one of the missing pieces might look like. Ask, *What colours will it have? Will it have a straight edge? What shape will it be? Will it be big or small?* Ask the children to find the missing piece and before putting it into its place, ask the children to say why they think this is the correct piece. Continue with the other pieces until you have completed the jigsaw together.

Explain to the children that there are some jigsaws on the tables with pieces missing. They need to find the pieces that are missing in the same way as they have just done with the floor jigsaw. As they work in their groups, question them to encourage them to think about the kind of pieces they are looking for. *Will it be big or small? What shape will it be? What colour will it be? Will it have any details?*

When the children have finished, repeat the activity, but this time spread the missing pieces around the groups so that they have to find them from different tables. You could also make very large jigsaws for the children to use outside at playtimes.

TEN PIN BOWLING

AREA OF LEARNING: MATHEMATICAL DEVELOPMENT. ELG: TO BEGIN TO RELATE SUBTRACTION TO 'TAKING AWAY'. NNS OBJECTIVE: TO BEGIN TO RELATE SUBTRACTION TO 'TAKING AWAY'.

LEARNING OBJECTIVES

To count numbers to 10; to begin to subtract by counting how many are left.

THINKING OBJECTIVE

To deduce and interpret.

THINKING SKILLS

The children will learn how to deduce the number of skittles knocked down by counting or calculating the difference between those knocked down and those standing. They will use a simple recording sheet and will interpret how many skittles were knocked down the most or least during the game.

WHAT YOU NEED

Ten skittles (or use the number of skittles compatible with the level of the children's ability, for example five might be more suitable for lower attaining children, or use the number of skittles to reinforce the number bond that you wish the

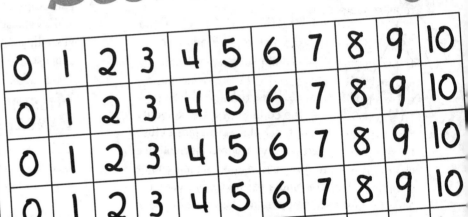

children to learn); an area outside against a wall; chalk; balls; pre-made score cards, marked into columns of squares, one square for each skittle (see illustration above).

WHAT TO DO

Go outside with the children and show them how to set up the skittles. Draw a line a suitable distance away and get them to stand behind it. Tell the children you want them to take it in turns to bowl the ball and try to knock down as many skittles as they can.

Give each child a score card. Tell them to colour in the appropriate number of skittles they knocked down on their sheet. Tell the children that you want them to calculate how many skittles have been knocked down by counting the number left standing and taking this away from the total number of skittles they started with. With lower attaining children, ask them to count how many skittles have been knocked down.

After a few games, take the children back indoors. Look together at the score cards and ask the children to interpret how many skittles were knocked down the most and the least.

A CHAIR FOR A BEAR

AREA OF LEARNING: KNOWLEDGE AND UNDERSTANDING OF THE WORLD. ELG: TO BUILD AND CONSTRUCT, WITH A WIDE RANGE OF OBJECTS, SELECTING APPROPRIATE RESOURCES, AND ADAPTING THEIR WORK WHERE NECESSARY.

LEARNING OBJECTIVE
To make a model from wood and card, selecting materials to use.

THINKING OBJECTIVE
To make judgements.

THINKING SKILLS
The children will be making judgements about size and material in this activity, before using these thinking skills to overcoming problems during and after the making process itself. They will discover that the legs of a chair need to be the same length for the chair to balance and that the ends of the chair legs need to be flat to stand evenly without wobbling. They will need to make judgements about what to do if they find that the legs are not strong enough to hold the size of the seat, or to judge how to hold the balsa wood still while they cut or saw.

WHAT YOU NEED
A copy of 'Goldilocks and the Three Bears'; three teddy bears of different sizes; square templates of three sizes; thick card; thin balsa wood; lengths of balsa wood thick enough to make legs that will stand; warm glue or non-toxic wood glue; snips; saws; sandpaper; tables.

WHAT TO DO
Tell the children the story of Goldilocks and the Three Bears. Talk to them about the Three Bears' chairs. Revisit which bear would have the biggest, middle-sized and smallest chair before asking the children to decide which bear they would each like to make a chair for.

Show the children the thick card and thin balsa wood and explain that these are the materials you want them to make their chairs from. Pass around the three teddy bears so that the children can decide what size the seat of the chair for their bear should be. Ask them to decide which material they think they should use for the seat of their chair and let them cut this from the thick card or thin balsa wood. Give the children the square shapes to draw round and let them cut these out with snips, which should

be suitable for both of the materials. Supervise the children closely to make sure they follow the safety rules for cutting materials.

Work with those children who need help to plan the length of each chair leg, and to think about how these will be cut and attached to the seat. Complete the making task together, helping the children to make judgements about the length of the legs, whether the ends will stand easily and how much glue will be needed. Evaluate the finished chairs for suitability, whether they wobble or will be comfortable for the teddy bears. Ask the children to say whether the legs on their chairs are the same length. Ask, *If the legs are not exactly the same length does this make the chair wobble?* If the legs are the same length and the chair still wobbles ask them if the ends of the legs are flat enough to make the chair more secure.

Extend the activity by getting the children to make tables and beds for a model Three Bears' house.

PANCAKE DAY

AREA OF LEARNING: KNOWLEDGE AND UNDERSTANDING OF THE WORLD. ELG: TO BEGIN TO KNOW ABOUT THEIR OWN CULTURES AND BELIEFS AND THOSE OF OTHER PEOPLE.

LEARNING OBJECTIVE
To learn that some people recognise Pancake Day and others do not.

THINKING OBJECTIVE
To form opinions.

THINKING SKILLS
The children will consider, or learn, who recognises Pancake Day and why, and begin to link this to religious beliefs. They will develop their own opinions about this religious celebration and begin to respect the beliefs of others.

WHAT YOU NEED
Pancake mixture; a means to cook pancakes; sugar; lemon; paper plates; plastic knives and forks.

WHAT TO DO
Before the lesson, check for any food allergies. Start by telling the children what Pancake Day is about. Explain that it takes place the day before Lent starts and that on this day many people give up treats for a few weeks to remember a special story about Jesus. Tell the children the story of how Jesus went into the desert for 40 days and nights to think about and overcome wrongdoings, and that today people give up something in remembrance of this.

Explain how it grew up as a tradition at this time that Christians would use up all the things in their pantry and fridge which would not keep over a number of weeks. Explain that in the past there were no fridges, so things that wouldn't keep well, like butter, milk and eggs, were mixed with flour to make a final meal before Lent.

In groups, mix together the ingredients and make pancakes for the children to share. As they eat, emphasise that it is only Christians who recognise Pancake Day. Many people from other religions do not. Ask the children to express their opinions about Pancake Day.

40

PHOTOGRAPHIC MEMORY

AREA OF LEARNING: KNOWLEDGE AND UNDERSTANDING OF THE WORLD. ELG: TO FIND OUT ABOUT PAST EVENTS IN THEIR OWN LIVES, AND IN THOSE OF THEIR FAMILIES.

LEARNING OBJECTIVE
To learn that life in the past was different from today.

THINKING OBJECTIVE
To interpret photographs.

THINKING SKILLS
The children will look at a range of photographs, some of the past and some modern-day shots. They will interpret both sets to find out about some of the things that people used to do, wear and the way they travelled in the past.

WHAT YOU NEED
Modern photographs of things that the children can relate to, such as people, cars, bicycles; photographs of people in the past enjoying a pastime together, such as a visit to the seaside, school sport's day or similar, which are black and white (try to find a sepia one if you can, too).

WHAT TO DO
Look at the modern photographs with the children and talk about what is happening in the pictures. Talk about the colours the children can see. Ask, *What are the people doing? What clothes are they wearing? What are their hairstyles like?* Perhaps some photographs

have cars or bicycles in them that the children can talk about too.

Then show the children the older photographs and see if they can note immediately that they are in black and white. Point out, therefore, that they cannot comment on the colours of the clothes that the people are wearing. Note the hairstyles, clothes and activities that the people are doing. Ask, *What are the cars like? Are they the same as we have today? What about the bicycles?* Compare the styles and shapes of clothes and cars with any of the modern photographs if you can. Use the opportunity, also, to develop the children's vocabulary by working on their understanding of *modern* and *old-fashioned*.

Finally, talk about how the older photographs help us to learn about the past. List all the things that the children have noticed about the differences in clothes, hairstyles, vehicles and the things that people do. Ask, *How is the past different to today?*

PIRATE ADVENTURE

AREA OF LEARNING: PHYSICAL DEVELOPMENT. ELG: TO SHOW AWARENESS OF SPACE, OF THEMSELVES AND OF OTHERS.

LEARNING OBJECTIVE
To find space independently, considering the space of others.

THINKING OBJECTIVE
To explain.

THINKING SKILLS
The children will have to decide for themselves whether there is enough room to travel along certain parts of a series of apparatus. They will need to understand the concept of space to explain where there are children, or where they themselves are, too close to others on the apparatus.

WHAT YOU NEED
A 'pirate's ship', constructed from different apparatus, including benches, ladders, climbing frames, ropes, planks, balancing beams, gymnastic tables, slides and mats; a loud bell.

WHAT TO DO
Put together the apparatus so that it is possible for a small group of children to explore it safely with them

all working on it at the same time.

Explain to the children that you have constructed a pirate's ship, and show them the apparatus. Tell them that the ship will set sail shortly and that you want them to check that everything is safe on the ship first. Explain that the rules are that only one child is allowed to be on one part of the ship at a time. Explain that each piece of apparatus is one part of the ship, for example a bench, a ladder, a rope. If they get too close to each other, or if there is more than one child on a part of the ship, you will sound the ship's bell. If they hear the bell they should stop immediately.

Find a starting point for each child so that they are safe when they start the game. Every time the children get too close to one another, sound the bell and ask them to look around and explain why you have done this. Point out where there are children too close to each other and ask them to move to a space that is further away from other children. Take this opportunity to ask the successful children to explain how they found a space for themselves.

COLOURING

AREA OF LEARNING: PHYSICAL DEVELOPMENT. ELG: TO HANDLE TOOLS WITH INCREASING CONTROL.

LEARNING OBJECTIVE
To learn to control paintbrushes, felt-tipped pens and crayons to fill colour evenly and within lines.

THINKING OBJECTIVE
To make decisions.

THINKING SKILLS
The children will decide what medium they wish to use to colour in a picture. They will select for themselves the appropriate size of tool for each part of their picture, according to the size of the space they have to colour, in order to colour it in evenly. Finally, they will think about where to start to keep within the line. Some evaluation at the end will be useful to allow the children to adapt their choices and processes another time.

WHAT YOU NEED
Suitable pictures to colour in which have both large and small spaces, and will not take too long to complete (enough for one for each child, and one for you to demonstrate on); paintbrushes of different sizes; watercolours; felt-tipped pens of different thicknesses; wax and pencil crayons; easels; tables.

WHAT TO DO
Show the children the range of pictures and colouring materials and remind them how the different materials are used to colour in. Ask the children to decide which material they want you to demonstrate with and move to the painting table together if this is chosen, or use an easel with the felt-tipped pens or crayons. Look at the picture together and ask the children where they want you to start. Decide together on the colour you will use. If the area the children have chosen is a small space, try to colour it in with a thick brush, pen or crayon, watching what happens and showing how difficult it is. Discuss with the children whether the tool you are using is the best. See if they can match a more appropriate-sized brush, for example, to the size of the space. Suggest this if they do not. Repeat the exercise with another section of the same size, showing how the better-sized tool is easier to use.

Move on to filling a large space. Ask the children how you can be sure to stay inside the line. Show them how to colour around the edge carefully first and how this will help them to stay inside the line when filling in the centre. Colour part of the large space in evenly and the other part erratically. Ask the children to say which is the best way to fill in the colour.

Give each child a picture to colour in and allow them to select their own medium. Let them colour in their pictures as an independent activity. Now and again, monitor what they are doing to make sure that they understand when to use thick and thin equipment and how to fill in colour evenly.

LINE DANCING

AREA OF LEARNING: CREATIVE DEVELOPMENT. ELG: TO RECOGNISE REPEATED SOUNDS AND MATCH MOVEMENTS TO MUSIC.

LEARNING OBJECTIVE
To move rhythmically to a piece of music.

THINKING OBJECTIVE
To interpret music.

THINKING SKILLS
The children will listen to a lively music track, feel the beat and interpret this to create sequences of movements, independently, in small groups and as a whole class. This will help them to develop their musical interpretation skills and their ability to respond to different types of music.

WHAT YOU NEED
A copy of a track by Shania Twain, S-Club or similar, which has a clear four-beat pattern; a tape or CD player; a large space.

WHAT TO DO
Play the music to the class and let them feel the beat. Let the children move independently to the music, interpreting it freely. Watch them as they move and collect their ideas. Introduce claps on the final or first beats, some turns, jumps and stamps, allowing the children to continue to interpret the beat and tempo of the music themselves.

Develop a sequence together, building on a basic four-beat sequence. Ask the children to form smaller groups and let them develop short line-dance sequences that they can repeat over and over again. Build each group's sequence into a class dance.

PATTERN LINKS

AREA OF LEARNING: CREATIVE DEVELOPMENT. ELG: TO EXPLORE COLOUR, SHAPE AND SPACE IN TWO DIMENSIONS.

LEARNING OBJECTIVE
To identify colour, shape and space in patterns.

THINKING OBJECTIVE
To give reasons.

THINKING SKILLS
The children will look carefully at different patterns on items and decide when and where patterns are repeated. They will then link the patterns that have something in common and say what the commonality is, for instance because the colour, shape or picture are the same. They will take part in group activities, drawing upon the information they gleaned from using their reasoning skills.

WHAT YOU NEED
Wallpaper, carpet squares with designs, gift paper, crockery, curtains and other items that have repeating patterns; a felt-tipped pen; printing blocks; paint; paper.

WHAT TO DO
Look at one of your gift paper or wallpaper patterns with the children and talk about the colour and shapes. Ask, *How many patterns are there?* Look carefully and ask the children to suggest if one pattern is repeated. Draw a ring around the pattern that is repeated, linking different instances of it with lines. Write the reason for the link above the lines, such as *Is the same pattern, Is the same colour, Is the same picture.*

Can the children find another pattern? Does that one repeat? Ask, *Is this pattern like the other pattern in any way? How is it the same, if so?* Try to get the children to link the two different patterns, and write above them how they link. Finally, notice together how the designs are always repeated at a similar distance away from each other.

Organise the following group activities. Provide a selection of items which contain patterns for the children to identify the links between the colours, shapes and pictures. Offer another group several lengths of wallpaper and ask them to match the lengths together to cover a space, matching the patterns accurately. Another group can use stamps and paint to design their own repeating patterns.

EXTENDING REASONING SKILLS

Area of learning and ELG, NLS or NNS objective	Activity title	Thinking objective	Activity	Page
Personal, social and emotional development ELG: To dress and undress independently	Getting dressed	To make judgements	Working out a suitable order in which to put on clothing when getting dressed	44
Communication, language and literacy ELG: To explore and experiment with texts NLS objective: To use a variety of cues when reading	Look out mouse	To infer; to give reasons and form opinions	Using picture clues to predict what happens next in a story, giving opinions and reasons for their inferences	45
Communication, language and literacy ELG: To use talk to organise, sequence and clarify thinking, ideas, feelings and events NLS objective: To be aware of story structures	Where is Father Bear?	To deduce	Positioning a teddy bear on a large map in relation to a character's movements being read to them from a story	46
Communication, language and literacy ELG: To use talk to organise, sequence and clarify thinking, ideas, feelings and events	Pizza please	To make decisions	Deciding which pizza toppings to order in a role-play	47
Mathematical development ELG: To count reliably up to 10 everyday objects NNS objective: To count reliably in other contexts	Swaps	To make decisions	Exchanging counters during a game to understand the meaning of value	47
Mathematical development ELG: To use language such as greater, smaller, heavier or lighter to compare quantities NNS objective: To use language to compare two quantities	Water bottles	To explain	Finding a way to measure which vessels hold more or less	48
Knowledge and understanding of the world ELG: To build and construct with a wide range of objects and adapting their work	Making shakers	To deduce	Making shakers, deducing the best method for getting rice into containers without spilling it	50
Knowledge and understanding of the world ELG: To investigate objects and materials by using all of their senses	Matchmaker	To deduce	Playing a matching game using the sense of touch	51
Physical development ELG: To handle tools safely and with increasing control	Negotiation	To make judgements	Judging how to use different tools	52
Physical development ELG: To recognise the importance of keeping healthy and those things which contribute to this	Happy food	To form opinions	Talking about which snacks are healthy and those which are not	53
Creative development ELG: To explore colour in two dimensions	Mixing colours	To make decisions	Making different colours from red, blue and yellow	54
Creative development ELG: To recognise and explore how sounds can be changed	Musical dominoes	To give reasons	Deciding how instruments are the same and different from the sounds they make	56

GETTING DRESSED

AREA OF LEARNING: PERSONAL, SOCIAL AND EMOTIONAL DEVELOPMENT. ELG: TO DRESS AND UNDRESS INDEPENDENTLY.

LEARNING OBJECTIVE
To learn to get dressed independently.

THINKING OBJECTIVE
To make judgements.

THINKING SKILLS
The children will think about the items of clothing they need to put back on when getting dressed after PE and decide which is the best order for these to be put on. They will need to make judgements about how, if they put on one item in the wrong order, it will affect another. After thinking about this as a class they will have the opportunity to decide on an order in small groups.

WHAT YOU NEED
A volunteer from the class with his PE kit; a flip chart or board; dolls and dolls clothes.

WHAT TO DO
Ask for a boy to volunteer to be a model to demonstrate the process of getting dressed. Make sure it is warm enough in the classroom, and ask the boy to get changed into his PE kit. Then ask him to get dressed again and together look at the clothes that have to be put back on. Ask the children to say what should be put on first. Help them to answer by asking questions, such as *Should it be socks and shoes?* Ask the model to put on his socks and shoes. Ask, *What do you think will happen when he tries to put on his trousers? Why do they think this?* Ask the boy to try to put his trousers on over his shoes to see if it is possible. When the children realise that it is too difficult, ask him to remove his shoes and put on his trousers before putting the shoes back on again. Ask, *Would it work if he put just his socks on first?* Discuss whether it is possible for girls to put on skirts if they have their shoes on already. Ask, *Why is this?*

Next, ask the children to decide together whether the boy should put on his shirt or jumper first. Ask, *Why should the shirt be put on first?* Discuss whether the shirt and jumper could be put on before the trousers, socks and shoes. *Why?*

On the flip chart list or draw pictures of the things that must always be put on before another item of clothing, for example socks before shoes, trousers before shoes and shirts before jumpers.

In small groups, ask the children to decide on an appropriate order for getting dressed. They can decide for themselves the order so long as the items agreed on the list are in the correct order. Draw pictures of the order in which the children decide to get dressed on the flip chart. They can then follow this each time they get changed for a physical development activity.

Finish by testing out the children's judgements by asking each group to dress dolls with the same items of clothing in the order they decided. Were they right?

DIFFERENTIATION
Guide lower attaining children through the process using dolls and dolls clothing, asking them to put clothes on in a particular order until they realise that it is always best to put shoes on almost last.

WHERE NEXT
Ask the children to complete Dress the Teddy on the computer to see if they are thinking about the order in which they are putting on each item of clothing. They can either do this individually or work in pairs to discuss their judgements.

Ask the children to get dressed in a different order each time after PE until they have found the best way.

ASSESSMENT
Note the children who apply the knowledge from this activity, and judge the order for getting dressed independently after PE activities better. Note whether these children get dressed faster as a result.

LEARNING OUTCOMES
Most children will think carefully for themselves about the order they put clothes on. They will judge that some items must always be put on first before another particular item of clothing.

FURTHER PERSONAL, SOCIAL AND EMOTIONAL DEVELOPMENT CHALLENGES
Inside out
Give the children items of clothing that are inside

out. Challenge them to find a way to turn them the right side out. Encourage them to watch each other and to make judgements about which is the easiest way to do this.

Dressing up

Give the children items of clothing and costumes to dress up in, either for themselves or to dress dolls in. Ask them to judge the best order for doing this. Ask questions to help them make judgements, such as *Should you put the hat on before the jumper or afterwards? Should sunglasses be on before the hat or afterwards, or does it not matter in this case?*

LOOK OUT MOUSE

AREA OF LEARNING: COMMUNICATION, LANGUAGE AND LITERACY. ELG: TO EXPLORE AND EXPERIMENT WITH TEXTS. NLS: TO USE A VARIETY OF CUES WHEN READING.

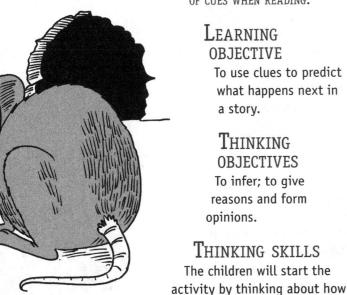

LEARNING OBJECTIVE

To use clues to predict what happens next in a story.

THINKING OBJECTIVES

To infer; to give reasons and form opinions.

THINKING SKILLS

The children will start the activity by thinking about how the title of a book helps them to infer what the story might be about. They will be asked to infer from their knowledge about what poses danger to mice in order to predict which character the mouse in the book is being told to watch out for. They will learn to use picture clues to help them infer what happens next in a story. The picture clues in the book are not obvious, so they will have to look very closely to see where the cat is coming from and the final page has a twist, which the children may or may not be able to infer. There is opportunity in the activity for the children to give their opinions and to give reasons for why they are inferring what they are.

WHAT YOU NEED

A copy of *Mouse, Look Out!* by Judy Waite (Little Tiger Press).

WHAT TO DO

Show the children the book *Mouse, Look Out!* Ask them to look at the front cover and title and suggest what they think the story might be about. Help them by asking questions, such as *Why do you think the mouse is being told to look out? Do you think there is any danger to the mouse from the picture and the title? Is the danger from a person or another animal?* If the children suggest a cat might be involved, ask them to say why they think this.

Read the first part of the story to the children, looking at and talking about what they can see. Ask them to look for clues in the pictures that might suggest what is going to happen next. Ask, *What character do you think will appear? What should we tell the mouse?* Read the speech on the first page, inviting the children to join in. Talk about why the print is larger than the rest of the page. Is it because it should be read with more expression? Practise this with the children.

Continue reading the story a section at a time, looking at the pictures and asking the children to predict from where the cat may appear. Question the children for reasons for their inferences.

When you get to the last page, note that you can see both the cat and the mouse. Ask, *Whose shadow can we see? Who could it be? Who do we need to warn to watch out now? What should we say to the cat? Did anyone infer that this twist might happen?*

End the lesson by asking the children their opinion about whether they like the story and the book. Ask them to give reasons for the opinions they give.

DIFFERENTIATION

For lower attainers, point out the shadow of the cat in the first picture so that the children's attention is drawn to it and so that they can make links between this and what happens on the next page. Tell higher attaining children that the ending is not as expected and invite them to predict possible endings by inferring what they can see in the picture.

WHERE NEXT

Read other stories with the children, using the clues in the pictures to ask them to predict what will happen next.

ASSESSMENT

Note the children who can interpret the pictures independently and use them to predict what may happen on the next page. Identify those children who still need direction to lead them towards an important part of a picture or, if they do see it, cannot link it to the next event.

LEARNING OUTCOMES

Most children will be able to infer what will happen next in a book by using the picture clues. They will learn to look carefully at pictures to help them with the comprehension and use this independently when reading other stories.

FURTHER COMMUNICATION, LANGUAGE AND LITERACY CHALLENGES

What's it about?

Look at a range of book covers, titles and pictures with the children. For each book, ask the children what they think the story is about. Read the story together to find out if they were right.

Back covers

Read the blurb on the back covers of some stories to the children and ask them to identify the key words that give us clues about what the stories are about. Ask them to infer possible characters and events and list these down under the book titles.

WHERE IS FATHER BEAR?

AREA OF LEARNING: COMMUNICATION, LANGUAGE AND LITERACY. ELG: TO USE TALK TO ORGANISE, SEQUENCE AND CLARIFY THINKING, IDEAS, FEELINGS AND EVENTS. NLS OBJECTIVE: TO BE AWARE OF STORY STRUCTURES.

LEARNING OBJECTIVE

To locate a person's position on a simple map.

THINKING OBJECTIVE

To deduce.

THINKING SKILLS

The children will produce a large map of a house and garden based on a story. They will position a teddy bear on the map as the story is read, deducing where the bear should be, and moving him, in relation to the character's movements in the book.

WHAT YOU NEED

Large pieces of paper; pens and crayons; a copy of *Peace at Last* by Jill Murphy (Macmillan Children's Books); a teddy bear.

WHAT TO DO

Read the story *Peace at Last* together and then make a list of all the places that Father Bear visits. Divide the class into groups and ask each group to produce a picture of one of the places that Father Bear visits. When all the groups have finished, put their pictures together to make a pictorial map of Father Bear's house and garden.

Read the first part of the story again. Invite a child to say where he or she thinks Father Bear is on the map at the start of the story. Put the teddy bear on this part of the map.

Read the rest of the story a section at a time and for each room that is mentioned, ask the children to place the teddy bear on the map where they think he is to be found. Ask questions to help the children, such as *Where is Father Bear now? How do you know? What features tell you that he is there?*

When you have finished, look at the map and count the number of places where Father Bear has tried to sleep during the story.

DIFFERENTIATION

Work with lower attaining children in small groups and use the pictures in the story to help them find where Father Bear is on the map. Talk about the things that are found in the pictures and direct the children to finding the same features on the map. Higher attaining children can work independently to locate Father Bear, recording where he is each time with a number to show the order of his visits.

WHERE NEXT

Repeat the activity with other stories involving characters moving from one place to another. Traditional tales would work well, such as 'Little Red Riding Hood', 'Snow White' and 'Hansel and Gretel', and modern ones, such as *We're Going on a Bear Hunt*.

ASSESSMENT

Note the children who deduce where Father Bear is each time by comparing the features in the story to those on their map.

LEARNING OUTCOMES

Most children will locate where Father Bear is on the map by deducing his position from the features in the story, by using either the pictures as clues or the text.

FURTHER KNOWLEDGE AND UNDERSTANDING OF THE WORLD CHALLENGES

Places to sleep

Look at a map of the local area or school grounds and ask the children to deduce where there would be good places for Father Bear to sleep. Why do they think these places are suitable? Is it because they are quiet, safe, comfortable or do they have some other reason?

Pizza please

Area of learning: Communication, language and literacy. ELG: To use talk to organise, sequence and clarify thinking, ideas, feelings and events.

Learning objective
To learn how to ask for a pizza.

Thinking objective
To make decisions.

Thinking skills
The children will consider the range of toppings available to have on a pizza of their choosing. They will decide which toppings they would like and have the opportunity to order their pizza.

What you need
A pizza takeaway menu which details different pizza toppings available; a flip chart or board.

What to do
Ask the children if they have ever had pizza. Explain what a pizza is if any of them don't know. Read the range of pizza toppings available for the children to choose from. Ask them to say which topping they would choose from the list. What if they could choose two? What would they choose then?

Tell the children what your favourite toppings would be and model how you would order this from the pizza takeaway. Model using *please* and *thank you* at the start and end of the conversation.

On the flip chart write down key word prompts to remind the children of how to place an order. Then invite a child to order their favourite pizza, choosing which toppings they would like. Tell them they should decide which toppings to order from the list before they order and then to order this politely from the pretend takeaway. Act out the role of the pizza takeaway place if this makes the activity easier for

the children to sequence. Repeat this, letting more children order pizzas.

Differentiation
Pair up with less able children, taking on the role of ordering the pizza to begin with so that you can model the language for them. Swap roles when you think the child is confident about what to say. More able children could order extras, such as different types of crust.

Where next
Set up a pizza delivery role-play area for the children to act out ordering and delivering pizzas to one another.

Assessment
Assess how well the children are able to choose the pizza toppings they would like from the list.

Learning outcomes
Most children will be able to make choices from a range of pizza toppings. Some will be able to successfully order their pizza.

Further communication, language and literacy challenges
Side order
Get the children to make meal plates of possible side orders that would go well with pizza. Tell the children they can include anything they like, from drinks, salads, crisps and chips, but they must decide on their own side orders. When they have finished, make judgements about whether the children have made healthy decisions or not.

Swaps

Area of learning: Mathematical development. ELG: To count reliably up to 10 everyday objects. NNS objective: To count reliably in other contexts.

Learning objective
To learn conservation of numbers.

Thinking objective
To make decisions.

Thinking skills
The children will develop the skill of exchanging through a fun game, swapping counters for others and understanding the meaning of *value*. They will need to decide for themselves what value different counters are worth, and when it is time to swap these during the game.

WHAT YOU NEED

Bronze, silver and gold counters; enough dice for the class working in groups of four; a large sheet of paper with three circles on it, labelled *bronze*, *silver* and *gold*; smaller pieces of paper with the same circles on (enough for one for each group of four).

WHAT TO DO

Show the children the bronze, silver and gold counters and ask them which they think is the most precious. Most will know that gold is the most precious, then silver and finally bronze.

Decide with the children how many bronze counters each silver one could be worth. Accept numbers that are realistic and that require the children to count to their own level. For example, children who can only count to 5 should choose a number between 1 and 5, while others could choose a number between 1 and 10. Do the same for the silver and gold counters, but this time make sure the children choose a different number to reflect the hierarchy of the counters' worth. Choose the same values when you play the game together, but once the children understand the rules choose different values depending on the abilities of the children.

Tell the children they are going to play a game with the counters. Divide the class into groups of four, ensuring each group has children of the same ability in it, and give each group a die and a paper with the three circles on. Tell them to write their chosen 'swap' number above the bronze and silver circles. Explain that they will throw the die and for each spot on the die the children can collect a bronze counter. They can swap their chosen number of bronze counters to collect a silver one, and then the right number of silver counters to swap for a gold counter. Tell them that the first group to collect a gold counter is the winner.

Supervise the groups to make sure that the swapping exercise is understood, or play the game together first using the large paper with the circles on to familiarise the children with the swapping.

DIFFERENTIATION

Play with silver and gold counters to begin with, then introduce the third bronze type once the children understand the process of exchanging. Higher attaining children can exchange numbers to 10 and start to relate this to coin values.

WHERE NEXT

Get the children to play the game using different colours or stickers, so that the children understand the idea of exchanging.

ASSESSMENT

Note the children who can count reliably and can decide for themselves whether they can swap a number of counters for one different coloured counter.

LEARNING OUTCOMES

The children will learn to exchange a number of counters that have the same value. They will decide for themselves how many to exchange and when.

FURTHER MATHEMATICAL DEVELOPMENT CHALLENGES

How many stickers?

Set up a swapping game for the children to play during a week. Set up Golden Time (where the children choose which activity they would like to do at the end of the week if they earn enough stickers for good behaviour). Agree with the children the sticker price for each particular activity they do during the week. As the week progresses, give the children stickers for good work and behaviour, and explain to them that the stickers can be swapped for a chosen activity at the end of the week. Get the children to decide which activity they would like to choose in advance so that you can work out how many more stickers each child needs to earn in order to be able to do their activity. It will also give you the chance to monitor that the children collect the stickers they need for the activity they have chosen to avoid disappointment.

10p piece

Get the children to exchange different coins to make 10p using a die. Explain that for each spot they throw they can collect 1p. They can swap this collection of 1p coins for the correct number of 2p coins, or 5p coins, with the aim being to make 10p. Extend to 20p or higher totals with higher attaining children.

WATER BOTTLES

AREA OF LEARNING: MATHEMATICAL DEVELOPMENT. ELG: TO USE LANGUAGE SUCH AS GREATER, SMALLER, HEAVIER OR LIGHTER TO COMPARE QUANTITIES. NNS OBJECTIVE: TO USE LANGUAGE SUCH AS MORE OR LESS, TO COMPARE TWO QUANTITIES.

LEARNING OBJECTIVE

To understand the language *full*, *empty*, *holds more* and *holds less* when comparing capacities for containers.

THINKING OBJECTIVE

To explain.

THINKING SKILLS

Through water play, the children will explore a number of different sized bottles to find out which holds more or less.

They will need to explain the measuring taking place, explaining the comparisons in the volume in two different containers.

WHAT YOU NEED

Bottles, cans and plastic containers, which hold different volumes of water; a water tray; a surface on which to order the bottles.

WHAT TO DO

Let the children play with the containers for a few minutes to begin with to develop their understanding of the terms *empty* and *full*. Explain that *full* means when the container will hold no more liquid or water, but that it is not overflowing.

Choose two containers, one that is obviously bigger and, therefore, will hold more than the other. Fill them both with water and ask the children to say which one holds more. Ask them to explain why they think this. (They may suggest it is because one container is bigger or fatter.) Ask the children if they can think of a way to show which container holds more by measuring with water. They may suggest filling the smaller container with water and pouring the contents into the larger one. If they do, explore how the same amount of water fills the smaller container full, to the top, where it fills the larger container only part full. Ask if the children can explain why the larger container is only part full. Is it because it holds more and the other container holds less? How do they know? Choose two more containers and compare them by pouring water. Continue until you are sure that the children understand that to find out which container holds more, they should pour the same amount of water from one to the other and compare how full each one is. The one which is the least full holds more water and the one that is full holds less. Make sure you ask the children to explain the measuring comparisons each time you make one.

Finish by asking the children to think of a way to find out which container holds less. They will need to think laterally to get to their explanation.

DIFFERENTIATION

Show higher attaining children how to measure the amounts of water in litres and half litres. Ask them to find out which containers hold more than half a litre, more than one litre, and more than half a litre but less than one litre, by filling them using a measuring jug. Ask them to explain what they did and the results they achieved. Limit the number of containers for lower attaining children so that they are able to explain that they compare two containers by pouring water from one to the other and that one is fuller than the other.

WHERE NEXT

Transfer the understanding of *full*, *empty*, *holds more* and *holds less* by filling containers and transferring sand. What do the children notice? Can they explain what they have found out?

ASSESSMENT

Note the children who understand the concepts of *full* and *empty* and can use this knowledge and understanding to explain which container holds more or less water.

LEARNING OUTCOMES

Most children will learn to explain the measuring involved when comparing the capacity of containers.

FURTHER MATHEMATICAL DEVELOPMENT CHALLENGES

Ten full bottles

Give the children a set of bottles and ask them to order them according to the amount of water they hold. Explain that they can do this by pouring the same amount of water from one to the others. They may see immediately which holds the least and most, but may need to compare two at a time to succeed in putting them in order. Ask them to explain how they solved this problem.

Sand containers

Fill containers with sand and ask the children to find out which one holds the most and least amount of sand. When they explain their process of measuring and comparing, listen to see if they have applied the pouring method of measuring.

MAKING SHAKERS

AREA OF LEARNING: KNOWLEDGE AND UNDERSTANDING OF THE WORLD. ELG: TO BUILD AND CONSTRUCT WITH A WIDE RANGE OF OBJECTS, SELECTING APPROPRIATE RESOURCES, AND ADAPTING THEIR WORK WHERE NECESSARY.

LEARNING OBJECTIVE

To make suitable shakers in the most effective and tidy way.

THINKING OBJECTIVE

To deduce.

THINKING SKILLS

The children will choose which shaker they want to make according to which sound they like. They will deduce which way is best for getting the rice and pulses into the containers without spilling any. They will need time to make decisions about this and to make a mess if necessary. This will help them to gain confidence to make decisions and to use the information for any similar activity.

WHAT YOU NEED

Empty, washed yoghurt pots, plastic drinks bottles and other containers with small necks; lids for the bottles and containers; dried pulses, rice and pasta shapes; ready-made shakers, made from the items listed above; a funnel.

WHAT TO DO

Explain to the children that they are going to make shakers to accompany a favourite story with sound. *We're Going on a Bear Hunt* by Michael Rosen (Walker Books) is a particular favourite for this type of activity.

Show the children the containers and the items used in each to produce the sounds. Then let them hear the sounds that each ready-made shaker makes. Allow the children to decide which sound they like best so that they can choose the things they want to use to make the shaker of their choice.

Set them a challenge. Explain that the cleaner has a very important party to go to that evening and won't have much time to clean the classroom when everyone has left. Tell the children that they have to try to make the shakers without making a mess.

Get out a bottle that has a fairly narrow neck, and try to pour rice directly from the packet into the neck without spilling any. Make a big act of not being able to do this without making a mess. Ask the children what you could do to pour the rice into the bottle more neatly. Encourage them to think laterally and make suggestions like choosing a container with a wider or bigger opening, like a yoghurt pot, or putting the rice grains in one at a time. Make a big fuss about it taking too long to do this if they suggest the latter. Can anyone think of another way, perhaps by using something available in the classroom to help?

Some children may remember their play in the sand tray at this point, when they use funnels to pour sand into bottles without spilling any. You may wish to ask questions to direct their thinking towards this.

Allow the children to explore the materials and containers and see if they can find ways for themselves of filling them without spilling anything, before giving them a funnel. When you do, make sure the funnel is too small for some of the dried peas and pasta shapes to pass through. Gather the children together and talk about the difficulties with the ready-made funnel. (There is only one so it will take a long time to pass the funnel around for everyone to use. Also, it is too small for the pasta shapes to pass through.)

Can the children think of anything else

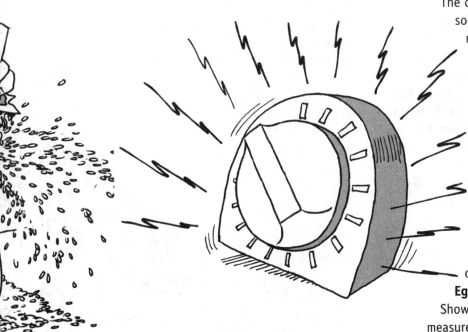

that will help them to make a funnel-like tool to help? You could show some children how to make a simple cone shape from paper to use as a suitable funnel to fill the containers.

DIFFERENTIATION
Some children may not have the control necessary to fill the bottles. Give them containers with wider openings but which still present them with the challenge required for learning. Give higher attaining children paper from which they must engineer a funnel. Let them do the activity last, giving them containers with smaller openings through which to pour their chosen fillings.

WHERE NEXT
Ask the children to fill small bottles with different coloured sand. The sand can be bought commercially, or colour some yourself using silver sand and food colourings. What techniques and materials will the children use? Provide higher attainers with materials from which they must make their own funnels, rather than letting them use those provided for other children.

ASSESSMENT
Watch the children as they complete the challenges and note those who use funnels to transfer their rice and pulses. Make a special note of those children who are creative and make their own funnels from paper and card to fit the container they are using.

LEARNING OUTCOMES
The children will learn to deduce how to solve a particular problem when making models. They will gain confidence to try to solve problems independently.

FURTHER KNOWLEDGE AND UNDERSTANDING OF THE WORLD CHALLENGES
Swapping water
Set up a game in an area of the classroom where the children transfer water and/or sand from large to small containers that have small necks. The child who fills the most containers with the same amount of water or sand is the winner.
Egg timers
Show the children a range of egg timers that measure time by transferring sand from one side to the other. Talk about how the small grains move through the small space, and about the shape of the containers to direct the sand in the desired direction. Use bottles and other small containers for the children to make their own timers. Ask them to find out how long it takes for the sand to flow from one container to another.

MATCHMAKER

AREA OF LEARNING: KNOWLEDGE AND UNDERSTANDING OF THE WORLD. ELG: TO INVESTIGATE OBJECTS AND MATERIALS BY USING ALL OF THEIR SENSES AS APPROPRIATE.

LEARNING OBJECTIVE
To use their senses to find matching objects and materials.

THINKING OBJECTIVE

To deduce.

THINKING SKILLS

The children will play a series of games which will develop their ability to identify different textures through using their sense of touch. They will deduce which fabrics and objects match using knowledge of pattern and texture, and following descriptions.

WHAT YOU NEED

A range of fabrics with different textures; objects with obvious patterns and which have interesting textures, such as sieves, wide-weft fabrics, embossed wallpaper, socks, flowerpots; a drawstring bag or covered box; a display board.

WHAT TO DO

Set up the following games to enable the children to explore a range of materials using their sense of touch:

Game 1

Put the range of fabrics in the drawstring bag or box, and display a matching set of fabrics on a board. Ask the children to feel the textured fabrics on the board one at a time and to find the corresponding fabric in the bag. As they are looking for the match, ask them to describe what they are looking for. Ask, *Are you looking for a rough, soft, fluffy or silky piece of fabric? How do you know that piece of fabric is the matching texture?*

Game 2

Put the objects in the drawstring bag or box and describe one of them to the children. Ask the children to find the object from the description, giving reasons for their deduction.

Game 3

With the same set of objects in the bag or box, ask a child to describe what they are feeling and ask another to find it from a set of matching objects.

DIFFERENTIATION

Play Game 2 first with lower attaining children, using objects that are very different to the touch. This will help them develop their deduction skills first before moving on to more difficult sensory comparisons. Higher attaining children should move to Game 3 first and then to the extension activities, below. This will require them to use more than one sense in their deductions.

WHERE NEXT

Play other feely bag activities where the children can use their senses to deduce what is in the bag.

ASSESSMENT

Watch the children as they play the games and note who uses their senses to consider the similarities and differences which will help them to deduce which texture matches which object or fabric.

LEARNING OUTCOMES

Most children will learn to use at least one sense to work out which object and fabric match which. Some will use more than one sense to deduce this.

FURTHER KNOWLEDGE AND UNDERSTANDING OF THE WORLD CHALLENGES

Which rubbing?

Make rubbings of the objects in your collection and display these on a board. Ask the children to deduce which rubbing was made from which object. Extend the activity by putting the objects in the drawstring bag or box. Ask the children to look closely at the rubbings and then to deduce by finding the matching texture which object matches each rubbing.

Sandcastles

Make a set of sandcastles and ask the children to deduce which mould made each one. Ask them to make a matching set in another sand tray to test out their thinking.

NEGOTIATION

AREA OF LEARNING: PHYSICAL DEVELOPMENT. ELG: TO HANDLE TOOLS SAFELY AND WITH INCREASING CONTROL.

LEARNING OBJECTIVE

To learn how to use various tools to join paper and card.

THINKING OBJECTIVE

To make judgements.

THINKING SKILLS

The children will look carefully at a collection of different tools and make judgements about the way they should be used in order to handle them safely. They will try out these safety rules themselves.

WHAT YOU NEED
A homemade book, joined together with staples; a collection of tools, including scissors, snips, staplers (with staples), sticky tape and holder, glue guns, a hole punch and paper clips; large pieces of paper and coloured pencils or crayons; a range of paper and card for making books.

WHAT TO DO
Show the children a homemade book that is joined together with staples. Ask the children to say how the staples were put into the paper. Ask, *What tool was used?* Let them identify this and tell them the name if they do not already know. Ask them to think about how the stapler should be used in order to keep safe. Listen to them judging how to use it and then show them how to use the stapler safely. Muse with them some of the things that could go wrong if it is not used correctly. Draw pictures on a large piece of paper that show a sequence of rules for using the stapler safely and put this in the centre of a table for reference.
Repeat this with the other tools in your collection, with particular emphasis on how these should be used and carried from one place to another safely. For each tool record in pictures how they should be used for the children to refer to during practical activities.
Set up tables with a range of paper and card, and one tool. Put the paper with the drawings of the safety sequence for the appropriate tool on the table too. In groups, let the children move from table to table making different things and joining the paper and card together using the tools on offer at each table. Monitor them closely to make sure that they are using the tools safely by following the rules and sequences they have agreed.

DIFFERENTIATION
Higher attaining children can make safety reference cards for other tools in the classroom with which they are familiar.

WHERE NEXT
Look together at construction tools, such as saws, hammers and screwdrivers, and judge the safety issues for their use.

ASSESSMENT
Note the children who can judge the safety implications of using tools and who can use this knowledge to decide a set of rules for use.

LEARNING OUTCOMES
The great majority of children will be able to judge for themselves how to use different tools safely, and thus be able to work and make choices independently about how to join paper and card.

FURTHER PHYSICAL DEVELOPMENT CHALLENGES
Staples or sticky tape
Set up a card-making activity and let the children judge whether to use sticky tape or staples to stick a cut-out picture to the front of a card. They should decide which to use and to make judgements about how they will use their chosen tool safely.

HAPPY FOOD

AREA OF LEARNING: PHYSICAL DEVELOPMENT. ELG: TO RECOGNISE THE IMPORTANCE OF KEEPING HEALTHY AND THOSE THINGS WHICH CONTRIBUTE TO THIS.

LEARNING OBJECTIVE
To learn which snacks are healthier than others.

THINKING OBJECTIVE
To form opinions.

THINKING SKILLS
The children will think about when they feel hungry and the changes that take place in their bodies to tell them this. They will consider the types of snack that are healthy and those that aren't, giving their own opinions to sort a variety of snacks into these two groups.

WHAT YOU NEED
A copy of the song 'Something Inside Me' by Kenneth Simpson in *Flying a Round*, edited by David Gadsby and Beatrice Harrop (Black); pictures and empty packets of snacks, such as biscuits, crisps, cakes and sweets, fruit, low-fat yoghurts, muesli bars.

WHAT TO DO
Teach the class the song and talk about what it is inside that tells them that it is time for them to eat.

Relate this to times when the children feel hungry. Identify with them when this usually happens and relate these times to the meals they eat in a day. Do the children feel hungry at other times? How do they know they are hungry? What happens in their bodies to tell them?

Talk about the need to eat a healthy and balanced diet, and that too many sweets and fatty foods are unhealthy. Explain that it is important for young children to eat some of these foods and that it is OK for them to eat sweets and cakes in smaller quantities.

Together look at the empty snack packets and pictures you have and separate them into healthy snacks and not so healthy snacks, basing the sorting according to the children's own opinions. Label each set *healthy* and *less healthy*. Discuss with the children their opinion about what they think are healthy snacks. Organise these for them to enjoy over the next few days.

DIFFERENTIATION

Help those who have difficulty understanding by telling them which foods are healthier than others. Relate this knowledge to their snack choices over the next few days to inform their opinions. Higher attaining children can start to think about the reasons for healthier choices in terms of added vitamins and less fat content. They should be encouraged to use these reasons when giving their opinions.

WHERE NEXT

Make healthy recipes together for snack time, for example fruit salad, vegetable fingers, muesli bars, making sure you heed any food allergies – especially to nuts.

ASSESSMENT

Note the children who are happy to give their opinions about what is a healthier snack. Note those who apply this opinion to their snack choices during the week. Make particular note of the children who give suitable reasons for their opinions in terms of healthy living, caring for the body or content of the food items.

LEARNING OUTCOMES

Most children will develop an awareness of their needs for staying healthy by forming opinions about what they should or should not choose for a healthier snack.

FURTHER PHYSICAL DEVELOPMENT CHALLENGES

Self-service meals

Collect pictures of food items and meals that are healthy and not so healthy, and use them in the role-play area with the children. Challenge the children to choose healthy meals, a balanced meal and not so healthy meals.

Snack time

Put out snacks and drinks for the children to enjoy. Let the children decide for themselves when it is time to have a snack.

They should be encouraged to say why they need to eat rather than just eating for the sake of it.

MIXING COLOURS

AREA OF LEARNING: CREATIVE DEVELOPMENT. ELG: TO EXPLORE COLOUR IN TWO DIMENSIONS.

LEARNING OBJECTIVE

To learn how to make colours by mixing red, blue and yellow.

Thinking Objective
To make decisions.

Thinking Skills
The children will make different colours by mixing red, blue and yellow paint and will decide which colours to put together when filling in spaces on a pattern. This activity can be set within any story involving patches of colour, such as *Elmer* or *The Patchwork Quilt*, or can be an individual and independent creative painting activity.

What You Need
A copy of the story *White Rabbit's Colour Book* by Alan Baker (Kingfisher Books); red, yellow and blue paints; mixing trays; water pots; paper with or without patterns drawn on it (enough for each child in the class); paintbrushes.

What to Do
Read the story *White Rabbit's Colour Book* to the class and talk about the colours that the rabbit made as he dipped his tail, and so on, into the different pots of paint.

Look at the red, blue and yellow paints and ask the children to say how they can make the other colours in the book using only these three colours. Does anyone know, for example, that if you mix red and blue it will make purple? Show the children how to mix the paints to make different colours, making sure they clean their brushes properly before mixing their next colour.

Prepare a sheet of paper with a pattern on for the children to fill with colour. This can be curved, straight, or a series of zig-zag lines, or a mixture of the three. Alternatively, let the children design a pattern for themselves if they are able. Show the children how to fill inside one of the spaces with the purple mixed paint. Mix another colour and decide which space to fill with this colour. Ask, *Shall I paint the space next to the first one? What will happen to the wet paint?* Explain that it is better to fill a space that is not next to the first one so that the first one has chance to dry.

Let the children paint inside their own patterns, mixing as many colours as they like and filling in the spaces. Ensure that the children decide for themselves which colours to paint next to each other. Ask the children why they put the colours they did next to each other. Was it because they were different or nearly the same?

When the paint is dry, the children could paint a pattern in contrasting colours next to each coloured space.

Differentiation
Let lower attaining children explore the range of colours they can make from only two different colours of paint before moving on to three. Give higher attaining children black and white paint in addition so that they can explore the tones and tints of colours. This will limit or extend the decisions about colour choices, respectively.

Where Next
Get the children to make pictures with tissue paper and glue. Ask them to stick overlapping coloured cellophane paper onto plain sheets of paper. Make tissue paper patterns by gluing pieces of tissue paper to white paper. They can paint over the top with water, letting the dye run from the tissue onto the white paper. When it is almost dry, they can remove the tissue to reveal the pattern underneath.

Assessment
Note the children who decide independently to combine a range of colours to make contrasting or varied patterns. Note those who understand that new colours are made by mixing others and that this will extend their choices and decisions.

Learning Outcomes
Most children will decide for themselves which colours to use to colour in their patterns. They will happily say why they have decided on the choices

they have. A few children will need support in this process, being content to colour in with almost the same colour, or putting similar colours next to each other.

FURTHER CREATIVE DEVELOPMENT CHALLENGES

Iced buns
Make some buns and decorate each one with designs cut from ready-made icing, for example a Christmas tree, a butterfly or flower shapes. You could also put a square of icing on top of each for the children to decorate onto. Show the children spray or bottles of colouring in red, blue and yellow and ask them to decide which ones to combine to make the Christmas tree the right colour, the butterfly purple and the flowers orange.

Make a rainbow
Get the children to use the food colouring to make rainbows on pieces of blotting paper. Ask them to decide which colour to use first before asking them to decide which and how to apply the second colour. As they do this, watch the colours spread into each other and change colour. Ask the children to give reasons why this is happening. Let them explore the colours and create their own carpet of colours.

MUSICAL DOMINOES

AREA OF LEARNING: CREATIVE DEVELOPMENT. ELG: TO RECOGNISE AND EXPLORE HOW SOUNDS CAN BE CHANGED.

LEARNING OBJECTIVE
To understand how to change the sounds that musical instruments make.

THINKING OBJECTIVE
To give reasons.

THINKING SKILLS
The children will consider the range of sounds different instruments make and use this knowledge to suggest how they are the same and how they are different. They will give reasons for their opinions in terms of the kind of sound that is being made, whether it is the same pitch, dynamic or tempo.

WHAT YOU NEED
A large set of musical dominoes that are divided

into two halves, with pictures of a percussion instrument on one side leaving the other side empty for the children to add a type of sound; a selection of percussion instruments which produce different sounds and which correspond with the instruments on the dominoes.

WHAT TO DO
Let the children explore the different sounds they can make on each of the instruments. While they are working, talk to them about what sort of sounds they are producing, encouraging them to explain in terms of whether the sounds are long, short, fast, slow, shake, tap, and scrape. This will model the language they will need later.

Tell the children that they are going to play a game with musical dominoes.

Give each group a set of dominoes and some writing materials. Working in groups of four, play a sound for the children to listen to and describe together. Ask each group to choose a domino with a picture of the musical instrument you used on it and to write the sound you made on the empty half of the domino. For example, the domino could have a drum on one side and the children could write *tap* on the other.

Explain to the children that the idea of the game is to match all the dominoes in their set together. Invite the children to match the first musical domino with their own sound, by either playing a sound on a drum or playing a different instrument to create a tap. If they choose to play a different sound on a drum, tell them they should choose one of their drum dominoes and add the type of sound they make on the empty half, matching the two drums on the dominoes together. If they decide to make a tapping sound on a different instrument, tell them they should choose a domino with a picture of the new instrument on it, adding the word *tap* and matching it with the *tap* half of the first domino.

Go around the groups to make sure the children understand how to play the game.

Ask questions to prompt them to explain the reasons why they are choosing the instruments or sounds they are, such as *Why did you choose to play the instrument in this way? How is it the same as the sound that that instrument made? Did you play this instrument in the same way?*

Continue with the game until the groups have matched all their dominoes.

DIFFERENTIATION

Limit the domino matches to the way the instruments are played with lower attaining children. This will limit their choices, but make it easier for them to give reasons for the sounds they have made. Higher attaining children should work with tuned percussion instruments as well so that they can think about higher and lower sounds. They should be expected to give reasons for how they changed the

musical elements as well as the way they played the instrument each time.

WHERE NEXT

Repeat the game, but this time ask the children to match differences in sounds or instruments. For example, if they tap the drum, the next person should use the drum to produce a different sound and add this domino to the first. If the first sound is made on a drum, a different instrument should be chosen to match the sound.

ASSESSMENT

Note the children who are able to give reasons for their choices. Can they explain how either their instrument or the sound is the same in some way?

LEARNING OUTCOMES

Most children will learn to give reasons for their choice of instrument and the sounds they make in some way. Some will go beyond this by giving reasons for how they matched the same type of sound.

FURTHER CREATIVE DEVELOPMENT CHALLENGES

Musical sound effects

Get the class to add sound effects to a favourite story. Choose one instrument only for the children to play, asking them to change the sound by playing it in a different way or changing the type of sound they produce. The children should give reasons for why they think their sound matches the effect the story requires.

Copy cat

Sing a song for the children to make the same or different sounds to, such as Verse 1 below which can be sung to the tune of London Bridge.

Who can play a sound like this?
Sound like this, sound like this,
Who can play a sound like this:
Tap, fast on a drum.

Play the sound you mention in the last line of the verse and tell the children they should make a similar sound by choosing the same instrument, playing it in the same way, or producing the same type of sound. They should answer your verse, by singing something similar to Verse 2, below:

I can play a sound like this
Sound like this, sound like this,
I can play a sound like this
Tap, fast on a drum.

The children's reasons for playing what and in the way that they have are included in the words of their verse.

ENQUIRY SKILLS

INTRODUCTION

Enquiry skills in the foundation stage develop the children's natural inquisitiveness. It is a cyclical process that builds in a structured way towards the children making sense of the world in which they live. It helps them to ask questions to identify what is happening and investigate how things work. They will develop the language skills necessary to describe what they have found out. Young children may not be able to define a problem themselves. It is important for them to know what the problem is and what they need to look for in order to find an answer to the problem. The skill goes beyond just identifying that there is a problem, although for less able children this may be as much as you can expect. With support, many children will be able to break down the problem so that they can identify which specific part needs to be addressed in order to solve it or to find the answer. When planning what to do, they will be thinking about how they will go about finding out about things. Research with young children often means looking and noticing what is happening, experiencing things by using their senses, noting changes and pattern and relationship within processes and by talking about what they see, feel, hear, taste and smell. They will decide what is the same and what is different between two things and consider this importance in helping them to draw conclusions about the world in which they live.

Enquiry in the Reception class relies on teachers modelling for children the enquiry process. Therefore,

rather than children anticipating consequences for themselves, the teacher needs to set up situations where they can begin to predict what they think might happen as a result of certain actions, which is the first step to anticipating consequences. These situations can be set within exploration of the natural world, by using their senses to investigate mixtures and changes in materials, or through considering the impact of their actions on others.

Finally, the children need to be able to test out their conclusions to find out whether what they thought would happen does. This helps them to realise that there is a cycle of processes to undertake during enquiry – they need to investigate, to have some idea or what they think may happen, to anticipate consequences and in order to inform eventual research to guide the testing out of predictions. Once this cycle is complete, some kind of consideration of how to use the information gained to improve ideas is needed. This starts the cycle again.

The enquiry skills in isolation are:
⊙ asking questions
⊙ defining a problem
⊙ planning research
⊙ predicting outcomes
⊙ anticipating consequences
⊙ testing conclusions
⊙ improving ideas.

INTRODUCING ENQUIRY SKILLS

Area of learning and ELG, NLS or NNS objective	Activity title	Thinking objective	Activity	Page
Personal, social and emotional development ELG: To understand what is right, what is wrong, and why	Caring	To anticipate consequences	Considering how to look after a pet and the consequences of forgetting to do these things	60
Communication, language and literacy ELG: To show an understanding of the elements of stories NLS objective: To be aware of story structures	Who was Noah?	To plan research	Comparing different versions of the same story, identifying the clues that will tell them if all the versions tell the same story	60
Communication, language and literacy ELG: To listen with enjoyment and respond to stories Personal, social and emotional development ELG: To consider the consequences of their words and actions for themselves and others	Behaving well	To anticipate consequences	Reading a story and saying what the consequences of certain actions could be	61
Communication, language and literacy ELG: To know that print carries meaning NLS objective: That words are ordered left to right and need to be read that way to make sense	Silly sentences	To define a problem	Identifying why sentences don't make sense	61
Mathematical development ELG: To use language to compare quantities NNS objective: To use language to compare two quantities	My feet	To ask questions	Asking questions to help find out similarities and differences between all their feet	62
Mathematical development ELG: To use language to describe the shape and size of solids NNS objective: To talk about, recognise and recreate patterns	Threading	To predict outcomes	Predicting and making patterns by threading beads	63
Knowledge and understanding of the world ELG: To ask questions about why things happen and how things work	Torch capers	To test conclusions	Discovering what makes a torch work	63
Knowledge and understanding of the world ELG: To investigate objects and materials by using their senses	Sandcastles	To anticipate consequences	Mixing sand and water to create the best consistency to make sandcastles	64
Knowledge and understanding of the world ELG: To begin to know about their own cultures and beliefs and those of other people	Harvest festival	To plan research	Researching the American festival of Thanksgiving	64
Knowledge and understanding of the world ELG: To investigate objects and materials by using their senses	Bottle skittles	To define a problem	Making skittles from bottles and testing them to see if they need to make any improvements	65
Physical development ELG: To handle tools safely and with increasing control	Cutting out	To anticipate consequences	Making a window cover in a card	65
Physical development ELG: To use a range of small and large equipment	Target practice	To test conclusions	Exploring which is the best way to throw different equipment at different targets	66
Creative development ELG: To match movements to music	How many beats?	To define a problem	Creating a dance by responding to music	66
Creative development ELG: To explore colour, texture and shape in two dimensions	Oil on water	To predict outcomes and test conclusions	Predicting patterns when oil is mixed with water	67

CARING

AREA OF LEARNING: PERSONAL, SOCIAL AND EMOTIONAL DEVELOPMENT. ELG: TO UNDERSTAND WHAT IS RIGHT, WHAT IS WRONG, AND WHY.

LEARNING OBJECTIVE
To care for living things.

THINKING OBJECTIVE
To anticipate consequences.

THINKING SKILLS
The children will consider what they need to do to look after a pet. They will anticipate what the consequences of forgetting to do any of the things they have suggested would be.

WHAT YOU NEED
A collection of pet care products; a flip chart or board.

WHAT TO DO
Show the children the pet care products and ask them what they think they are for. Talk about how the food bowl is suitable for the pet to feed from and why. Discuss the importance of giving pets enough water to drink. Talk about each item in your collection. Make a list on the flip chart of all the things that they should do to look after a pet, using the items in your pet care collection as prompts. Ask prompt questions, such as *What do animals need? How can we care for them? How often should we feed them? Where can they sleep? Will that be a comfortable place? How can we help them to keep warm?*

Then ask what the consequences of forgetting each thing on the list would be. Ask questions to encourage the children's thinking, based on the list, such as *What would happen if we forgot to feed a pet?*

Repeat the activity for different types of pets and for plants and flowers.

WHO WAS NOAH?

AREA OF LEARNING: COMMUNICATION, LANGUAGE AND LITERACY: ELG: TO SHOW AN UNDERSTANDING OF THE ELEMENTS OF STORIES, SUCH AS MAIN CHARACTER, SEQUENCE OF EVENTS AND OPENINGS. NLS OBJECTIVE: TO BE AWARE OF STORY STRUCTURES.

LEARNING OBJECTIVE
To understand the main elements of the story of Noah.

THINKING OBJECTIVE
To plan research.

THINKING SKILLS
The children will look at a number of books that all tell the same story. They will think about how to find out if the books all tell the same story, identifying those things which will give them clues (text and illustrations). In groups, the children will research a different book and report back on the story elements, for example what the story was about, what order events happened in and what characters appeared.

WHAT YOU NEED
Different books which tell the story of Noah and which contain lots of illustrations; a flip chart or board.

WHAT TO DO
Listen to, or read, the story of Noah with the children. Then, show them the range of books you have and explain that they all tell the story of Noah. Ask the children, *How can we find out whether the story is the same when it is told in the different books?* Listen to the children's suggestions. Guide them towards comparing the illustrations in the books. Read the relevant text by the illustrations to the children to help them find out. Together, research the

illustrations in all the books to see if the same things appear in the drawings. Ask, *Can we tell how the story goes from the pictures?*

Divide the class into groups and give each group a different book. Look with them at the illustrations and retell the story. While you work with one group, other groups can be engaged in self-initiated tasks, such as playing with a toy Noah's Ark and acting out the story, or acting out the story in a Noah's Ark role-play area. When all the groups have read their books, organise a plenary session for the children to retell the story they heard in their groups to the rest of the class. Sequence the story that each group tells in pictures on the flip chart. Using the pictures, decide together whether the story was the same in each of the books.

Tell the children that the story of Noah is told in a number of sacred texts, including the Bible and the Jewish Torah, and that it is important to people of different religions. Explain that this is why it always contains the same characters and events, and is told in the same order.

Behaving well

AREA OF LEARNING: COMMUNICATION, LANGUAGE AND LITERACY. ELG: TO LISTEN WITH ENJOYMENT, AND RESPOND TO STORIES. NLS OBJECTIVE: TO BE AWARE OF STORY STRUCTURES, AND THE WAYS THAT STORIES ARE BUILT UP AND CONCLUDED. AREA OF LEARNING: PERSONAL, SOCIAL AND EMOTIONAL DEVELOPMENT. ELG: TO CONSIDER THE CONSEQUENCES OF THEIR WORDS AND ACTIONS FOR THEMSELVES AND OTHERS.

Learning objective
To predict possible consequences in a story.

Thinking objective
To anticipate consequences.

Thinking skills
The children will listen to a story and try to think about what the consequences of certain actions or behaviour by the characters might be. Once they are practised in this, the children can move on to relating this to their own behaviour when playing together in the classroom, or when outside on the playground. Some children may think about their behaviour at home and consider how they can keep themselves safe.

What you need
A copy of *Suddenly!* by Colin McNaughton (Picture Lions).

What to do
Read the first part of the story to the children and every time you get to the part where the text says *suddenly...* ask them to consider the possible consequences of the wolf's actions. Ask the children questions to help them anticipate what will happen, such as *What is the wolf trying to do? What will Preston do? What might the consequences of Preston's actions be?*

Read the next page to see if the children's thinking was the same as the author's each time. Continue in this way, talking together about the last page as you reach it and see if the children can anticipate what might happen at the end of the story.

Ask the children to think about times when they need to consider the impact of their actions on others. For example, talk about the times when someone has refused to allow a friend to join their game, or someone has called someone else a name or has ignored a request for help. This could form the basis of several circle-time activities where the children consider rules for different areas in the classroom, the playground and when out and about with their parents and friends.

Silly sentences

AREA OF LEARNING: COMMUNICATION, LANGUAGE AND LITERACY. ELG: TO KNOW THAT PRINT CARRIES MEANING AND, IN ENGLISH, IS READ FROM RIGHT TO LEFT AND FROM TOP TO BOTTOM. NLS OBJECTIVE: THAT WORDS ARE ORDERED LEFT TO RIGHT AND NEED TO BE READ THAT WAY TO MAKE SENSE.

Learning objective
To learn that in English we read from left to right for the text to make sense.

Thinking objective
To define a problem.

Thinking skills
The children will need to identify problems when reading, explaining why text that they have read doesn't make sense. Once they have defined the problem – because the sentences are not in the correct order, or a word has been substituted – they will be able to read the text in the correct order to make sense of it.

What you need
Any big book with which the children are familiar and which contains simple sentences that they can read themselves.

WHAT TO DO

Read the first part of the book to the children. Allow them to join in with familiar words and sentences to get them involved in the story.

On one page, read the sentences in the wrong order so that the text does not make sense. Ask the children what is wrong with what you have just read, and if necessary read it again. Help them by asking, *Why doesn't it make sense? Have I read the words in the correct order? Which way should the words be read?* Invite a child to read the words in the right order and ask the children if the text makes sense now. Continue in this way, every so often reading a couple of sentences in the wrong order so that the story does not make sense and inviting the children to say why and what you need to do to make it make sense.

On occasions, substitute another word for one written in a sentence so that it obviously does not make sense. Ask the children which word is stopping the sentence from making sense. Invite them to think of a substitute(s) so that the sentence will make sense.

In a small group afterwards, show higher attaining children how the order of words can be changed to turn a sentence into a question. Explain that because the sentence or question is always read from left to right, it always makes sense.

MY FEET

AREA OF LEARNING: MATHEMATICAL DEVELOPMENT. ELG: TO USE LANGUAGE TO COMPARE QUANTITIES. NNS OBJECTIVE: TO USE LANGUAGE TO COMPARE TWO QUANTITIES.

LEARNING OBJECTIVE

To learn that people have different sized feet and how to measure this.

THINKING OBJECTIVE

To ask questions.

THINKING SKILLS

The children will look at their feet and notice things about them. These will be turned into questions that can be asked to find out what is the same and what is different about all their feet. They will go on to ask independent questions regarding each other's feet. This skill can be used to ask questions about other things using mathematical language.

WHAT YOU NEED

A shoe measurer; large sheets of paper, divided into columns of different shoe sizes (enough for the class to work in groups); writing materials; pictures of feet; glue sticks.

WHAT TO DO

Ask the children to take off their shoes and socks and sit in a circle with their feet straight out in front of them. Together, count the number of toes they each have. Say the rhyme 'This little piggy went to market' together, holding onto the corresponding toes as the rhyme is told.

Ask the children what they can tell you about their feet. For each of their suggestions, present this to another child as a question. For example, if one child says *I have ten toes*, you could ask another, *How many toes do you have?* If a child says *I have two feet*, you could ask the same question of another child, querying *How many feet do you have?* Continue until you have modelled several questions for the children.

At this stage invite questions from the children to help them find out more things about each other's feet. These might include, *How many toes do you have on each foot? How many toes altogether? Does everyone have the same number of toes? Is one toe bigger than another?* Think together whether the children have the same sized feet. Help them by asking, *When you go to buy shoes, can you just buy a pair off the shelf? What do you need to do first?* Most children will know that they need to have their feet measured first. If not, ask the children to recall what they do when they go to a shoe shop. What does the person in the shop ask first?

Divide the class into groups. Explain that each child in the groups should measure their feet and record the shoe size they take as a pictogram. Give the children the recording paper and pictures of feet and ask them to stick the pictures in the appropriate columns to record their shoe size.

Repeat this activity for other things, such as hand size or the height of different children, inviting the children to ask questions using mathematical vocabulary, such as *greater* or *smaller*.

THREADING

AREA OF LEARNING: MATHEMATICAL DEVELOPMENT. ELG: TO USE LANGUAGE TO DESCRIBE THE SHAPE AND SIZE OF SOLIDS. NNS OBJECTIVE: TO TALK ABOUT, RECOGNISE AND RECREATE PATTERNS.

LEARNING OBJECTIVE
To thread beads according to a repeating pattern.

THINKING OBJECTIVE
To predict outcomes.

THINKING SKILLS
The children will look at different patterns and predict which patterns are being made to match which. They will use this skill of predicting to create their own patterned designs for friends to predict and finish.

WHAT YOU NEED
Six pre-made cards with bead patterns on them (make some that have beads threaded randomly and some that have patterns of repeating colours or shapes); individual beads that match those used on the cards; laces.

WHAT TO DO
Show the children the cards with the bead patterns on and identify which beads from your collection have been used to make the patterns on each card. Talk about whether there is a pattern that repeats or not on each card. Focus the children's thinking by asking, *Can you see a bead the same colour? Is there one the same shape or size? If it repeats, does it repeat by colour or by shape and size of the beads?*

While the children are still looking at the cards start to thread beads together to match one of the patterns. After you have done enough, ask the children to predict which pattern you are making. Match the threaded beads against the card to check their predictions. Move onto another pattern and repeat the process. Then invite a child to thread another set of beads, and ask the rest of the class to guess which pattern is being made.

Give the children a chance to make their own bead patterns for others to predict which bead should be threaded on next. Or ask the children to finish making patterns that have been started by their friends. Can they predict which bead should be threaded next? Note the children who can predict the colour and shape of the next bead and thread this on.

TORCH CAPERS

AREA OF LEARNING: KNOWLEDGE AND UNDERSTANDING OF THE WORLD. ELG: TO ASK QUESTIONS ABOUT WHY THINGS HAPPEN AND HOW THINGS WORK.

LEARNING OBJECTIVE
To talk about how a torch works.

THINKING OBJECTIVE
To test conclusions.

THINKING SKILLS
The children will think about how a torch works, testing out their conclusions by turning torches on and off to see if they were right.

WHAT YOU NEED
A collection of torches that can be taken apart, including some topical ones such as Bob the Builder or Thomas the Tank Engine; stickers of the children's favourite characters.

WHAT TO DO
Look at a torch with the children and talk about how it works. Ask, *How can we make the light come on? How do we turn it off again?* When the children have come up with some ideas, pass the torches round and let them test their conclusions on how to turn each one on and off. Ask them to describe what they are doing. Ask, *Were you right? What happens when the torch is turned on? What happens when it is turned off? What is making it work? What do you think is happening inside the torch?*

Ask the children to design a torch for a favourite TV or book character. Perhaps a Disney cartoon character or one from a favourite film, such as *Toy Story* or *101 Dalmatians*. Show the children what happens when a sticker of a character is put over the front of the torch, where the light shines through. Let them do this and then let them play torch tag by shining the torch on the ceiling, turning it on and off before they are tagged by each other. Ask, *How do you know which is your light?*

Make a display of the torches you have made. During the plenary invite the children to show and say how they turn their torch on and off, and why they chose the design that they did.

SANDCASTLES

AREA OF LEARNING: KNOWLEDGE AND UNDERSTANDING OF THE WORLD. ELG: TO INVESTIGATE OBJECTS AND MATERIALS BY USING ALL OF THEIR SENSES AS APPROPRIATE.

LEARNING OBJECTIVE
To explore a material using their senses.

THINKING OBJECTIVE
To anticipate consequences.

THINKING SKILLS
The children will need to think ahead about the texture of sand which will be most successful for building sandcastles from. They will be asked to anticipate the consequences of adding water to dry sand, and how much water to add to get the right consistency.

WHAT YOU NEED
Sand; a bucket; a water tray.

WHAT TO DO
Ask the children to play with the dry sand and talk about what it feels like. Do they think it will make a sandcastle? If necessary, ask a group to try this out. When it doesn't work, ask them to say what they need to do to make the sand suitable for making sandcastles. Help them to come up with the answer that they need to add water. Then get a bucket of water and ask them how they think you should make the sand wet. Ask, *Should we pour the water onto the sand?* Wonder with them what might happen if you pour all the water into the sand. If the children fail to anticipate the consequences of this, pour all the water in and invite someone to try and build a sandcastle from the very wet sand. What do they notice? If the children do anticipate that the sand will be too wet and will still be unsuitable to make sandcastles from, ask how you can find out exactly how much water to mix with the sand.

Use trial and error, mixing in water a bit at a time and asking the children to try to build sandcastles until you find the best consistency.

HARVEST FESTIVAL

AREA OF LEARNING: KNOWLEDGE AND UNDERSTANDING OF THE WORLD. ELG: TO BEGIN TO KNOW ABOUT THEIR OWN CULTURES AND BELIEFS AND THOSE OF OTHER PEOPLE.

LEARNING OBJECTIVE
To find out how different people celebrate harvest.

THINKING OBJECTIVE
To plan research.

THINKING SKILLS
The children will think about how Christians celebrate harvest festival and why. They will then plan how they can research the American Thanksgiving celebrations in November.

WHAT YOU NEED
A selection of harvest festival foods, such as vegetables, tinned food, bread, empty packaging, herbs, flowers and pictures of fish and meat; a laminated picture of an American Thanksgiving dinner; a water-based pen.

WHAT TO DO
Talk with the children about the meaning of the word *harvest*. Discuss why Christians celebrate harvest festival, and show the children the vegetables, packaging, flowers and pictures you have collected and talk about the idea of how all these things are gathered together and stored for the long winter.

Explain to the children that you are going to use a picture to research where the food comes from in an American Thanksgiving dinner. Look at the picture of the Thanksgiving food. Talk about where each item of food came from. Put a ring round those things that are grown. Look at the things that do not have a ring and talk about the ingredients that they contain. Identify the grown ingredients that went into making these foods. Explain that the celebration is to remember the food that was gathered by the settlers when they first went to America. Explain that the settlers held a celebration every year to give thanks to God for the food. Make a display of all the ingredients that are in a Thanksgiving dinner. Compare it to the harvest festival displays in school.

BOTTLE SKITTLES

AREA OF LEARNING: KNOWLEDGE AND UNDERSTANDING OF THE WORLD. ELG: TO INVESTIGATE OBJECTS AND MATERIALS BY USING ALL OF THEIR SENSES AS APPROPRIATE.

LEARNING OBJECTIVE
To learn that they can find things out by using their senses.

THINKING OBJECTIVE
To define a problem.

THINKING SKILLS
The children will define an initial problem before setting about solving it. They may define an additional problem in their initial solution, which will also need solving.

WHAT YOU NEED
Empty plastic drinks bottles; sand; water; balls.

WHAT TO DO
Tell the children that you want to make a set of skittles to use in a game. Stand up the bottles in a pattern and ask the children if they think these will be suitable to use as skittles. Ask, *What if it was a very windy day and we were playing the game outside? What would be the problem with using these bottles?* Make sure the children define the problem – that the bottles would fall over too easily.

Then explore with the children how they can make the bottles more stable. Let them try, in small groups, filling some bottles with sand or water, or anything else they suggest, and let them test out which makes the bottles more stable to use as skittles. If possible, let the children go outside to test their 'skittles' by playing a game to see how

many they can knock over. Ask, *Are some skittles too stable now and make the game too difficult? Why is this? Is it because there is too much sand or water, and this has made them too heavy to be knocked over?* See if the children can define this second problem together and solve it by adding or removing an amount of sand and water until they have a suitable set of skittles to play with. Some children may use lateral thinking and suggest finding heavier balls to knock the skittles over with.

CUTTING OUT

AREA OF LEARNING: PHYSICAL DEVELOPMENT. ELG: TO HANDLE TOOLS SAFELY AND WITH INCREASING CONTROL.

LEARNING OBJECTIVE
To cut out a piece of cellophane the right size.

THINKING OBJECTIVE
To anticipate consequences.

THINKING SKILLS
The children will think about the size of cellophane they will need to cut to cover a given space. They need to anticipate that if they cut the cellophane too small it will not cover the space. This will lead them to the conclusion that they need to cut the cellophane slightly bigger than the window to make it work.

WHAT YOU NEED
A pre-made card with a character inside that shows through a window cut into the front, the window being covered with cellophane; cards with a window cut out in the front (one for each child); matching sized window templates (one for each child); cellophane paper cut into manageable sizes and to prevent too much waste; scissors; glue sticks.

WHAT TO DO
Explain to the children that they are each going to make a card which shows a character inside through a window on the front. Show them the ready-made card and how the character shows through the cellophane window from the inside.

Ask the children to draw a picture of a character on the pre-cut piece of paper. Choose any context for the children's characters, depending on your topic or the time of the year.

Using the finished card, focus the children's attention on the piece of cellophane stuck over the cut-out window. Give each child a ready-made card with a window cut out. Explain that you want them to make a cellophane window for their card.

Let the children choose the colour of cellophane they want. Before they start, ask them to say what size they think they need to cut their cellophane. Ask, *Should you just cut it, or do you need to measure it first? How can you measure the size?* Show them the window template. Ask if they cut out the cellophane to the same size as the template whether they think it will be the right size to fit the window in their cards. Some will say yes, in which case let them cut out the cellophane and discover for themselves that it is too small. Others may anticipate that this will be too small and that they need to cut the shape slightly bigger.

Demonstrate to the children how to cut the cellophane to the right size. Put the shape on top of the cellophane and, holding both tightly between two fingers, cut around the shape to leave some cellophane sticking out over the template. Glue the cellophane into position on the inside of the card. Get the children to make other cards to extend their understanding.

TARGET PRACTICE

AREA OF LEARNING: PHYSICAL DEVELOPMENT. ELG: TO USE A RANGE OF SMALL AND LARGE EQUIPMENT.

LEARNING OBJECTIVE
To learn to control beanbags, balls and quoits.

THINKING OBJECTIVE
To test conclusions.

THINKING SKILLS
The children will decide which is the best way to send a variety of throwing equipment to hit different targets. They will test out their conclusions and then see if they can develop further ideas about the most effective way to throw equipment to hit targets, again testing out their conclusions.

WHAT YOU NEED
Throwing equipment, such as beanbags, balls and quoits; targets, such as hoops, skittles, buckets and baskets.

WHAT TO DO
Take the children outside or into a large area and organise the targets for them to explore. Let them use beanbags, balls and quoits to try to knock over the skittles, to land in the baskets and buckets and to both land and stop inside the hoops.

After a few minutes, gather the children together and ask them to say whether they think it is easier to get a quoit, ball or beanbag to land inside a hoop.

Ask for their reasons. Test out their conclusions by asking for volunteers to throw each piece of equipment and comparing which is the easiest to land inside a hoop without it rolling out. Let the volunteers have several goes with each piece. Were their conclusions right? Ask the children, *Do you think you can send the objects in a different way to make them land more accurately?* For example, throwing a quoit like a frisbee so that it lands flat and won't roll, rather than underarm where it probably will roll?

Conduct the same process for the other throwing equipment and targets. Gather the children's ideas about which they think is the best piece of throwing equipment for landing in the basket and bucket, and for knocking over the skittles. Test out their conclusions before investigating whether they can improve things by adapting the way they send the beanbags, balls and quoits. Is the same equipment still the most effective for the different targets? Let the children test out their conclusions independently.

HOW MANY BEATS?

AREA OF LEARNING: CREATIVE DEVELOPMENT. ELG: TO MATCH MOVEMENTS TO MUSIC.

LEARNING OBJECTIVE
To move in response to music.

THINKING OBJECTIVE
To define a problem.

THINKING SKILLS
The children will need to consider an initial problem before going about solving it. They will listen to a piece of music and be motivated to move in time to this. They will consider their movements and begin to think of different sequences of moves to make up a country dance.

WHAT YOU NEED
A piece of country dancing music with four or eight beats.

WHAT TO DO

Explain to the children that you want to make up a country dance to perform to some of the other classes in school, perhaps as an assembly. Ask, *What do we need to do before performing the dance? Do you know what the steps are? Will you need to learn them?*

Listen to the music together and tell the children that you want them to make up a dance to this piece of music. Explain that they will work together to make up different dance steps and sequences that will fit the music and make the dance interesting to watch. Explain that their task is to make up an interesting sequence of dance moves. Play the first half of the music again and encourage the children to clap along to it. Talk about the pattern of a country dance. Explain that each sequence of music usually has eight beats. Play the second half of the music, counting along together in phrases of eight beats.

Explore with the children some of the steps used in country dancing, such as moving in a circle, skipping round or walking with a partner, and walk through some of these moves counting to eight at the same time. Encourage the children to change to a new movement after eight beats.

As a class, choose some of these moves and agree a pattern for the dance. Write the pattern down for the children to remember the sequence, using a picture sequence for this.

OIL ON WATER

AREA OF LEARNING: CREATIVE DEVELOPMENT. ELG: TO EXPLORE COLOUR, TEXTURE AND SHAPE IN TWO DIMENSIONS.

LEARNING OBJECTIVE

To create patterns.

THINKING OBJECTIVE

To predict outcomes and test conclusions.

THINKING SKILLS

The children will learn to predict what they think will happen when oil is mixed with water. They will refine their predictions by looking at a range of products and noting what happens when these are mixed with water. They will test out their predictions by making patterns with marbling inks, which are oil based and therefore will float on top of the water. They will be encouraged to predict what their pattern will be like to reflect the movement of the water.

WHAT YOU NEED

Rectangular tray deep enough to hold two centimetres of water, with space left at the top; cooking oil; food colouring; marbling inks; A4 sheets of paper which will absorb oil; wooden dowelling or spoon to mix.

WHAT TO DO

Show the children the tray of water and the food colouring. Ask the children to predict what will happen if you pour some of the food colouring into the water. Test out their conclusions by pouring a drop into the water, mixing it in and noting what happens.

Change the water in the tray and ask the children to predict what will happen if you pour a little oil onto it. Note how the oil floats on top. Then drop a sheet of A4 paper on top of the water and after a couple of seconds lift it off. Show the children how the paper has collected the oil.

Next, ask the children what they think will happen if you mix some of the cooking oil with the food colouring and pour this onto the water. Again, test out their conclusions. Agree that the oil has changed colour and that it still floats on top of the water and has collected onto the paper. Note the coloured pattern you can see this time. Ask, *Is it the oil or the food colouring that gives the pattern the colour?*

Put fresh water in your tray again. Invite the children to choose a colour they like from the marbling inks. Pour their choice on top of the water and again, put a sheet of paper on top. Lift it off and look at the pattern. Ask the children to say what the pattern is like. Do this again, but this time, after you have swirled the mixture around, ask the children to predict what sort of shapes they think will appear on the paper. Swirl again if necessary and soak up the pattern with the paper. Note with the children whether the pattern on the paper looked like they thought it would. Repeat until you have made several different patterns.

EXTENDING ENQUIRY SKILLS

Area of learning and ELG, NLS or NNS objective	Activity title	Thinking objective	Activity	Page
Personal, social and emotional development ELG: To work as part of a group or class	Sharing food	To define a problem	Sharing apples fairly when there are more children than apples	69
Communication, language and literacy ELG: To write their own names and other things such as labels and captions NLS objective: To write labels or captions for pictures and drawings	Writing signs	To improve ideas	Making signs to give clear messages and instructions	69
Communication, language and literacy ELG: To use talk to organise events NLS objective: To learn that words can be written down to be read again for a wide range of purposes	Baggage claim	To define a problem	Anticipating problems that could occur with baggage on an aeroplane journey, and acting a role-play to see how these problems can be overcome	70
Communication, language and literacy ELG: To show an understanding of how information can be found in non-fiction texts NLS objective: To re-read frequently a variety of familiar texts	Creatures	To plan research	Researching creatures and animals that could be hiding in different habitats	72
Mathematical development ELG: To use everyday words to describe position NNS objective: To use everyday words to describe position	Getting from here to there	To ask questions	Asking questions to a bear that is lost in order to help him find his way home	73
Mathematical development ELG: To relate subtraction to 'taking away'	How many?	To define a problem	Identifying what they need to find out to solve a problem	74
Knowledge and understanding of the world ELG: To identify features in the natural world	Through a window	To improve ideas	Considering what features look like when viewed from different perspectives	75
Knowledge and understanding of the world ELG: To find out about, and identify, some features of living things	Planting	To test conclusions	Investigating if it matters which way up bulbs are planted	76
Knowledge and understanding of the world ELG: To begin to know about the cultures of other people	Dragon boats	To plan research	Developing cultural knowledge by finding out about dragon boats and then making a boat themselves to act out a role-play	77
Physical development ELG: To handle objects with increasing control	Threading	To predict outcomes	Lacing a shoe and predicting whether the pattern will look like its laced counterpart when it is laced in different ways	78
Physical development ELG: To handle tools, objects and materials safely and with increasing control	Making books	To anticipate consequences	Making books and thinking about the consequences of not planning ahead	79
Creative development ELG: To recognise and explore how sounds can be changed	Tambourine sounds	To plan research	Exploring the sounds that different instruments can make	80
Creative development ELG: To recognise repeated sounds and sound patterns and match movements to music	Repeating patterns	To ask questions	Asking questions to organise repeating patterns in a song	81

Sharing food

AREA OF LEARNING: PERSONAL, SOCIAL AND EMOTIONAL DEVELOPMENT. ELG: TO WORK AS PART OF A GROUP OR CLASS, TAKING TURNS AND SHARING FAIRLY, UNDERSTANDING THAT THERE NEEDS TO BE AGREED VALUES AND CODES OF BEHAVIOUR FOR GROUPS OF PEOPLE, INCLUDING ADULTS AND CHILDREN, TO WORK TOGETHER HARMONIOUSLY.

Learning objective
To learn to share.

Thinking objective
To define a problem.

Thinking skills
The children will think about the number of apples they have and note that there are not enough for them to have one each. They first need to define this problem and then that of having to cut the apples fairly to share them out.

What you need
Four apples for each group of six children; a knife; chopping board; a risk assessment, taking account of food allergies.

What to do
When most of the children are engrossed in other adult-focused and self-initiated play activities, gather focused groups of six children, one group at a time, to enjoy an apple snack. Put four apples in the centre of a table and explain that you have four apples for them to share for a snack. Ask them to say whether there is a problem with the number of apples you have to share between them. Does anyone notice that there are not enough apples? Ask them how the apples could be shared so that everyone has some.

Follow the children's instructions and cut the apples accordingly. If they say to cut the apples in half, do and then share these out noting that there are still some pieces left over. Before you get to the end of the sharing task, note whether anyone defines this problem - that there will be some left over still to share and that it cannot be shared unless it is cut again.

Differentiation
Use three apples with lower attaining children so that they can be cut in half and there will be enough for everyone. They should still be encouraged to define the problem, however. Higher attaining children can investigate a number of different apples to share (four, five and seven) and suggest how these should be cut.

Where next
Repeat the activity with other things that can be shared, such as bananas or pears.

Assessment
Listen to the children as they work out what the problem is. Note those who then anticipate whether they have cut the apples so that everyone in the group has a fair share.

Learning outcomes
Most children will begin to identify when there is a problem and what this is. They will start to anticipate the consequences of their ideas, whether there will be enough pieces for everyone to have a fair share.

Further personal, social and emotional development challenges
Drinks on the house
Ask the children to think of a way to share four cartons of juice between six children. Note the problem with the children before identifying how to share the juice out fairly.
Fruit segments
Share out fruits that are naturally divided in different ways, for example grapes and oranges. Ask the children to say how they could divide these fruits into equal shares and to think of the problems.

Writing signs

AREA OF LEARNING: COMMUNICATION, LANGUAGE AND LITERACY. ELG: TO WRITE THEIR OWN NAMES AND OTHER THINGS SUCH AS LABELS AND CAPTIONS. NLS OBJECTIVE: TO WRITE LABELS OR CAPTIONS FOR PICTURES AND DRAWINGS.

Learning objective
To write signs to label different areas in the airport role-play area.

Thinking objective
To improve ideas.

Thinking skills
The children will make signs for an airport role-play area. They will consider how well these can be seen and how clear the messages they give are, before improving their ideas and making them clearer or more precise in their instructions.

What you need
Pictures of airports with typical signs; large sheets of card or paper in different colours; string to hang these with; paint; felt-tipped pens; paper.

WHAT TO DO

Show the children the pictures of airports and draw their attention to the signs that can be seen. Ask the children, *What sort of signs can you see? What are they telling passengers? Do the signs have words only or do some have arrows to show the direction passengers need to go in?* Look at any signs that show a direction and note whether the arrows are straight, at an angle or are bent at right angles.

Tell the children that you want them to make some signs to create an airport role-play area. Make a list together of the signs that you want to include and decide who will do which sign. Allocate each child or group of children a sign, depending on the ability of the children.

When they have finished, hold up one of the signs from the back of the classroom and ask the children whether it can be seen from a distance. Ask questions for the children to appraise the sign, such as *Is it clear to read? Are the instructions telling the passenger where to go clear?* Talk about the colours that have been used. Have the children chosen a favourite colour or one that can be seen clearly?

Talk about how they can improve their signs. Can they make the writing bigger, clearer, in a different colour, on a different coloured background? Encourage the children to try these ideas out and to compare the results with their original signs. Ask them to choose the version they think is the best and ask them to draw pictures to show what the sign says. They can glue the matching picture to the sign so that children who are not yet reading can use the picture as a prompt.

DIFFERENTIATION

Ask lower attaining children to write shorter words that might be found on signs in the departure lounge, such as *Exit*. They can work together as a small group to work on words within the same context. They will also not have the problem of fitting long words onto their piece of paper. Let higher attaining children work on longer words. This will make them remember the letters and decide how to make words fit onto their piece of card. They could also work on signs containing more than two words.

WHERE NEXT

Get the children to make signs for other areas in the classroom or school.

ASSESSMENT

Listen to the children's evaluation of their signs and note those who can think how to make improvements independently, perhaps suggesting how to make the sign clearer to read from a distance. Do any children

think about keeping the sign small so that it is easy to hang up?

LEARNING OUTCOMES

Most children will consider how and why signs are written and think of ways to improve their own signs to fit the purpose identified.

FURTHER COMMUNICATION, LANGUAGE AND LITERACY CHALLENGES

Name cards

Help the children to find a picture on the computer, from a simple clipart program, and insert this into an empty page. Invite the children to type their name next to their picture to make a name card. Are they happy with the finished label? Show them how to change the colour and style of the writing. Help them to improve their ideas and print them out to make a name card for the table, drawer/tray or cloakroom peg.

Signs here and there

Go for a walk around the local environment and photograph some of the signs that give the name of a street or building. Discuss these with the children and ask them how they would make improvements to make the signs more attractive. Perhaps they could add a picture or symbol. Scan some of the photographs into the computer and let the children make any improvements to the signs by adding pictures or changing the colour.

BAGGAGE CLAIM

AREA OF LEARNING: COMMUNICATION, LANGUAGE AND LITERACY. ELG: TO USE TALK TO ORGANISE EVENTS. NLS OBJECTIVE: TO LEARN THAT WORDS CAN BE WRITTEN DOWN TO BE READ AGAIN FOR A WIDE RANGE OF PURPOSES.

LEARNING OBJECTIVE

To read simple signs and labels.

THINKING OBJECTIVE

To define a problem.

THINKING SKILLS

By learning about what happens to people's luggage

when they travel by aeroplane, the children will start to define problems that could occur with locating luggage once a plane has landed. Once they have identified the difficulties they will take part in a role-play to understand how the problems are overcome.

WHAT YOU NEED

A space to act as a baggage claim area away from the classroom, for example an empty classroom or school hall; cases and bags (enough for one for each child); luggage labels; signs directing the children where to find the baggage claim area.

WHAT TO DO

Tell the children a story about what happens to luggage when people go on an aeroplane journey. Explain how bags and suitcases are checked in, loaded onto the plane and taken off again at the other end. Identify together what the problem might be for passengers when they get to the other end of their journey – that they need to find out where their cases are when they have been taken off the plane. Ask, *How will they find their cases?*

Explain how cases are all taken to the baggage claim area where their owners pick them up. Can the children think of another problem here? Ask the children how they think the owners know where to go to get their cases. Ask, *Do they ask someone? Do they wander around until they find their case? Does someone bring their case to them?* Tell them that there are signs that tell passengers where to go to collect their cases. Explain how the information on the signs tells passengers where to go to collect their cases.

When they get to the baggage claim area, what other problem do the children think passengers are likely to have? Ask, *How will they know which case belongs to them?* Explain to the children how people know what their cases look like, but that sometimes two cases could look the same, so people tie labels onto their cases with their name on.

Give each child a case or bag and tell them that when they come back in after playtime they will have

to find it. Identify with the children the things they need to know about their cases in order to find them. They should write their name on a luggage label and tie this to their case.

When the children are out to play, take all the cases to your chosen baggage claim area. Put up the signs for the children to follow from the classroom to the baggage claim area. Make sure that the signs have pictures of cases on them as well as written information, for those children who cannot read yet. Put up several which take the children in a roundabout route to the area.

When the children come in from play, pretend to go on a plane journey. When you have landed, pretend that they need to collect their cases. Ask them what the problem is. Where do they have to go? What is there that tells them where to collect their cases? Agree together that the signs tell them where to go. Together, follow the signs to the baggage claim area. Ask the children what the problem is now. Get them to identify the correct colour and style case that is theirs and to check on the labels whether they belong to them.

DIFFERENTIATION

Higher attaining children should be given cases which are alike so that they have to check by reading the labels to identify their cases. Lower attaining children should be escorted to the baggage claim area to make sure they are reading the signs properly. Check if they understand that to overcome the problem of finding their cases, they need to read the signs to tell them which way to go.

WHERE NEXT

Make baggage claim tickets from stickers and air tickets that the children can use to check in with at the check-in desk. Let the children take these to the baggage claim area to exchange for the correct number of cases. If they have two tickets, they can collect two pieces of luggage.

ASSESSMENT

Note the children who realise that they need to know certain things when going on an aeroplane journey – that they need to locate and follow signs, find and collect their luggage. Who knows that they need to locate the signs and read these to get to the right place to find their cases?

LEARNING OUTCOMES

Most children will realise that there are problems related to finding luggage when travelling, which they need to identify and solve if they are to find the cases that belong to them.

FURTHER COMMUNICATION, LANGUAGE AND LITERACY CHALLENGES

Passports

Tell the children that you want them to make a passport for themselves. Decide together the things that they will need to include on their passport. The back page could include a photograph and personal details. Ask the children to note how much space there is to fit all this information in and if they can think what the problem here might be. Tell them to decide how big to make their writing before starting the task in order to fit all their details on. Finally, decide together how to make the pages to add stamps of the countries they intend to visit.

Departure gate

Set up signs that will take the children to an airport departure gate. Label five within the classroom, the corridor, and in the hall. Talk to the children about what they need to do after they have checked in (go to the departure gate to board their aeroplane). Ask, *How will you know which is your aeroplane?* Look together at the problem. Identify what they need to know to find their aeroplane. List these on a flip chart or board. Find which departure gate is on their ticket. Look for signs that give directions. Read and follow the signs to the correct gate.

CREATURES

AREA OF LEARNING: COMMUNICATION, LANGUAGE AND LITERACY. ELG: TO SHOW AN UNDERSTANDING OF HOW INFORMATION CAN BE FOUND IN NON-FICTION TEXTS TO ANSWER QUESTIONS ABOUT WHERE, WHO, WHY AND HOW. NLS OBJECTIVE: TO RE-READ FREQUENTLY A VARIETY OF FAMILIAR TEXTS.

LEARNING OBJECTIVE
To read simple sentences.

THINKING OBJECTIVE
To plan research.

THINKING SKILLS
The children will read simple sentences in a book and plan research to think of the possible insects, birds and small animals that could be hiding in various habitats. They will learn to look for these things in books, using pictures and labels to collect possible ideas. They will need to consider the size of their findings to decide whether they would manage to hide in the different places shown in the book.

WHAT YOU NEED
Buster's Day by Rod Campbell (MacMillan Children's Books); simple books containing pictures and names of insects, birds and small animals.

WHAT TO DO
Look at the front cover of the book with the children and talk about what the story may be about. Explain that it is about all the things that Buster does on one day. Look at the first picture and ask the children, *What do you think Buster is helping with in the picture?* Tell the children to look for clues in the picture. Read the sentence opposite the picture, *'I'll help with the washing,' says Buster.* Ask for a volunteer to lift the flap and see what is in the washing machine. Ask the children what Buster could put into the washing machine. Listen to the children's suggestions and decide if they are all things that are washed in the washing machine. Agree that we wash clothes in the washing machine.

Look together at the second picture and talk about the things that are kept in a fridge. Ask another volunteer to lift the flap and see what is in the fridge to check the children's suggestions.

Continue like this until you get to the page where Buster goes into the garden. Invite the children to suggestion what could be hiding under the leaf. Ask, *What size does it need to be? Could it be a cat or a bird?* Agree that it will be some kind of insect. Ask the children how they could go about finding out about some creatures that could be hiding under the leaf. Accept that they will already know some insects. Explain that you want them to find others that they may not be familiar with. Ask, *Where could you research the information? What kind of book do you need to use?* Divide the children into four groups to research different insects using appropriate books, or let the children find the books they will need from your collection. After a short amount of time call the groups back together and ask them to pool their research. Then lift the flap and see if anyone found this insect during their research.

Ask the groups to go away and research again for what animals might be in the nesting box and in the flower bed.

DIFFERENTIATION
Let lower attaining children research the insects only. Ask higher attaining children to research nocturnal animals that could be under the flap on the last page of the book. Take them to the library and let them find some of the books they will need with your help.

Ask them, *How can you find out the names and types of nocturnal animals that there are?*

WHERE NEXT
Ask the children how they can find the words of some of the items that might be found in the bathroom, kitchen and bedroom in the book.

Use other simple story books as a basis to research some of the items mentioned in them.

ASSESSMENT
Note the children who realise that information is found in non-fiction books. They may be ready to research using an index or contents page. Talk to the children to find out if they know that information books help them to find out or research different things.

LEARNING OUTCOMES
Most children will understand that non-fiction books will help them plan research to find out about a favourite or familiar topic.

FURTHER COMMUNICATION, LANGUAGE AND LITERACY CHALLENGES
Ten green bottles
Ask the children how they could go about finding out as many things as possible that can be found in a green bottle. Ask, *Where could you find the information? Who could you ask?* Possible suggestions include a visit to a supermarket, looking in a food or mail-order catalogue, collecting empty bottles (which contained safe contents) from home.

Topic vocabulary
Plan research for finding the names of things connected with a current topic. For example, ask different groups of children to plan research to find the names of different types of transport – water, air, road and rail; or shades of yellow, red, blue, green and orange paints.

GETTING FROM HERE TO THERE

AREA OF LEARNING: MATHEMATICAL DEVELOPMENT. ELG: TO USE EVERYDAY WORDS TO DESCRIBE POSITION. NNS OBJECTIVE: TO USE EVERYDAY WORDS TO DESCRIBE POSITION.

LEARNING OBJECTIVE
To give instructions about how to get from one place to another.

THINKING OBJECTIVE
To ask questions.

THINKING SKILLS
The children will ask a sequence of questions to a bear that is lost in order to help him find his way home.

WHAT YOU NEED
A map of the local area or play mat; a play phone; a teddy bear.

WHAT TO DO
Look at the play mat or map of the local area together and identify some of the features on it. Show the children the teddy bear and explain that Bear is lost and needs to find his way home, or back to school. Ask, *What problem does Bear have? How has he got lost? Why can't he find his way home?*

Pretend that Bear has a phone. Tell the children he is able to describe where he is so that they can direct him home. Pretend to be Bear phoning the children on his mobile phone. Invite the children to ask Bear a question to try to identify first where he is. Describe an area on the map which tells the children where he is and ask them to put him on the map. Then ask them to ask a question to locate his home.

Tell the children you want them to work out a route for Bear to get home. Invite the children to give him the first instruction, for example *Walk along the road until you get to the end. Turn right at the end of the road.* Ask a child to move Bear so that he is following the instructions.

Pretend to be Bear again and call the children, telling them that you are at the end of the road and what you can see now. Invite the children to give the next instruction. Pretend to go the wrong way, moving Bear on the map accordingly. Invite the children to ask where Bear might be now. Make sure you are happy that the children are asking questions which use positional language. For example, *Are you next to a playground? Have you just walked past a post office? Have you crossed over the road? Have you gone under a bridge?* Finish when Bear has reached his home.

DIFFERENTIATION
Let the children move Bear around the play mat as each direction is given. Model the language of position for them as he is moved from one place to another, describing where he is walking and what he is going over and under, for example. Higher attaining children should be encouraged to relate his route again afterwards, using the relevant positional vocabulary.

WHERE NEXT

Repeat the activity with stories that the children know with characters who travel from one place to another.

ASSESSMENT

Ask an additional adult to tick off on a list of the class when the children ask a question using positional language.

LEARNING OUTCOMES

Most children will learn to ask questions to find out someone's position.

FURTHER MATHEMATICAL DEVELOPMENT CHALLENGES

Obstacle madness

Set up an obstacle course for the children to direct a partner through. They should describe the pathways using positional language, including *along, under, over, round, through, by.*

Where are you?

Invite a child to pretend he or she is standing somewhere on the map or play mat. The other children should ask yes/no questions to find out where this child is standing. Make sure they use positional language in their questions, such as *Are you standing next to the park?* or *Are you standing under a bridge?*

HOW MANY?

AREA OF LEARNING: MATHEMATICAL DEVELOPMENT. ELG: TO BEGIN TO RELATE SUBTRACTION TO 'TAKING AWAY'. NNS OBJECTIVE: TO BEGIN TO RELATE SUBTRACTION TO 'TAKING AWAY'.

LEARNING OBJECTIVE

To find out how many are left by taking away.

THINKING OBJECTIVE

To define a problem.

THINKING SKILLS

In this activity the children will be defining a problem by breaking it down into steps in order to solve it. They will identify the information they have by discussing the problem.

WHAT YOU NEED

A packet of biscuits; a plate; a copy of the story *A Wolf at the Door!* by Nick Ward (Scholastic); Little Red Riding Hood's basket, cakes and toy animals for the Further mathematical thinking challenge.

WHAT TO DO

Read the story *A Wolf at the Door!* to the children and note the characters who come to Little Bear's house. Notice the cakes that Little Bear enjoys in the first picture and talk about who is eating the cakes in the subsequent pictures.

Tell the children that you want them to pretend that Little Bear gave each of his visitors a biscuit when they came to his house. Explain that you want them to find out how many biscuits he would have left when all his visitors had had one.

Start by emptying the biscuits onto a plate, making sure you have the number you want in order to match the task to the children's previous learning (ten is a good number to start with, however). Define the problem together by asking the children, *What do we already know?* Agree with the children that they know there are ten biscuits. Ask, *How can we work out how many biscuits Little Bear will have left when all his visitors go home?* Follow the children's suggestions and ideas.

Check their answers by asking some children to play the part of the characters in the story. Read the story again, with the children acting out the visitors each receiving a biscuit. After each visitor has taken a biscuit, count the number of biscuits that are left on the plate. Line the visitors up in front of the class. Ask the children, *If Little Bear gave his visitors a biscuit each, how many biscuits did Little Bear have left for the next day? How do you know?* Of course the plate is empty.

Explain to the children what they have done. That they worked out how to solve the problem by deciding what they already knew, identifying what they needed to find out and thinking about how they could find the answer. Remind them that they then checked their answer.

DIFFERENTIATION

Use fewer characters and biscuits with lower attaining children. Give higher attaining children more biscuits to work with and ask them to give each visitor two biscuits each time. Encourage them to take away by counting backwards, as well as counting how many are left each time.

74

WHERE NEXT

Repeat the activity using more than ten biscuits. Tell the children that one of the characters has brought his brother along to play. Ask, *How many characters are there now?* Think with the children how they can work this out. They can ask someone to play the brother and count from the beginning again, or they could add on one. Let them work out how many biscuits would be left on the plate this time.

ASSESSMENT

Note the children who are beginning to identify the process of solving problems by defining what they know, what they need to find out and how they will do this. Note those who realise the importance of checking their answers.

LEARNING OUTCOMES

Most children will begin to solve simple problems. Some will begin to do this independently and some will do so with help.

FURTHER MATHEMATICAL DEVELOPMENT CHALLENGES

Red Riding Hood's basket

Tell the children a story about Red Riding Hood walk through the wood with a basket of cakes (decide the number of cakes matched to your children's learning level). Explain that, as she goes through the wood, she meets a certain number of toy animals, to whom she gives a cake each. Ask the children to work out how many cakes she has left in the basket when she gets to Grandma's house. Ask them to define the problem by identifying what they know, what they need to find out and how they will do it. How will they check their answer? Encourage them to give each toy animal a cake each and to count how many are left each time.

THROUGH A WINDOW

AREA OF LEARNING: KNOWLEDGE AND UNDERSTANDING OF THE WORLD. ELG: TO IDENTIFY FEATURES IN THE NATURAL WORLD.

LEARNING OBJECTIVE

To identify features in the natural world from different points of view.

THINKING OBJECTIVE

To improve ideas.

THINKING SKILLS

The children will think about what features look like when seen from a car, a sideways view, before considering what they might look like from above. They will use this information to improve their ideas about how to draw these different perspectives.

WHAT YOU NEED

Large sheets of paper; drawing materials; paint and paintbrushes.

WHAT TO DO

Talk about the things that can be seen from a car window. Ask, *What do things look like?* Together draw some of the things the children have seen from a car window from a sideways view. Ask, *What if you were on a train? What would you see then? Would you see the same view? What about a boat? What view of things might you see from a boat in the middle of the ocean?* Ask the children who have been in an aeroplane to say what they saw out of the window. Ask, *Did you see a tree like the one you have drawn? What about houses and cars? What did they look like?* Ask the children to draw some clouds and bird's-eye views of trees and houses to improve the children's ideas about how things look from different points of view.

Ask the children to pretend they are in a car. Ask them to paint views from a window. Then get them to pretend they are in a boat, an aeroplane or a train. Ask, *Would the same paintings be all right for these views?* Then ask them to paint different pictures of the things they would see from the air.

Set up journeys by car, train, boat and aeroplane in the role-play area over the next few days. Ask the children to choose the correct pictures for the views they would see from each of these modes of transport.

DIFFERENTIATION

Stick to cars, trains and boats with lower attaining children and ask them to improve on their drawings showing what they would see from each of these. Higher attaining children should be challenged to improve on their ideas of what views are like from aeroplanes by drawing other things from a bird's-eye point of view.

WHERE NEXT

Look at pictorial and aerial maps with the children and identify some of the features on them.

ASSESSMENT

Look at the children's paintings and drawings and assess whether they have improved on their ideas about what views look like from different modes of transport.

LEARNING OUTCOMES

Most children will learn that features will look different from a different viewpoint. This will help them improve their drawings of features when drawing maps.

FURTHER KNOWLEDGE AND UNDERSTANDING OF THE WORLD CHALLENGES

From where am I looking?

Show the children the photographs of different views and ask them to say whether they were taken from a car, aeroplane, train or boat. How do they know? Ask them to draw additional views for one of the modes of transport.

PLANTING

AREA OF LEARNING: KNOWLEDGE AND UNDERSTANDING OF THE WORLD. ELG: TO FIND OUT ABOUT, AND IDENTIFY, SOME FEATURES OF LIVING THINGS.

LEARNING OBJECTIVE

To learn how to plant bulbs and seeds.

THINKING OBJECTIVE

To test conclusions.

THINKING SKILLS

The children will work with you to plan and carry out a simple investigation to find out if a bulb will grow upwards if it is planted upside down. They will test out what they thought and begin to say whether what happened was what they thought would happen.

WHAT YOU NEED

Pictures of flowers; bulbs; pots; fibre.

WHAT TO DO

Show the children the pictures of the flowers. Then show them the bulbs and explain that this is how the flower grew, by planting the bulb. Wonder with the children where the flower will grow from. Ask, *Will it grow from the top of the bulb? Will it grow from the bottom?* Talk about any leaves and discuss which part of the bulb they will grow from. Agree with the children where each part of the flower will grow from the bulb, talking about the roots and the shape of the bulb.

Tell the children that you want them to grow flowers from the bulbs. Show them the pots and the fibre, explaining how this needs to be slightly damp. Ask the children to say which way up the bulbs should be planted. Should they always be upright? Wonder with them what would happen if one bulb is planted upside down. Will the bulb still grow and the flower appear, or will the flower grow downwards into the ground? Ask the children to suggest how they could test this out. Suggest that in one of the pots they could plant a bulb upside down to see.

Let the children plant a bulb each in the pots. You could plant some in pots that will fit on tables and shelves, and one or two in bigger pots to put outside in the garden or playground.

Wait for the bulbs to grow and note whether they all have flowers. Does the one that is planted upside down still have a flower that grows upwards like the others? Were the children right to think that the flower would grow down? Or were any children right who thought the flower would grow the same as the others and that it doesn't matter which way up the bulb is planted? Talk about why it is important to test out conclusions to see if you are right.

DIFFERENTIATION

Ask higher attaining children to research how the bulb would have looked as it started to grow. Help them to find pictures that show how the stem begins to first grow downwards, and then bends to grow upwards.

WHERE NEXT

Plant different seeds with the children. Look at the shape and size of these. Ask them to say whether it matters which way up they are planted. Can they see which is the top and which is the bottom of the seed? Grow the seeds to see how well they grow and to test out the children's conclusions.

ASSESSMENT

Write down the children's predictions about whether the bulbs will still grow normally when planted upside down and note those who get the prediction right.

LEARNING OUTCOMES

Most children will learn that when they give a prediction, it is useful to test out conclusions to check if they were right.

FURTHER KNOWLEDGE AND UNDERSTANDING OF THE WORLD CHALLENGES

Planting on paper

Ask the children to say whether they think seeds will grow on paper. Make a model of a lawn by growing cress seeds on layers of newspaper. Watch as they grow and ask the children if the test matches their conclusions. Grow other seeds on paper. Ask the children to predict which ones they think will grow and to test out their conclusions. Decide which seeds would be good for making models, for example a desert island made from papier-mâché.

DRAGON BOATS

AREA OF LEARNING: KNOWLEDGE AND UNDERSTANDING OF THE WORLD. ELG: TO BEGIN TO KNOW ABOUT THE CULTURES OF OTHER PEOPLE.

LEARNING OBJECTIVE

To learn about a Chinese celebration.

THINKING OBJECTIVE

To plan research.

THINKING SKILLS

The children will listen to a story and look at pictures, using these as a basis for researching what dragon boats look like. They will use their research to make boats to act out the dragon boat races themselves in as realistic a way as possible.

WHAT YOU NEED

A picture of dragon boat racing; a copy of the traditional tale of Ch'u Yuan (www.henleydragons.com tells the tale well – see 'About dragon boating'); a tape containing drum sounds; a range of drums; several large cardboard boxes; paint; coloured paper.

WHAT TO DO

Show the children the picture of dragon boat racing and tell them the story about Ch'u Yuan and the origins of Chinese dragon boat races. Explain that these now take place every year around the world.

Talk about and recall significant aspects of the story of Ch'u Yuan. Talk about how people believed that the calling and beats made on drums helped to keep the fish and demons away.

Tell the children that you want them to build two dragon boats and to act out the dragon boat racing. Ask, *How can you go about finding out what your dragon boats should look like? What sort of things do you need to know about the boats and the things people use them for?* Look at the picture again and describe some of the boats together. Ask questions to help the children, such as *What shape are they? How big are they? Are they decorated in a special way?* Ask the children how this helps them to research what their boats should look like.

Together, plan and design two boats identifying the materials you will need. Let the children use large cardboard boxes, paint and papers to make and decorate the boats. When the boats are finished, invite the children to take part in a dragon boat race.

Ask the children to think about the kind of sounds they will need to make, referring back to the story of Ch'u Yuan Ask, *What can you use to make these sounds?* Talk about the different sounds made by different types of drum, such as large and small drums, or plastic drums and those made with hide.

Invite some children to play the drums while others paddle the boats in a pretend dragon boat race. Evaluate with them whether their research has helped them to make realistic boats and to act out the race realistically.

DIFFERENTIATION

If necessary, let lower attaining children copy some of the things they see directly from the picture to help them. Higher attaining children can look in books and use a range of ideas to help them in their research. Let them use this research to develop their own creative and imaginative ideas.

WHERE NEXT

Get the children to plan some research into Chinese music to use with their dragon boat race or any other Chinese celebrations the class participates in.

ASSESSMENT

Assess how well the children use the picture as a basis for their research. Make a note of those children who identify other sources they could use.

LEARNING OUTCOMES

Most children will learn that pictures and stories are useful to help them plan research to find out about the world in which they live. Some will be able to use other sources to help them with their research.

FURTHER KNOWLEDGE AND UNDERSTANDING OF THE WORLD CHALLENGES

The school fête

Get the children to plan some research to find out the kinds of things people do at a school fête. Use different types of sources, such as showing the children some pictures and photos, asking older children to come to the class to talk about previous school fetes, reading stories together. Use the information to make a display about some of the things that can be enjoyed at a school fête, and set up some of the games that can be played at them, such as guessing the doll's name.

Paddle or row

Show the children a short extract from a video of a famous boat race, for example the Oxford and Cambridge boat race or one from an Olympic games. Talk about the number of people in each team, the size of the boat and the way the people make the boat move forward. Wonder with the children whether there is always the same number of people in the boats, and whether they always use oars to make the boats move. Ask, *Do you think there are other ways to make a boat move?* Discuss with the children how they can find out. Look at pictures and books together to find the answer.

THREADING

AREA OF LEARNING: PHYSICAL DEVELOPMENT. ELG: TO HANDLE OBJECTS WITH INCREASING CONTROL.

LEARNING OBJECTIVE

To learn to thread laces in a shoe.

THINKING OBJECTIVE

To predict outcomes.

THINKING SKILLS

The children will look carefully at a laced shoe and then decide whether the different ways you lace a shoe will mean that this pattern will be the same, predicting the outcome each time.

WHAT YOU NEED

Shoe laces; a pair of shoes, one threaded in a criss-cross pattern and one unlaced.

WHAT TO DO

Ask the children to look at the pattern of the lacing on one of your shoes. Talk about this pattern and how the lace criss-crosses over itself. Unthread your lace and show them how to do this by threading the lace

across the two holes at the top, closest to your shin, and starting to thread it in a criss-cross pattern. After lacing it through one hole on each side, ask the children to predict whether this will look right when it is finished. Agree with them that this cannot be right because the lace ends will finish at the bottom, near the toe of the shoe, when they should be at the other end near the shin to tie.

Thread the lace again, starting at the bottom, or toe-end, of the shoe, and threading through the bottom two holes to start, threading each end from under the hole and inviting a child to pull the lace through. Then criss-cross the lace down through the next two holes. Ask the children to say whether they think this will look right this time. Thread another shoe but this time ask the children to start the lace off for you.

DIFFERENTIATION

Work individually with lower attaining children and point out to them how the lace patterns match. Ask them to predict whether the pattern will look the same each time you lace another hole. Higher attaining children should be invited to say which holes you should lace next. Ask them questions, such as *Does it matter which side is laced next or will either hole still make the same pattern?*

WHERE NEXT

Start the children off on lacing their own shoe. Do the first criss-cross for them and then let them use their prediction skills to work out how to finish it. They should predict whether or not they will get this correct before they thread the final holes.

ASSESSMENT

Note the children who correctly predict whether the pattern will look the same as the first shoe.

LEARNING OUTCOMES

The children will learn how to lace shoes in a criss-cross pattern by predicting whether a pattern being laced on a shoe looks right.

FURTHER PHYSICAL DEVELOPMENT CHALLENGES

Lace it up

Get the children to lace shoes in different ways. Give them pairs of shoes with one laced in a certain way and the other unlaced. Start the children off and challenge them to predict how the lace is threaded through before finishing the lacing.

MAKING BOOKS

AREA OF LEARNING: PHYSICAL DEVELOPMENT. ELG: TO HANDLE TOOLS, OBJECTS, CONSTRUCTION AND MALLEABLE MATERIALS SAFELY AND WITH INCREASING CONTROL.

LEARNING OBJECTIVE
To use tools to make books.

THINKING OBJECTIVE
To anticipate consequences.

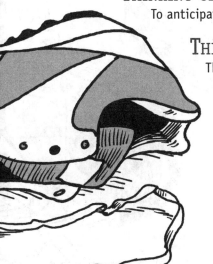

THINKING SKILLS
The children will watch a book-making process and will be encouraged to think about the consequences of not planning ahead. For example, not measuring and lining up the paper before stapling or putting holes in it.

WHAT YOU NEED
Pieces of paper of different sizes; a stapler and staples; a hole punch; treasury tags; string; ribbon.

WHAT TO DO
Explain to the children that they will be making books this week on the making table. Look at the range of materials you have collected for them to make these from.

Show the children several sheets of paper that are different sizes. Ask them to say whether these would be suitable to make a book from. Ask, *What is wrong with the sheets of paper? Do they all need to be the same size?* Agree with the children that the book will look different to usual books if paper of different sizes is used. However, some children may decide that this looks interesting. Let the children decide what they want their finished book to look like.

Next, shuffle the paper into a pile ready to staple. Make sure that several pages are askew. Ask the children to anticipate what the book will look like if you staple the pages together now. Staple them together so that the children can see how some paper has not been caught and that some pages have dropped out. Show them how untidy the pages look. Agree that the paper needs to be in line and straight to make the book look neater. Staple another set of paper together to make a book with the pages straight and together. Compare the two and agree which one the children like best and why.

Ask the children to use this knowledge to plan how to make holes in the book with the hole punch that are straight and tidy, and that are easy to thread ribbon or string through. Show them what happens if the holes are made in each piece of paper separately and how they are not in line with one another. Explain that this will make it very difficult to thread the ribbon, string or treasury tags through the holes.

Finish by completing the book. Make holes through several pieces of paper at a time, showing the children how it looks neat and straight, and let them choose whether to use ribbon, string or treasury tags to join the pages into a book. Leave the resources available on the table for independent group book-making tasks.

DIFFERENTIATION
Make books individually with less able children, putting different sizes of paper together and showing them what happens when you staple them together. Challenge more able children to anticipate what will happen when stapling books with a centre fold.

WHERE NEXT
Let the children make a range of books in the same way and use them for writing in, or displaying the children's work in.

Look at different books together and note how these are made.

ASSESSMENT
Note the children who understand the need to shuffle the paper straight before joining the pages. Talk to the children as they make their own books to find out who anticipates the consequences of not preparing the pages before stapling or making the holes.

LEARNING OUTCOMES
Most children will be able to make books independently, using staples and a hole punch. Many will understand the need to make the papers straight before trying to join them into a book.

FURTHER PHYSICAL DEVELOPMENT CHALLENGES

Filing system

Together, make loose-leaf pages to go into a fact file linked to a current topic. This could be about animals, themselves, plants and flowers or nursery rhymes. Let the children anticipate what will happen if they do not measure carefully where to punch the holes before they put their pages into the file.

Name labels

Ask the children to make labels for their coat pegs by punching holes into cards and hanging them from the pegs with ribbon threaded through the holes. Encourage the children to say what will happen if they do not punch the hole in the correct place.

TAMBOURINE SOUNDS

AREA OF LEARNING: CREATIVE DEVELOPMENT. ELG: TO RECOGNISE AND EXPLORE HOW SOUNDS CAN BE CHANGED.

LEARNING OBJECTIVE

To learn how to change sounds by the way an instrument is played.

THINKING OBJECTIVE

To plan research.

THINKING SKILLS

The children will explore all the different sounds they can make on different instruments. They will think about the way these are played and will then use this research to make different sounds on one instrument.

WHAT YOU NEED

A range of percussion instruments; different beaters and brushes.

WHAT TO DO

In small groups, let the children explore the sounds the different instruments make. After a few minutes, bring the children back together and choose a triangle, inviting a child to show it makes a sound. Invite the children to say if they know a different way to make a sound on the triangle. Repeat the different ways the sounds can be made on the triangle for the children to listen to.

Ask them to say whether they think they could make a different type of sound with a different beater. Ask, *How can we find out?* Explain that they can find out by exploring the range of beaters in the collection. Allow them to do this for a few minutes in groups, before coming back to report on their findings. Choose a drum next. Ask the children how they can go about finding out how many different sounds they can produce on this instrument. Again, allow them to try their ideas out in groups.

DIFFERENTIATION

If the children have not used instruments for a while, or this is their first time, concentrate on how to produce the sounds rather than researching the changes in musical elements. Higher attaining children should be encouraged to research instruments where different ways of playing them is not immediately obvious, for example maracas and Indian bells.

WHERE NEXT

Set up everyday objects for the children to research the sounds they make, such as crisp packets, different papers, tins and card cartons.

ASSESSMENT

Note the children who use their research plan to systematically explore the range of sounds the instruments can make. Note those children who research the musical elements in addition to the different ways of producing the sounds.

LEARNING OUTCOMES

Most children will follow the research plan to explore the full range of sounds that can be produced on each instrument.

FURTHER CREATIVE DEVELOPMENT CHALLENGES

Tambourine sounds

Individually, or in small groups, get the children to explore the range of sounds that can be made with a tambourine. Plan the research together first by thinking about the different ways that instruments can be played, the ways that sounds can be changed and identifying beaters and other resources that can be used to produce different sounds.

REPEATING PATTERNS

AREA OF LEARNING: CREATIVE DEVELOPMENT. ELG: TO RECOGNISE REPEATED SOUNDS AND SOUND PATTERNS AND MATCH MOVEMENTS TO MUSIC.

LEARNING OBJECTIVE
To recognise repeating patterns and use them as prompts to sequence movements.

THINKING OBJECTIVE
To ask questions.

THINKING SKILLS
The children will learn to ask each other questions which will help them to play along to repeating patterns in a song.

WHAT YOU NEED
A copy of 'March of the Siamese Children' from *The King and I* by Rodgers and Hammerstein; a selection of instruments, such as drums, tambourines, woodblocks.

WHAT TO DO
Play the music, letting the children clap along to it at will. You will notice some will start to pick out the crotchet, quaver/quaver rhythm and start to clap along to this. If they do not, do this yourself until they are all copying and joining in with this repeating rhythm.

Give half the class an instrument each and invite them to play the repeating rhythm along to the music. Tell the others they should clap along. Explain that you will swap the instruments over at the end. When the music has finished, invite the group who were clapping to ask the instrumentalists questions to help them play the instruments in time to the music when it is their turn. If they cannot think of

any questions, model these for them, such as *Is it easy to keep the rhythm? Do you need to listen to the music carefully? Which bit of the rhythm is harder to play? How should I hold the instrument? Do I need to tap the instrument hard or gently?*

Swap over the instruments and let the second half of the class play them. When they have finished, invite the other half to ask questions about how they felt. Model again if they think of no questions, such as *Did you like playing the instruments? Did you find it easy to keep the rhythm? How hard was it to listen to the tune and play at the same time?* Finish by letting all the children have an instrument to play the repeating rhythm accompaniment.

DIFFERENTIATION
Work with lower attaining children afterwards in a small group, inviting them to ask questions about whether the other group liked playing the instruments.

WHERE NEXT
Set up the activity as a small independent group task during self-initiated play activities. Invite the children to ask each other questions about their performances.

ASSESSMENT
Ask an additional adult to list some of the questions the children ask each other. Ask them to note the names of the children alongside. Organise those who did not ask a question to listen to another piece of music and invite them to ask each other about the parts they liked best and why.

LEARNING OUTCOMES
All the children will learn to ask questions, either questions that invite a response about how other children liked the music, or more specific questions to help them perform the accompaniments themselves.

FURTHER CREATIVE DEVELOPMENT CHALLENGES
Repeating tunes
Listen to the tune again and invite the children to ask each other questions about whether they liked the tune or not. Invite the children to close their eyes and think about how the children in the song might be moving. Invite them to question each other to describe what they saw in their heads. Play the music again and let the children pretend to be one of the Siamese children and move to the music. Challenge them to change their movements when the tune changes, either by changing direction or the way they are marching.

CREATIVE THINKING SKILLS

INTRODUCTION

Young children are adventurous with their ideas and often do not let practicalities get in the way. They design freely and see no reason why their favourite book or TV character cannot form the basis for a bed or a chair. With this in mind, the activities in this chapter are organised so that the children are given the opportunity to really think outside the box. However, the skills the children will learn come second to their using them in a creative way. The activities aim to give the children enough space to let their imaginations run wild. Sometimes the children may want to think in a different way to solve a problem or when working out how to approach a task. Activities in this chapter give the children familiar tasks but give them the freedom to understand why things are approached in the way that they are. For example, the children will learn the practical skill of folding. They will learn that it is a way of giving something a design or structure, but that it is also a way to pack things away neatly to make them easier to handle next time you want them. This development of lateral thinking is a way of developing the children's independence, allowing them to use their initiative and take responsibility for their own learning.

Questions such as *What will happen if...* are considered during the activities, which give the children the opportunity to hypothesise about certain situations. Questions such as *What will happen if I put this here?* will lead the children to hypothesise about their designs and creative ideas. They will consider this when combining colours, dance movements or deciding whether to glue or staple paper or collage materials when making a picture.

By considering how items are designed and made, the children will consider how they can extend ideas by incorporating some of them into their own work. For example, when looking at fans, they will consider how to use the folding techniques employed in their own designs when making objects or decorations from folding paper.

The creative thinking skills are:
⊙ creating ideas
⊙ imaginative thinking
⊙ finding alternative innovative outcomes/lateral thinking
⊙ hypothesising
⊙ extending ideas.

INTRODUCING CREATIVE THINKING SKILLS

Area of learning and ELG, NLS or NNS objective	Activity title	Thinking objective	Activity	Page
Personal, social and emotional development ELG: To work as part of a group, taking turns and sharing fairly	Taking turns	To extend ideas	Understanding how to play a game fairly	84
Communication, language and literacy ELG: To use language to imagine and recreate roles and experiences NLS objective: To re-read frequently a variety of familiar texts	Aeroplane	To think imaginatively	Using role-play to develop imaginative thinking	84
Communication, language and literacy ELG: To show an understanding of the elements of stories NLS objective: To understand how story book language works	Story line	To think imaginatively	Making up a class or group story	85
Mathematical development ELG: To use language to compare quantities NNS objective: To use language to compare two quantities	Is it taller?	To extend ideas	Putting themselves in height order	85
Mathematical development ELG: To use developing mathematical ideas to solve problems NNS objective: To compare two lengths by making direct comparisons	Hats and belts	To think laterally; to extend ideas	Selecting suitable resources to measure round things	86
Knowledge and understanding of the world ELG: To find out about past and present events	The photographer	To hypothesise	Looking at photographs from different periods from the past and deciding which are oldest	86
Knowledge and understanding of the world ELG: To find out about some features of living things, objects and events	It's a small world	To think imaginatively	Imagining the world in which small creatures live	87
Knowledge and understanding of the world ELG: To use information and communication technology to support learning	Music live	To create ideas	Recording a radio programme, to include music and talk, on tape	88
Physical development ELG: To travel around, under, over and through balancing and climbing equipment	Over and under	To create ideas	Creating obstacle courses	88
Physical development ELG: To recognise the changes that happen to their bodies when they are active	Work out	To hypothesise	Learning the importance of warming up and cooling down before and after exercise	89
Creative development ELG: To use their imagination in dance	Wellington splash	To create ideas	Creating a sequence of dance movements	89
Creative development ELG: To express and communicate their ideas, thoughts and feelings by using a variety of musical instruments	Sounds like	To create ideas	Composing sound to accompany an extract from a favourite film	90

TAKING TURNS

AREA OF LEARNING: PERSONAL, SOCIAL AND EMOTIONAL DEVELOPMENT. ELG: TO WORK AS PART OF A GROUP OR CLASS, TAKING TURNS AND SHARING FAIRLY.

LEARNING OBJECTIVE
To learn how to share and take turns.

THINKING OBJECTIVE
To extend ideas.

THINKING SKILLS
The children will learn to think about the feelings of others during this activity. They will decide together fair rules for taking it in turns to play with a new toy or game, and sharing it amicably. They will then extend the idea of fairness, pulling names out of a hat to organise the order of turns that each child will take at the new toy or game.

WHAT YOU NEED
A new toy(s) or game, which you know all of the children will want to play with; the name of each child written on a small piece of paper; a hat.

WHAT TO DO
Show the children the new toy or game and talk about all the things they can do when playing with it. Ask, *Who would like to have a turn? How many children can play at any one time?* Wonder with the children how they can make it fair so that everyone who wants to have a turn can do so. Make decisions about how the turns will be organised. What if everyone has a very short turn today, and from tomorrow the class can organise turns so that everyone has a go for a much longer time?

Invite the children to say how they could organise today's turn taking. Encourage ideas, and then suggest that each child should have five minutes each at the game so that there is time during the day for everyone to have a turn. (Adapt the length of time for the number in your group. Five minutes will allow 12 children per hour to have a turn and, therefore, 36 during a three-hour morning session. This should provide enough time for full-time and part-time attendees to have a go.)

Invite the children to suggest how they can make sure that people change over at the right time. Agree that an adult should organise this, using a timer that rings a bell. The children will need a prompt to make sure they are ready for their turn each time.

Next ask the children how they could decide the order in which the children will take turns. Show them the hat and the names written on the pieces of paper, then put all the names into the hat. Ask the children what they could do with the hat and the names. At their prompt, pull the first name out of the hat and invite that child to have the first turn. Set the timer going. Pull the next name out of the hat and invite that child to be ready for the next turn. As the bell sounds at the end of each turn, pull the next name out of the hat in preparation until all the children have had a turn.

AEROPLANE

AREA OF LEARNING: COMMUNICATION, LANGUAGE AND LITERACY. ELG: TO USE LANGUAGE TO IMAGINE AND RECREATE ROLES AND EXPERIENCES. NLS OBJECTIVE: TO RE-READ FREQUENTLY A VARIETY OF FAMILIAR TEXTS.

LEARNING OBJECTIVE
To imagine what it is like on an aeroplane and to take part in a number of activities that air passengers might.

THINKING OBJECTIVE
To think imaginatively.

THINKING SKILLS
The children will have their imaginations sparked by listening to a talk about what it is like to fly on an aeroplane. They will then create their own aeroplane, using their imaginations, and will then take part in various role-plays, acting out different situations and taking part in different activities while on board.

WHAT YOU NEED
A number of chairs; a TV and video player; videos of the children's favourite programmes and some of different countries around the world; books and comics; a trolley with real drinks; food trays similar to those found on aeroplanes; fruit.

WHAT TO DO
Ask an older child or adult to come into the classroom and talk about a time when they travelled on an aeroplane. Ask them to talk about what kind of activities they did, how they ate dinner, what they had to drink, what jobs the flight attendants did.

Afterwards, talk with the children about the different people that were on board the aeroplane and the kinds of things they did. Tell the children that you want them to create the inside of an aeroplane. Explain how it usually has seats organised in rows and that these can be two rows of three seats with an aisle in between, or seats of three, five and three with two aisles dividing the rows, depending on the size of the aeroplane. Let the children decide for themselves how they want to organise these. Leave the other equipment around for the children to find, giving them the freedom to find the things they want to include themselves. This will develop their imaginative thinking further.

Allocate roles and set up different activities for the children to take part in. For example, on one day, organise the children inside the aeroplane so that they can watch favourite programmes or videos about different destinations around the world. This will link to 'Knowledge and understanding of the world' activities. On other days, leave a range of familiar books and comics for the children to read. Organise snack time to take place in the aeroplane so that the children begin to understand the difficulties of eating and drinking from a tray in a small space. Let the children take turns to play the roles of the flight attendants and pilot, pouring drinks or telling the passengers details of the flight, speed, altitude and flight path.

STORY LINE

AREA OF LEARNING: COMMUNICATION, LANGUAGE AND LITERACY. ELG: TO SHOW AN UNDERSTANDING OF THE ELEMENTS OF STORIES, SUCH AS MAIN CHARACTER, SEQUENCE OF EVENTS, AND OPENINGS. NLS OBJECTIVE: TO UNDERSTAND HOW STORY BOOK LANGUAGE WORKS AND TO USE SOME FORMAL ELEMENTS WHEN RETELLING STORIES.

LEARNING OBJECTIVE
To make up a story with a main character and a sequence of events.

THINKING OBJECTIVE
To think imaginatively.

THINKING SKILLS
The children will think imaginatively to make up a story.

WHAT YOU NEED
A flip chart or board.

WHAT TO DO
Tell the children that you are going to make up a story together that will include a main character and a sequence of events. Explain that you want them to use their imaginations to make an interesting story.

Start the story with an opening you either want the children to learn, or one that they are familiar with, such as *Once upon a time...* and write this on the flip chart. Invite the children to say who the main character will be and write their name and draw a picture of what the children think they look like underneath. Continue the story with *One day...* and let the children suggest what the character did. Then write the next part, such as *As* [the main character's name] *looked around...* and invite the children to say what the setting for the story is. Next write *As* [the main character's name] *looked around he/she/it noticed...* Continue following the children's lead and writing what happens to build up the story. Make up other stories with those who want to continue.

IS IT TALLER?

AREA OF LEARNING: MATHEMATICAL DEVELOPMENT. ELG: TO USE LANGUAGE SUCH AS 'GREATER', 'SMALLER', 'HEAVIER' OR 'LIGHTER' TO COMPARE QUANTITIES. NNS OBJECTIVE: TO USE LANGUAGE SUCH AS LONGER OR SHORTER TO COMPARE TWO QUANTITIES.

LEARNING OBJECTIVE
To compare height and length.

THINKING OBJECTIVE
To extend ideas.

THINKING SKILLS
The children will work out a way of ordering a group in height order by comparing sizes. They will extend their ideas by transfering this to length, before using their knowledge of comparative language to think of ten things that are taller, longer, and shorter than themselves. Some of these things they will find in the local environment and some will be based on previous learning experiences.

WHAT YOU NEED
Large sheets of paper; paint; a large floor space to make the pictures; a display space.

WHAT TO DO

In small groups, ask the children to organise themselves in order of height. Suggest they start from the shortest or tallest child and work from there. Give them time to think about how they can do this for themselves. Many will start to compare themselves to a neighbour to see whether they are taller or shorter, but may not be able to transfer this to finding out whether anyone else in the class is taller or shorter. The children will probably know immediately who is the tallest and shortest in their group, but may find it more difficult to find out the order of heights in between.

Model the language as the children organise themselves by asking, *Who is shorter? Who is taller? Who needs to stand next to this person?*

When each group have got the idea of ordering themselves by height, ask them to order themselves by length, modelling the language for this: *longer* and *shorter*. If they are struggling to do this, suggest they do this by lying on the floor. Does anyone realise that the tallest will also be the longest, and so on, or do they start the comparisons over again?

When you are sure the children understand the comparative language of length, ask the whole class to organise themselves by height and watch as they extend the idea and think for themselves how to do this.

As a small group or individual task, ask the children to think of ten things that are taller, shorter and longer than they are. Identify some of these from the immediate environment, such as a door, window, tree, house, cupboard or PE bench. Finish by asking the children to paint actual-sized pictures of some of these things to add to a display.

HATS AND BELTS

AREA OF LEARNING: MATHEMATICAL DEVELOPMENT. ELG: TO USE DEVELOPING MATHEMATICAL IDEAS TO SOLVE PROBLEMS. NNS OBJECTIVE: TO COMPARE TWO LENGTHS BY MAKING DIRECT COMPARISONS.

LEARNING OBJECTIVE

To identify resources for measuring round things.

THINKING OBJECTIVE

To think laterally; to extend ideas.

THINKING SKILLS

The children will use their understanding of measures to find out how long they need to make something to fit around their heads. They will think laterally by deciding for themselves how to measure around their heads in a practical activity, choosing from a range of resources. They will extend the idea by making belts to fit in the same way.

WHAT YOU NEED

Crêpe and tissue paper in different colours; strips of card; tape measures, ribbon and string; a flat ruler; a stapler; PVA glue; two pre-made hats made from these materials, one which is too big and one which is too small; fabric, paper clips.

WHAT TO DO

Show the children a simple hat made from crêpe or tissue paper. Put it on your head and show them that it is too big. Put the other hat on to show that it is too small. Tell the children that you want them to make a hat for themselves, but one that fits!

Undo one of the hats and show the children how it is made. Then, give each child a strip of card and invite them to choose a favourite colour of tissue or crêpe paper to glue around the strip. When they have done this and the glue is dry, ask the children to think of a way to find out where they need to join the strip so that it fits their head. Ask, *How can you make sure that it will not be too big or too small?* Some children will put the strip around their head and ask you to hold it in place and staple the ends together. This is fine, but either challenge them to think of another way, or pretend to lose your place so that this way is shown to be not so reliable.

Extend the children's thinking by getting them to link the need for something which is flexible to measure around their heads. Show the children the ribbon, string and tape measures. Can anyone suggest how these could be used to measure their heads? Why are these better than measuring with a flat ruler?

Extend the activity by getting the children to make belts from fabric to fit around their waists. They can use paper clips to join the two ends of the belt together.

THE PHOTOGRAPHER

AREA OF LEARNING: KNOWLEDGE AND UNDERSTANDING OF THE WORLD. ELG: TO FIND OUT ABOUT PAST AND PRESENT EVENTS.

LEARNING OBJECTIVE
To find out about the past from a photograph.

THINKING OBJECTIVE
To hypothesise.

THINKING SKILLS
The children will look at photographs from different periods in the past and hypothesise which photographs are modern and which are old.

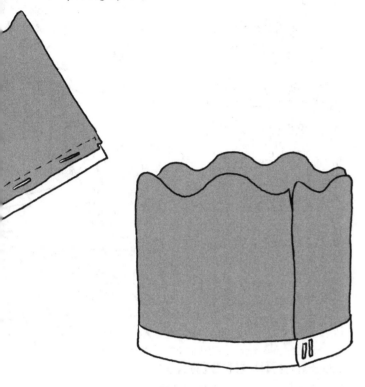

They will use clues such as fashion, hairstyles, car designs and what people are doing and decide which photograph is oldest as a result of their thinking.

WHAT YOU NEED
Photographs of people from different periods in the past, for example the fifties, seventies and nineties, which show fashions, hairstyles, vehicles and pastimes; modern photographs showing the children during activities recently.

WHAT TO DO
As a class, look at photographs together of recent activities that the children have done, and which they will remember doing. Talk about what they are doing in the photographs and get them to look carefully at the things in the picture. Ask, *What are you wearing? What are your hairstyles like? What things are you doing? How do we know that these photographs are modern or recent?* Explain that it is because of the quality of the photograph as well as the answers to the questions you have just asked.

Let some children go to their self-initiated play activities while you work with others in small groups, looking at some of the older photographs in your collection. Let the children comment on the fashions, the hairstyles and the other things in the pictures which look different to them. Note whether the photographs are in colour or black and white. Ask, *Which is the oldest photograph? How do you know?* Perhaps you have a sepia photograph in your collection, or one that has been coloured by hand. Hypothesise with the children whether these photographs are modern or reflect things that happened in the past. How do the children know?

Look at two photographs from the past that are very different, perhaps one in colour and one in black and white. Talk about the things the children can see and invite them to hypothesise which is the oldest. Ask, *How do you know this person is older than this person? Why do you think this?* If you have any photographs in original frames, talk about these and hypothesise which is the oldest frame. Ask, *What does this photograph frame tell you about its owner? Which is the oldest? How do you know? Is it made from plastic or wood? Which is the most modern?*

IT'S A SMALL WORLD

AREA OF LEARNING: KNOWLEDGE AND UNDERSTANDING OF THE WORLD. ELG: TO FIND OUT ABOUT, AND IDENTIFY, SOME FEATURES OF LIVING THINGS, OBJECTS AND EVENTS THEY OBSERVE.

LEARNING OBJECTIVE
To think about where small creatures live.

THINKING OBJECTIVE
To think imaginatively.

THINKING SKILLS
The children will go on a safari to find all the creatures that live in the school or grounds before imagining what the world looks like from their perspective.

WHAT YOU NEED
An extract from the film *Honey, I Shrunk the Kids* (Disney) where the children are lost in the grass.

WHAT TO DO
Take the children for a walk around the school or the grounds noting all the natural features, like hedges, trees, ponds, grass and flowerbeds. Note human features too, such as fences, walls, the playground and seats. Talk to the children about all these areas

and imagine with them what creatures live there. Ask the children, *Who do you think visits the tree? What creatures live under the hedge or in the long grass? Do you think any creatures would live on the playground?*

Go on a class safari and look for small creatures in these places. Note with the children the range of creatures there are, and whether they live alone or in groups. On return to the classroom, ask the children to imagine what each creature's world looks like to them. Ask questions to help them think about this, such as *What does the grass look like to a spider? How tall is it to an ant? What about the tree? How far does the walk from the bottom of the tree to the top seem for an ant or a spider? What about the worms who live under the hedge? How long does it take for them to get from one end to the other?*

Play the children the extract from *Honey, I Shrunk the Kids* where the children are lost in the garden. Focus the children on thinking about the height of the grass, how the shape of it looks and the thickness of each blade. Let the children choose one feature from among the grass on the extract and draw the creatures that they think would live on or in this. Invite them to write thought bubbles reflecting what the creatures are thinking about their habitat. You could develop this activity further in a dance activity.

MUSIC LIVE

AREA OF LEARNING: KNOWLEDGE AND UNDERSTANDING OF THE WORLD. ELG: TO USE INFORMATION AND COMMUNICATION TECHNOLOGY TO SUPPORT THEIR LEARNING.

LEARNING OBJECTIVE
To learn to use a tape recorder to record sounds.

THINKING OBJECTIVE
To create ideas.

THINKING SKILLS
The children will create their own radio show, from introducing songs as a DJ would, to choosing their own music to include in their show. They will be responsible for recording their show onto a tape.

WHAT YOU NEED
A radio; a flip chart or board; a tape recorder and tape; music CDs and CD-player.

WHAT TO DO
Tell the class that you want them to create their own radio show. As a class, listen to the radio and identify the kinds of things DJs say when introducing records. Practise some of the things the children may

like to say when introducing a record. For example, *Coming right up is a track from my favourite album,* or *The next record has been requested by Class X from Main Road Primary School.*

Then discuss and identify the kinds of records the children would like to include. This could be a favourite recorded song, a piece of music or one that the children want to sing themselves. Let them decide and make their own selection and record these on the flip chart.

Gather together the music the children want to include on their radio show for the next lesson. Work with the children and organise the resources they will need, and then in small groups, ask them to choose a song, introduce it and record it onto the tape. When all the groups have contributed to the tape, listen to the whole thing so the children can hear their creation.

OVER AND UNDER

AREA OF LEARNING: PHYSICAL DEVELOPMENT. ELG: TO TRAVEL AROUND, UNDER, OVER AND THROUGH BALANCING AND CLIMBING EQUIPMENT.

LEARNING OBJECTIVE
To travel safely on a range of balancing and climbing apparatus.

THINKING OBJECTIVE
To create ideas.

THINKING SKILLS
The children will create their own obstacle courses on which they can practise a range of balancing, travelling and climbing movements. They will decide for themselves how to organise the PE apparatus to make as many different obstacle courses as they can.

WHAT YOU NEED
A range of apparatus for climbing and balancing to make an obstacle course from, including gymnastics tables, planks, ladders, beams, benches and mats; a flip chart or board and writing materials.

WHAT TO DO

Tell the children that you want their ideas for an obstacle course which will make them move in a set of predetermined directions, for example going up, along, over, through and down various pieces of apparatus. Set up their ideas and let them move along the obstacle course, checking that all the directions of movement are possible.

See how many different obstacle courses the children can come up with over a week. At the end of each session, talk about what they liked about the obstacle course. Would they like to keep this one the next day? Is there anything they would like to change? Can they make any parts more challenging? Are there any bits too difficult? Is there somewhere that can be used as a creative role-play part? Make sure the class agree and then draw the obstacle course for the next day, labelling the apparatus you will use to make it.

WORK OUT

AREA OF LEARNING: PHYSICAL DEVELOPMENT. ELG: TO RECOGNISE THE CHANGES THAT HAPPEN TO THEIR BODIES WHEN THEY ARE ACTIVE.

LEARNING OBJECTIVE
To learn what happens to their bodies during exercise and the importance of warming up and cooling down.

THINKING OBJECTIVE
To hypothesise.

THINKING SKILLS
The children will note the changes in their bodies after exercise. After an initial warm-up activity, they will hypothesise about what will happen to their bodies after more exercise and then consider whether

their hypotheses were correct. They will link this to the importance of warming up and cooling down before and after exertion.

WHAT YOU NEED
An extract of lively music, such as a pop song with a steady and regular repeating beat; a suitable music player.

WHAT TO DO
Do a gentle warm-up with the children to get their muscles working. Explain, if appropriate, what they are doing and why, but do not go into too much detail at this point.

Tell the children that they are going to do a fitness routine. Play them the extract of music, and ask them to think about the type of movements they could do to the music. Do not spend too long on this, as the children need to stay warm. However, do spend a few moments hypothesising with the children about what they think will happen to their bodies as they move about to the music. Things to think about include getting out of breath, getting hotter, beginning to sweat and their legs aching.

When they have had suitable opportunity to express their hypotheses, let them move freely to the music, developing suitable routines that fit it. Ask, *Were your hypotheses right? What has happened to your bodies so far?* Practise some more routines, acting as the leader yourself the first time, and then inviting other children to play the leader to extend some of your ideas. At the end of the session, invite the children to lie very still while they think about how their bodies have changed after exercise. Link this to their hypotheses and to the need to warm up at the beginning of PE lessons. Also explain the importance of what they are doing now, that cooling down so that the body can return to its usual state is just as important.

WELLINGTON SPLASH

AREA OF LEARNING: CREATIVE DEVELOPMENT. ELG: TO USE THEIR IMAGINATION IN DANCE.

LEARNING OBJECTIVE
To create movements based on a particular scenario and to sequence these movements.

THINKING OBJECTIVE
To create ideas.

THINKING SKILLS
The children will listen to a story about splashing around in puddles. They will reflect on this and

use the context to create their own dance ideas to recreate the splashing movements. They will take this one step further, creating a sequence of dance movements.

WHAT YOU NEED

A copy of *Alfie's Feet* by Shirley Hughes (Red Fox Picture Books); a flip chart or board; a large space; a suitable piece of music for the children to move around to; a camera.

WHAT TO DO

Before the lesson read the story *Alfie's Feet* to the children and talk about what it is like to splash in puddles. Together, think of all the words to describe the movements, such as *stamp, splash, stomp, jump, hard* and *kick* and record these on the flip chart. Look at some of the illustrations in the book to help the children think of the words, if necessary.

Move to a large space and play the music, letting the children move freely to it, exploring the pulse. When the children have warmed up sufficiently, ask them to pull on an imaginary pair of Wellington boots and to move to the music again. Tell them to pretend that the hall, or space in which they are moving, is covered in puddles. Remind the children of the classroom discussion and the words they came up with for moving in puddles. Play the music again and let the children create their own ideas for splashing in the puddles, perhaps jumping in with two feet, or stamping with one foot. Use hoops to help the children use all the space if necessary.

Watch the children as they move and choose some that are moving in interesting ways, for example lifting their knees up very high and stamping down, to demonstrate to the rest of the class. Evaluate some movements together for a few minutes and then put a series of them together and practise this sequence as a class. Get the children to practise the sequence over and over again to the music, until they remember how it goes. Take photographs of the children's movements.

Back in the classroom, use pictures of the different

moves to organise the dance into a sequence. Talk to the children how they want to organise this. Perhaps changing them around to add interest. Repeat the dance over the next few weeks, adapting and extending the children's ideas.

SOUNDS LIKE

AREA OF LEARNING: CREATIVE DEVELOPMENT. ELG: TO EXPRESS AND COMMUNICATE THEIR IDEAS, THOUGHTS AND FEELINGS BY USING A VARIETY OF MUSICAL INSTRUMENTS.

LEARNING OBJECTIVE

To express feelings and mood through composing sounds.

THINKING OBJECTIVE

To create ideas.

THINKING SKILLS

The children will watch an extract of a favourite film with the sound turned off. They will consider how the extract makes them feel, and create sounds to reflect these feelings and emotions.

WHAT YOU NEED

A copy of *The Jungle Book* (Disney) on video; a TV and video; a selection of instruments.

WHAT TO DO

In small groups, watch an extract from the film *The Jungle Book*. Almost any extract will do, but certainly the parts where Mowgli and Baloo meet the monkeys, where the snake hypnotises Mowgli, and where the elephants are on parade are suitable. Leave the sound turned down. Talk to the children about what they can see. Ask, *What sounds do you think are going on all around? What do you think Mowgli is feeling? How could you express these feelings as a sound?* Let the children explore the instruments and add sounds to the extract.

When all the groups have composed their own ideas, watch each extract together as a class, letting the children play their compositions. Afterwards, watch the extracts again with the sound turned up to see if the children's compositions reflected the mood of the film music.

EXTENDING CREATIVE THINKING SKILLS

Area of learning and ELG, NLS or NNS objective	Activity title	Thinking objective	Activity	Page
Personal, social and emotional development ELG: To continue to be interested, excited and motivated to learn	Rewards	To create and to extend ideas	Setting up a reward system for good working habits	92
Communication, language and literacy ELG: To use talk to organise, sequence and clarify thinking, ideas, feelings and events NLS objective: To understand how story book language works	Comic characters	To think imaginatively	Making up a story from pictures	93
Communication, language and literacy ELG: To write their own names and captions and to form simple sentences NLS objective: To understand that writing can be used for a range of purposes	Character study	To think imaginatively	Making up a character for a story	94
Communication, language and literacy ELG: To interact with others and taking turns in conversation NLS objective: To use knowledge of familiar texts to re-enact the main points of a story	Noah's Ark	To think imaginatively	Making a role-play area to re-enact a story	95
Mathematical development ELGs: To count reliably up to 10; to use mathematical ideas to solve practical problems NNS objectives: To count reliably up to 10 everyday objects; to solve simple problems in a practical context	Blackberries and apples	To think laterally and to extend ideas	Counting blackberries and apples	97
Mathematical development ELG: To use language to describe the shape and size of flat shapes NNS objective: To use language to describe a flat shape	Take two triangles	To think laterally; to hypothesise	Making pictures, patterns and shapes from other shapes	98
Knowledge and understanding of the world ELGs: To look closely at similarities, differences, patterns and change; to investigate materials by using all of their senses	Plasticine shapes	To extend ideas	Making different shapes from Plasticine and other materials	99
Knowledge and understanding of the world ELG: To find out about some features of living things	Colour garden	To create ideas	Designing, and finding suitable plants for, a garden of colours	100
Knowledge and understanding of the world ELG: To look closely at similarities, differences, patterns and change	Hidden robots	To hypothesise	Thinking about camouflage in pictures	101
Physical development ELG: To handle malleable materials safely and with increasing control	Paper decorations	To extend ideas	Making decorations by folding and pleating paper	102
Physical development ELG: To show awareness of space, themselves and others Creative development ELG: To use their imagination	Photo fit	To create ideas	Creating dances based on a circus character	103
Creative development ELG: To explore colour in two dimensions	Concentric circles	To extend ideas	Painting using circles and mixing colours, using the paintings of Kandinsky as inspiration	104

REWARDS

AREA OF LEARNING: PERSONAL, SOCIAL AND EMOTIONAL DEVELOPMENT. ELG: TO CONTINUE TO BE INTERESTED, EXCITED AND MOTIVATED TO LEARN.

LEARNING OBJECTIVE
To understand how rewards can motivate learning.

THINKING OBJECTIVE
To create and to extend ideas.

THINKING SKILLS
The children will consider the way that rewards are currently measured in the classroom, or will learn of a new reward system. They will have input into the activities they are offered in class 'golden time', creating their own ideas for a new reward each week. They will extend their ideas by thinking of different ways to show how close they are to getting their next class golden time, thinking of new replacements for stickers as rewards.

WHAT YOU NEED
Stickers to award to the children; a flip chart or board; large toy bricks; a space to build these in.

WHAT TO DO
If you have individual golden time with your class, talk with the children about how they are awarded this. If you do not, start awarding the children a sticker every time they do something that shows a good attitude or good behaviour. For example, completing a piece of work on time, making a particular effort to present it neatly, co-operating in a group, or helping someone to find something they need. At the end of the week the stickers can be exchanged for 'golden time' – time when the children can choose a special activity in which to take part. Let the award scheme run for a few weeks until the children get the idea of golden time and sticker rewards.

After a few weeks, explain to the children that you want to extend the award system and develop a class golden time. Explain that every time the children are awarded a sticker, they should add a brick to a collection in the classroom with the intention of building a wall. Tell them that when the wall is built, the whole class will be awarded golden time. Explain how many bricks there will need to be in the finished wall.

List all the things that the children would like included as possible golden time when the wall is built. This may be a visit to the local park, a picnic or watching a favourite video. Take a vote and make a note of the chosen activity so that the children know what they are working towards. Leave other ideas on the list for the children to choose the next time the class has earned class golden time. Over the next few days, as the children are awarded a sticker, invite them to add a brick to create the wall.

When the wall is built, organise the activity chosen by the class for class golden time. Make this a very special occasion and make sure the children know what this is for.

Extend the children's ideas by organising a planning activity where the children create new ways of displaying their rewards that have been awarded for class golden time. Ideas to think about could include making a large flower by adding petals, in autumn having leaves falling from trees, building models of cars, adding stars to a night sky (where the rewards are petals, leaves, car components and stars respectively). Let the children come up with their own ideas for rewards and ways of displaying them and record these ideas for the class to choose the ones they like best. Over the next few weeks, use the children's ideas instead of stickers for displaying rewards for awarding class golden time.

DIFFERENTIATION
Work with less able children in a smaller group and let them choose from a range of given ideas for rewards, or let them adapt these. Make the collection of rewards as practical as possible, for example building a car from a construction kit where the children get a wheel, axle or seat as a reward, so that the children are actively building something. Higher attaining children should be encouraged to find their own way of collecting their rewards early on in the activity, using their own ideas for collecting rewards to act as leads and to provide ideas for others in the class. These ideas can be shared during class sharing time.

WHERE NEXT

Each time you plan a display, explain to the children that as it is added to over a number of days this will go towards earning them class golden time. When the display is finished, the children will have earned golden time for the class.

Let the children nominate each other for stickers for particular acts of kindness. This will encourage them to work towards completing the wall much faster and give them some responsibility for developing and managing their own behaviour.

Find a way of rewarding those children who make a particular contribution to the wall every day. It is important that every child is given recognition at some point during each term.

ASSESSMENT

Keep two tick lists – one to note the children who create their own ideas for collecting rewards and one for those who extend the ideas of others to make it suitable for the activity.

LEARNING OUTCOMES

Most children will use the ideas of others to create a suitable way to collect rewards. Some will create new ideas, which will also contribute to a class display.

FURTHER PERSONAL, SOCIAL AND EMOTIONAL DEVELOPMENT CHALLENGES

Target skills

Identify a particular attitude, skill or behaviour you want the children to learn during the week. Ask the children to think of a way of collecting recognition for these standards. For example, if they are learning to take turns, they could collect snakes and ladders to add to a blank 100 square to make up the game, and when the game is complete they can have class golden time. You may wish to set up some kind of exchanging so that there are not too many snakes and ladders, for example for every ten stickers earned a child can swap it for a snake or a ladder. Ask the

children to suggest activities that can be earned for different numbers of snakes and ladders. For example, if they collect one snake or ladder, they can play on the adventure playground for five minutes; if they earn ten snakes and ladders, they can choose their favourite games to play on the Friday morning or afternoon.

Sticker collection

Every time the children are filling in their individual sticker chart, invite them to create a new design. They may wish to turn their stickers into leaves for a tree, windows on a block of flats or to form the shell for a snail. Link this to Matisse's painting 'The Snail' if you wish. Let the children share or extend each other's ideas, too.

COMIC CHARACTERS

AREA OF LEARNING: COMMUNICATION, LANGUAGE AND LITERACY. ELG: TO USE TALK TO ORGANISE, SEQUENCE AND CLARIFY THINKING, IDEAS, FEELINGS AND EVENTS. NLS OBJECTIVE: TO UNDERSTAND HOW STORY BOOK LANGUAGE WORKS AND TO USE SOME FORMAL ELEMENTS WHEN RETELLING STORIES.

LEARNING OBJECTIVE

To tell an unknown story from pictures.

THINKING OBJECTIVE

To think imaginatively.

THINKING SKILLS

The children will read pictures to gain an understanding of what is happening in a story. They will then make up their own stories based on the pictures, describing the characters and surroundings and imagining what is happening and what characters are saying. They will finish by looking at how different groups told the story in order to understand that everyone uses their imagination differently.

WHAT YOU NEED

A selection of comic strips or picture books with no or few words that tells a story; a large sheet of paper.

WHAT TO DO

As a class, look at one of the picture books or comic strips, briefly talking about the characters in it and what they are doing. When you have an overview of what the story may be about, encourage the children to talk about it. Use questions to guide their thinking and help them organise their thoughts. Start with the first picture and ask, *Can you describe the first character? What might they be saying or thinking in this picture? Why do you think this?*

Focus on the pictures one at a time and encourage the children to use their imagination to describe what they think is happening in each picture. Ask questions to focus their thinking, such as *Is a new character being introduced? Are the characters talking to each other? Are they friends or not? What might happen next?*

Develop the children's thinking further by talking about the possibilities for changing the end of the story. Can the children think of a different ending? Discuss endings with which the children are familiar first, such as *and they all lived happily ever after*, or *he gives a big yawn and falls fast asleep*. Look at the final sentences in different stories to help them with ideas, if appropriate.

In smaller groups, choose different picture books or comic strip and talk with the children about what is happening. Give all the groups a set of pictures. Repeat the activity, talking about the characters, what they are doing and what they may be saying and thinking. Draw individuals into the activity by targetting your questions appropriately. Stick the pictures to a large sheet of paper and write the children's ideas about what is happening underneath each one. Read the finished picture story together with the group.

Share the different group stories at the end of the lesson for the children to note how they all used their imagination differently.

DIFFERENTIATION

Give lower attaining children a very structured picture book, which has a time-sequenced story. This will encourage them to structure their thinking into a now, then and last type sequence. The one central character can meet different characters or do different things on each page. Higher attaining children should be encouraged to imagine what their characters are thinking and saying and to write thought or speech bubbles for some of their characters.

WHERE NEXT

Put up picture sequences for the children to act out as a literacy group activity.

ASSESSMENT

Listen to the children's stories and note those who are merely describing what is happening in the pictures and those who are thinking imaginatively to make up individual and unique ideas.

LEARNING OUTCOMES

Most children will be able to make up a story using a sequence of pictures to help structure their thinking and ideas. They will think imaginatively to make up a completely different story from the same set of pictures.

FURTHER COMMUNICATION, LANGUAGE AND LITERACY CHALLENGES

Puppet show

Ask the children to use a comic strip to make up a story for puppets. Challenge them to think of a good starter, some dialogue based on what happens and a good ending. Let them perform their stories to each other at the end of the day.

Radio soap

Let the children act out one of the stories to tape. This will make them realise the importance of dialogue in stories. Act as narrator so that you can guide the action and help the children structure the performance.

CHARACTER STUDY

AREA OF LEARNING: COMMUNICATION, LANGUAGE AND LITERACY. ELG: TO WRITE THEIR OWN NAMES AND CAPTIONS AND BEGIN TO FORM SIMPLE SENTENCES, SOMETIMES USING PUNCTUATION. NLS OBJECTIVE: TO UNDERSTAND THAT WRITING CAN BE USED FOR A RANGE OF PURPOSES.

LEARNING OBJECTIVE
To write captions for story characters.

THINKING OBJECTIVE
To think imaginatively.

THINKING SKILLS
The children will need to think imaginatively to draw a picture of a made-up character. They will need to think of a suitable name that reflects the character they have conjured up and write this as a simple caption under their picture.

WHAT YOU NEED
Large sheets of paper; crayons and pencils.

WHAT TO DO

Organise the children into groups or pairs. Invite them to close their eyes for a moment and to think of a character for a story. As they think, remind them of some of the characters who appear in stories they have heard of. Then in their groups, ask the children to negotiate who their character will be and to draw them. As they work, talk to the children about what their character looks like. Ask, *What are they wearing?* Ask questions about what type of character it is, such as *Do they smile a lot? Do they sometimes get angry?* Ask the children to think about some of the things the character likes to do and ask them to draw things that show this. For example, if it is a boy who likes football, the children could draw a football in their picture. Finally, challenge the children to think of a suitable name for their character which closely depicts what the character is like or reflects the way the character looks. Ask them to write the character's name underneath the picture.

DIFFERENTIATION
Ask less able children to link their character to stories with which they are familiar. Find dressing-up clothes and ask the children to dress as their character before extending it to an imaginary character on paper. Higher attaining children should be encouraged to write a simple description of their character.

WHERE NEXT
When you next write a story with the children, draw some of the characters they want to include. This will help them to picture the characters in their heads as they make up stories.

ASSESSMENT
Note whether drawing the pictures helps the children to imagine different things their characters may get up to, thus sparking their imagination.

LEARNING OUTCOMES
Most children will be able to imagine what characters look like and how their appearance often gives them their character. They will use their imagination to give their characters names. Some will be able to start to write simple sentences to describe their characters.

FURTHER COMMUNICATION, LANGUAGE AND LITERACY CHALLENGES
A wolf at the door
Get the children to create other characters to include in books that they already know. For example, read *Kipper's birthday* by Mick Inkpen (Hodder Children's Books) and ask the children to think of additional guests for the party.
Picture this
Read any unfamiliar story to the children and ask them to choose one of the characters and imagine what they look like. Ask them to draw a picture of the character from their imagination.

NOAH'S ARK

AREA OF LEARNING: COMMUNICATION, LANGUAGE AND LITERACY. ELG: TO INTERACT WITH OTHERS, NEGOTIATING PLANS AND ACTIVITIES AND TAKING TURNS IN CONVERSATION. NLS OBJECTIVE: TO USE KNOWLEDGE OF FAMILIAR TEXTS TO RE-ENACT THE MAIN POINTS OF A STORY.

LEARNING OBJECTIVE
To act out some parts of the story of Noah.

THINKING OBJECTIVE
To think imaginatively.

THINKING SKILLS
The children will think about some of the activities that the characters in the story of Noah did when they were building and sailing the ark. They will

think imaginatively, using language to organise their thoughts and to imagine different actions, conversations and events that the characters would have taken part in.

WHAT YOU NEED
A space in the classroom or outside to create the different areas of the story; materials to make the ark from, such as cardboard boxes, wooden poles, string; carpentry tools, such as a workbench, wood, screws and nails; soft toys and model animals; straw; drink and food containers.

WHAT TO DO
Remind, or tell, the children the story of Noah's Ark. Identify with them all the role-play possibilities in the story that they could organise in the classroom. Develop these together, planning and making the different areas.

In smaller groups, let the children play in their chosen area, imagining what the different people from that part of the story would be doing and saying. For example, set one group up to role-play making the ark. Let them use carpentry tools (under supervision) to pretend to make this. Let them add things to the cardboard frame, such as masts tied with string or rope, or pretend to hammer the wood into place. Another group could act out caring for all the animals – cleaning them out, feeding and watering them, grooming them. Leave the children to use their imagination, but be on hand to ask what and why they are doing things, to supervise for safety or to help with difficult construction. Those in the home area will need less supervision and support because they will be in a more familiar situation.

Encourage the children to think about how the people in their part of the story might be feeling. Help them to reflect on and consider how they might feel about the water rising, for example, and encourage them to incorporate this into their role-play.

DIFFERENTIATION
Give lower attaining children specific situations to imagine in order to keep their thinking focused. For example, give them the job of making sure that there are no holes in the ark's frame, or getting breakfast ready for the others when they have finished the animal cleaning chores. Question them to imagine what they could say to let Noah know that the ark is watertight, or to let Noah know when breakfast is ready. Encourage higher attaining children to imagine more unusual situations, such as sailing through a storm in the ark, or seeing different creatures in the water.

WHERE NEXT
Let the children use the different role-play areas to act out the story of Noah as you read it. Use this as a prompt for the children to identify other resources needed to role-play the story.

ASSESSMENT
Listen to the children's conversations in their groups to see how well they are using their imaginations to make up story lines for the characters. Intervene with questions to develop this further with those children who are not playing a full role.

LEARNING OUTCOMES
Most children will be able to imagine what was happening behind the scenes in the story of Noah. Some children will think up imaginary storylines to extend the story and imagine what the characters saw from the ark when they were sailing around looking for land. With your support, all children will be able to use imagination to act out the story of Noah's Ark.

FURTHER COMMUNICATION, LANGUAGE AND LITERACY CHALLENGES
Sailing away
Get the children to act out other stories, rhymes and poems that are set on the sea. For example, *The Owl and the Pussycat* by Edward Lear. Challenge the children to imagine what it was like on the island and to create the scenery. Set up the wedding scene of the owl and the pussycat.
Pirate adventure
Turn the ark that the children made in the main activity into a pirate ship and get them to imagine and act out different pirate adventures. This will inevitably develop into imaginary battles if you are not careful, so try to channel the children's imaginations by giving them treasure to find.

BLACKBERRIES AND APPLES

AREA OF LEARNING: MATHEMATICAL DEVELOPMENT.
ELGs: TO COUNT RELIABLY UP TO 10; TO USE DEVELOPING
MATHEMATICAL IDEAS AND METHODS TO SOLVE PRACTICAL
PROBLEMS. NNS OBJECTIVES: TO COUNT RELIABLY UP TO 10
EVERYDAY OBJECTS, THEN BEYOND; TO COUNT IN TWOS; TO
COUNT IN TENS; TO SOLVE SIMPLE PROBLEMS IN A PRACTICAL
CONTEXT.

LEARNING OBJECTIVE
To count to 10 and beyond.

THINKING OBJECTIVE
To think laterally and to extend ideas.

THINKING SKILLS
The children will count the number of apples they are given one at a time, trying hard not to miscount. They will then consider whether there is an easier way to count these, extending their skills beyond counting in ones and then extending their thinking and processes further by counting blackberries.

WHAT YOU NEED
Around 20 apples and 50 blackberries (which you may have picked with the children to reinforce their understanding of what *harvest* means).

WHAT TO DO
Ask the children to sit in a circle and put the apples in the centre. Wonder how many apples there are altogether. Invite a child to line the apples up and then count together how many there are. Ask the children if this would be a good way to count the apples if there were lots more. Can they think of a different way of ordering them to make the counting easier? Invite them to show you how they could order the apples in a different way and count them together again. If they did not do this before, invite the children to put the apples into pairs and to count them in twos. Then suggest they put them into groups of ten and ask the children to say if they are easier to count now.

Organise the children into smaller groups and tell them that you want them to count the apples again. By working with smaller groups, you can differentiate the number of apples according to ability and let the children organise the apples in the way that they wish. Give the groups some blackberries and telling them to be careful not to get juice on their fingers, or perhaps handling them yourself, ask the children to use the ideas learnt so far to count how many blackberries there are.

DIFFERENTIATION
Ask lower attaining children to count apples only, showing them how they can organise the apples into groups of two, five or ten to make it easier to keep count. Give higher attaining children a second group of apples and ask them to find a way of gauging how many apples there are in the second group without counting them all. This will require them to compare the two groups and to find out how many more one group has than the other by assessing more or less.

WHERE NEXT
Cut the apples into slices and add the blackberries to make and eat a blackberry and apple crumble. Ask the children to count the number of apple slices you have put into the crumble. Can the children think of a way to make sure there are the same number of apple slices and blackberries in the crumble?

ASSESSMENT
Note the children who are clear about how to organise the apples to make counting them easier. Note which higher attaining children are thinking laterally to find out how many apples are in the second group, by counting how many more or less there are than in the first group.

LEARNING OUTCOMES
Most children will find a way of counting the apples by organising them into groups, or counting one at a time if necessary.

FURTHER MATHEMATICAL DEVELOPMENT CHALLENGES
How many seeds?
Count the number of seeds in a melon together. Challenge the children to use their ideas from organising the counting of apples and blackberries to find a way of counting the seeds quickly. Many, including lower attaining children, will organise the seeds into groups of ten. Higher attaining children will count in tens to find how many seeds there are.

Counting cubes

Ask the children to count different numbers of cubes, which are easier to count in tens and twos when organised thus. Develop the more able children's understanding of numbers from 10 to 20 by showing them how to count one ten and other units.

TAKE TWO TRIANGLES

AREA OF LEARNING: MATHEMATICAL DEVELOPMENT. ELG: TO USE LANGUAGE TO DESCRIBE THE SHAPE AND SIZE OF FLAT SHAPES. NNS OBJECTIVE: TO USE LANGUAGE TO DESCRIBE A FLAT SHAPE.

LEARNING OBJECTIVE

To learn the name *triangle*.

THINKING OBJECTIVES

To think laterally; to hypothesise.

THINKING SKILLS

The children will use different triangles to make pictures, patterns and other shapes. By putting them into different positions – edge to edge, corner to corner and overlapping – the children will create different shapes, pictures and patterns depending on the number and type of triangles they use. The children will hypothesise whether certain pictures can be made from the triangles before trying this out for themselves.

WHAT YOU NEED

A good number of different-coloured, plastic triangles of different sizes and types, such as isosceles, right-angled and equilateral; sheets of white paper.

WHAT TO DO

Before the lesson, cover the tables with white paper so that the shapes will show up and place a selection of triangles in the centre of the tables. Ask the children to gather around one of the tables and to consider if they can make pictures, shapes and patterns with two triangles. Invite a child to make their idea. After a few children have made shapes with two triangles, talk about whether these have been made by joining the sides or corners together. Ask, *Do the triangles fit together? Have you made a different shape, such as a square or a rectangle? Have you made a picture of something like a bow-tie or an egg timer?*

Show the children two right-angled triangles. Ask them to hypothesise, or to think in their heads, whether these will make a different triangle. Invite a child to try this. Ask the children to hypothesise if they can make a star. Again, invite a child to try this.

Give them a clue that they may have to make this by putting one triangle on top of another. Repeat this with other shapes and pictures. Draw these on a piece of paper so the children can try to visualise how to put the triangles together first.

Finish off the session by explaining the group activity to the children. Invite them to make as many different shapes, pictures and patterns as they can with their selection of triangles. Tell them they should try just two triangles to begin with, but then to use as many triangles as they like. Photograph the designs the children make to use in a class display of triangles.

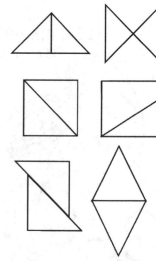

DIFFERENTIATION

Make pictures and shapes with triangles for lower attaining children to copy to begin with. Show them how to turn the triangles around to make different shapes and talk to them about what they have made. Work with higher attaining children, asking them to hypothesise whether they can make certain shapes from certain types of triangles before letting them check their hypotheses out.

WHERE NEXT

Use other shapes with the children to make patterns and shapes with.

ASSESSMENT

Note those children who do not understand how to make other shapes with triangles and give them pictures to match or copy.

LEARNING OUTCOMES

Most children will think laterally to make different shapes with the triangles. Some will be able to hypothesise which shapes can be made before trying this out for themselves.

FURTHER MATHEMATICAL DEVELOPMENT CHALLENGES

Meccano shapes

Ask the children to join five Meccano strips of the same size and get them to move them around to make different shapes. Challenge them to make a star shape and get them to draw all the shapes they were able to make.

Border designs

Ask the children to use the triangles to make border designs for the triangle display. Let them think laterally about how they can make these shapes fit on the paper. Will they need to use large or small triangles? Are the children able to work out how to make the same shapes and designs with different sized triangles?

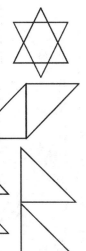

PLASTICINE SHAPES

AREA OF LEARNING: KNOWLEDGE AND UNDERSTANDING OF THE WORLD. ELGs: TO LOOK CLOSELY AT SIMILARITIES, DIFFERENCES, PATTERNS AND CHANGE; TO INVESTIGATE MATERIALS BY USING ALL OF THEIR SENSES AS APPROPRIATE.

LEARNING OBJECTIVE

To learn that things change shape when rolled, squeezed and squashed.

THINKING OBJECTIVE

To extend ideas.

THINKING SKILLS

The children will listen to a poem and use it as a basis to create different shapes from Plasticine. They will extend these ideas by shaping models from other materials, including papier-mâché and plaster of Paris.

WHAT YOU NEED

A copy of the poem 'Plasticine' by Wendy Cope found in *Twinkle, twinkle, chocolate bar* compiled by John Foster (OUP); Plasticine; plaster of Paris; papier-mâché; digital camera.

WHAT TO DO

Read the poem 'Plasticine' by Wendy Cope and talk to the children about the different shapes and models that it talks about. Give each child a piece of warm Plasticine, read the poem again and after each verse talk about the vocabulary used to describe the piece of Plasticine. Ask, *How did the author change its shape? Did she pull it or push it? What did she do?* Using the discussion that should follow these questions as a guide, let the children squeeze, squash and roll their piece of Plasticine into as many shapes as they can. Photograph each shape with a digital camera, print these out and invite the children to give each one a name. Label each photograph with its name.

Organise the children into smaller groups and let them work individually to explore papier-mâché and plaster of Paris in a similar way to make models and sculptures. Talk to them about what they are doing to change the materials into the shape of their creations. Are they squeezing, squashing and rolling? Are they doing anything else?

DIFFERENTIATION

Limit lower attaining children to exploring the Plasticine to begin with so that they understand the different ways they can change the shape of this malleable material. Move them onto the different materials to extend their ideas as soon as you are sure they are comfortable with the Plasticine. Higher attaining children should be challenged to make modern sculptures with interesting shapes and designs. Talk with them about the form of each one as they extend their ideas.

WHERE NEXT

Make bricks from clay and when they are dry let the children build a wall for Humpty Dumpty or the small world toys. Let the children extend their ideas to make other things from clay.

ASSESSMENT

Make a note of the children who can extend their ideas to other media, such as papier-mâché and plaster of Paris. Note those who work together to change the shape and form of their sculptures.

LEARNING OUTCOMES

Most children will be able to extend their ideas for models from Plasticine to other media. Some will need help with this transition to papier-mâché and plaster of Paris.

FURTHER KNOWLEDGE AND UNDERSTANDING OF THE WORLD CHALLENGES

Group sculpture

Prepare a large quantity of papier-mâché for the children to explore in groups. Ask them to work together to create a group sculpture, perhaps a recognisable creature or object or perhaps a piece of modern art with interesting shape and form. Talk to them about what they did to the papier-mâché to change the shape and form of the sculpture as it was made.

Cooking is fun

Extend the children's ideas to cooking bread and biscuits. Let the children's imaginations run wild to create and make biscuits and bread in different shapes and sizes.

COLOUR GARDEN

AREA OF LEARNING: KNOWLEDGE AND UNDERSTANDING OF THE WORLD. ELG: TO FIND OUT ABOUT, AND IDENTIFY, SOME FEATURES OF LIVING THINGS.

LEARNING OBJECTIVE

To combine vegetables, fruits, flowers and sculptures to make a garden of colours.

THINKING OBJECTIVE

To create ideas.

THINKING SKILLS

The children will think about the different colours of plants and garden furniture to design a garden of different colours. They will work in groups to combine plants and objects of the same group colour to make a part of the overall garden.

WHAT YOU NEED

Planters; flower and vegetable catalogues; seeds and bulbs of the children's choosing; windmills, glass balls, vases, garden ornaments and sculptures; trellis; outdoor paint and paintbrushes.

WHAT TO DO

Show the children the empty planters and explain that you want them to make a garden of different colours. Tell them that they will be working in groups, and that each group will create a different coloured garden. Explain that you want them to paint the planters different colours and plant vegetables and flowers of the same colour in them. Show them the flower and vegetable catalogues at this point so they can see the colours and varieties. Let them choose the colours they want for the garden, but try to include green to incorporate the vegetables and red to include fruits.

Take the children to a garden centre and help them to pick out the flowers, bulbs and plants that will fit into the colour scheme that they have decided upon as a group. Buy trellis and matching coloured paint if you are unable to find trellis to match your colours. Buy seed packets of fruit and vegetables the same colour as the children's planned garden.

On return to the classroom, show the children how to plant the seeds and bulbs. You could plant strawberries in a red pipe with holes cut in the side, for instance. Insert trellis, painted in a matching colour, into the planters for any climbing plants. Place matching coloured ornaments and sculptures,

garden ornaments and windmills between the plants. Encourage the children to keep watch as the multi-coloured garden grows.

DIFFERENTIATION

Use bedding plants with lower attaining children to create immediate gardens of colour. Extend learning for higher attaining children by asking them to find scented or tactile plants to add an extra dimension to their garden.

WHERE NEXT

Invite the children to bring things in from home to add to the gardens.

Use broken tiles and, under adult supervision and making sure they wear gloves to protect their fingers, let the children set these into plaster of Paris to make names for the garden. You will need to organise the children into pairs and make sure that they finish one letter at a time so that the plaster does not set before they have finished.

ASSESSMENT

Note the groups who are creative with their designs and who use a range of plants and garden ornaments to create their part of the coloured garden.

LEARNING OUTCOMES

Most children will use their creative ideas to design and make a garden that is colourful and interesting to look at. Some will go further and think about other senses their garden might stimulate.

FURTHER KNOWLEDGE AND UNDERSTANDING OF THE WORLD CHALLENGES

Sound gardens
Encourage the children to make gardens that incorporate sounds, such as water features, wind chimes, bells and rustling ferns and pines.

Textured gardens
Create gardens together that have interesting textures. Use cactus, driftwood, bark, stones, shells and any other things the children think of. You may wish to limit the children to stone and rock, or wood only, to really challenge their creative ideas.

HIDDEN ROBOTS

AREA OF LEARNING:
KNOWLEDGE AND
UNDERSTANDING OF THE WORLD.
ELG: TO LOOK CLOSELY AT
SIMILARITIES, DIFFERENCES, PATTERNS
AND CHANGE.

LEARNING OBJECTIVE
To learn to look closely at colours and compare them with their background.

THINKING OBJECTIVE
To hypothesise.

THINKING SKILLS
The children will think about the colour of some pictures before hypothesising whether they can be seen easily when set in different surroundings.

WHAT YOU NEED
A copy of *Harry and the Robots* by Ian Whybrow (Gullane Children's Books); sheets of paper; paint; paintbrushes; palettes for mixing.

WHAT TO DO
Read the story *Harry and the Robots* to the children. Focus on the robots Harry made and ask the children to describe some of the shapes, colours and components that he made them from. Then look at the last picture in the book where Harry has the robots together in the garden. Ask the children, *Can you see the robots easily? Which one can be seen the easiest? Which one is most difficult to see?* Talk about why some robots can be seen clearly and some can't. Ask, *Is it because they look very different to the background? Are the colours very different?* Help the children to hypothesise which type of background would be best to hide the robots for a game. *What sort of background would we need to have? What colour should it be so that the robots could not be seen easily?*

When you are sure that the children understand how to hypothesise the kind of background they need in order to hide the robots, ask them to draw or paint pictures in which the robots will be hidden. Give them colour copies of two or three robots from the book and tell them to stick these to their paper before painting the surrounding landscape. Tell them they can choose any landscape for this, but encourage them to plan this in a sketchbook before they draw and paint the final picture.

DIFFERENTIATION
Ask less able children questions to direct their thinking towards the hypothesis that in order for an object to blend into its background, the colours need to be similar. Ask higher attaining children to change the colours of pictures of other objects and animals so that they blend into different backgrounds.

WHERE NEXT
Look at army camouflage with the children and talk about how this makes soldiers and equipment blend into their background so that they cannot be seen easily.

Go on a safari with the children to find small creatures in the immediate environment. Before going, talk about whether the children think these creatures will be easy to find. Talk about where to look and how closely they need to look. Encourage them to think about the colours of the creatures and the colours of their surroundings. Which creatures do the children think will be the easiest to spot? Why?

ASSESSMENT
Note the children who successfully identify which robots can be seen easily and are able to hypothesise why.

LEARNING OUTCOMES
Most children will hypothesise by the end of the activity that things of similar colour will blend into

their background more easily than those that have very different colours.

FURTHER KNOWLEDGE AND UNDERSTANDING OF THE WORLD CHALLENGES

Spots and stripes

Cut out pictures of zebras, tigers, and leopards. Ask the children to hypothesise whether they think it would be easy to see these animals in the world. Display each type of animal together as one big picture against their natural background and ask the children to count how many animals they can see. What do they think now? Was this easy to do? Ask those who thought it would be easy to see these animals in the wild to hypothesise again. Have they changed their minds?

Rainbow fishes

Draw pictures of different coloured fish, octopus and shell creatures, and hide them among a large picture of a coral reef with seaweed. Hypothesise with the children whether it is easy to see these. Watch video clips of sea creatures moving about a coral reef and see if the children think it is easy to see the creatures.

PAPER DECORATIONS

AREA OF LEARNING: PHYSICAL DEVELOPMENT. ELG: TO HANDLE MALLEABLE MATERIALS SAFELY AND WITH INCREASING CONTROL.

LEARNING OBJECTIVE
To develop the skills involved in folding.

THINKING OBJECTIVE
To extend ideas.

THINKING SKILLS
The children will look at different things that have been designed by using a folding process, such as fans or lampshades. They will learn the skill of folding and pleating before extending their ideas about how pleating can be used to make different items.

WHAT YOU NEED
A collection of items that are made from folding paper, fabric or other materials, such as fans, lampshades, screens or concertina books; a pleated shirt front; a pleated skirt; strips of gummed and crêpe paper cut into different widths and lengths; glue and stapling equipment.

WHAT TO DO
Show the children a fan and talk about how this has been made by folding paper. Explain that the special way that it has been folded is called *pleating*. Show the children how to fold a piece of paper into pleats to make a concertina. Then look at other items from your collection that have pleats, such as the lampshades and any decorated items you have. Look around to see if anyone is wearing a pleated skirt. If they are, point this out to the rest of the class. Alternatively, show the children the skirt and shirt front and note how they are pleated to make the effect. Look at the concertina book and note how it has been folded to give it its shape and organisation.

In groups, ask the children to make decorations, fans and books from the paper strips. Let them decide what they want to make and help them to do the pleating. Show them how to use staples and glue to secure their finished fans and decorations into shape. Give them the opportunity to extend their ideas by joining two structures together, to make a half-circular shape. Display the finished products to show the range of things the children have made.

DIFFERENTIATION
Model the folding with lower attaining children so that they understand the idea of how the pleats are made. Invite higher attaining children to extend their ideas by looking at and making other things which use pleating, such as umbrellas and parasols. Look at the frame together and think about how these help give the open umbrellas their shape and rigidity.

WHERE NEXT

Explore together the different ways of folding paper to make decorations for the classroom at different times of year, perhaps for the Christmas tree.

Get the children to make Chinese and Japanese screens from rigid frames and appropriate fabric. Invite the children to decorate these with designs that reflect Chinese or Japanese culture, such as writing or exotic animals and flowers.

Set up an ironing activity in the home role-play area for the children to iron and fold clothes in. Focus on the different ways that particular items of clothing can be folded. Link it to caring for their own possessions when changing for physical activities or hanging coats up after play.

ASSESSMENT

Note the children who can use the idea of pleating to make their own fans, books and decorations. Help them to extend their ideas by letting them create their own decorations.

LEARNING OUTCOMES

Most children will understand the basic idea of pleating and will use this to extend their ideas to create a range of products by folding paper.

FURTHER PHYSICAL DEVELOPMENT CHALLENGES

Plaiting, twisting and weaving

Take the children on a walk around the local area to see if there are any things that have been made by plaiting, weaving and twisting. Explain to the children that things to look out for include garden fences, willow structures, iron flower trellis, basket weave and climbing plants. Take pictures of any finds. Back in the classroom look at other things that are made by twisting, plaiting and weaving, such as string, hair, plaited loaves, fabrics, curtain tiebacks and baskets. Provide the children with string, rope and thick knitting wool to weave, plait and twist into tassels to hang from coat hangers as mobiles. You could also let them use everyday materials, like evergreen leaves,

fir and thin branches to weave a screen from.

Fold it up

Show the children a folded map, tablecloth, towels and sheets. Unfold them and ask the children to refold them to make them look tidy. Can the children extend their ideas by thinking of a better way to fold the items up so that they look smarter?

PHOTO FIT

AREA OF LEARNING: PHYSICAL DEVELOPMENT. ELG: TO SHOW AWARENESS OF SPACE, OF THEMSELVES AND OF OTHERS. AREA OF LEARNING: CREATIVE DEVELOPMENT. ELG: TO USE THEIR IMAGINATION IN DANCE.

LEARNING OBJECTIVE

To make up a dance by responding to music.

THINKING OBJECTIVE

To create ideas.

THINKING SKILLS

The children will move freely to two different pieces of music, creating ideas for their own movements and ideas based on a circus character of their choosing. They will think about how to pose to have their photograph taken and incorporate this as an idea into their dance.

WHAT YOU NEED

A copy of 'The Syncopated Clock' and 'The Typewriter', available on the CD *The Typewriter – Leroy Anderson Favourites* (Red Seal).

WHAT TO DO

Play the 'The Syncopated Clock' and let the children move freely to the music as a warm-up activity. When they are suitably warm ask them to move again, but this time to try out just one or two of their warm-up ideas. Then ask each child to share their idea(s) with the rest of the class, making sure that everyone has a turn.

Introduce the idea of the circus at this point and the idea of the circus stars moving around the circus ring. Tell the children that every so often the people will stop while the audience takes their photograph. Invite the children to decide which person they will be and to move again in time to the music, every so often stopping to pose for photographs.

Play the children 'The Typewriter' next and invite their suggestions about who or what this piece of music may be depicting. They may suggest acrobats, trapeze artistis, clowns or some other member of the circus. Do not restrict their ideas, but let them pretend to be a member of the circus of their own choice. Again, invite them to move to this piece of music using a suitable movement and to pose for a photograph every so often. If the children do not remember to do this, be the photographer and act as a prompt for them to pose for you.

Once you are sure the children have got the idea divide the class into two. One group should act as photographers, while the other group can move to the music and act out their circus roles. They can swap over at intervals to have a turn at each activity.

DIFFERENTIATION
Move around with lower attaining children, prompting their ideas by reminding them when to stop and how to hold a pose. Ask more able children to work together to develop a group dance.

WHERE NEXT
Use other pieces of music for the children to develop their ideas to. Develop sequences of travels and pose-type movements.

ASSESSMENT
Assess how well the children respond to the music and whether they come up with creative and original ideas for their movements and poses. Note the way they move and whether this reflects the music.

LEARNING OUTCOMES
Most children will create ideas for movement and poses, building in responses to the music to depict the actions of certain characters, based on the children's own ideas.

FURTHER CREATIVE DEVELOPMENT CHALLENGES
Music to dance to
Play other pieces of music and choose those that spark the children's interest to move and dance to. Organise activities so that the children can try out their ideas to the different pieces of music before choosing the piece they like best.

CONCENTRIC CIRCLES

AREA OF LEARNING: CREATIVE DEVELOPMENT. ELG: TO EXPLORE COLOUR IN TWO DIMENSIONS.

LEARNING OBJECTIVE
To learn to mix paints to make different colours.

THINKING OBJECTIVE
To extend ideas.

THINKING SKILLS
The children will look at how an artist has created a painting with circles and use this as a basis for their own designs. They will extend the ideas to make their

own pictures. They will also mix paints and extend this skill during their painting.

WHAT YOU NEED
A print of *Concentric Circles* by Kandinsky; powder or poster paint in primary colours; paper, rulers; black felt-tipped pens.

WHAT TO DO
Look with the children at the painting *Concentric Circles* by Kandinsky and talk about the colour and shapes he has used. Ask questions to aid the discussion, such as *How has the artist organised the circles to make his painting? How has he divided the painting? How many circles has he painted? How did he mix colours to make new ones? How did he make orange?*

Show the children how to use a ruler to divide up a piece of paper into squares. Use a black felt-tipped pen to mark the lines. Then let the children mix paint to make the different colours they want to use and to make concentric circles like Kandinsky in each square. Let the children cover their paper with concentric circle designs if they wish, so as not to restrict their ideas.

Let the children extend their ideas to make paintings using straight lines, rectangles and squares and to fill these with colours.

DIFFERENTIATION
Give less able children freedom to cover the paper with different colours if this is what they want to do. Higher attaining children can use other shapes as a basis for their paintings.

WHERE NEXT
Let the children use these skills to make Elmer the Elephant designs with paint.

Extend the children's ideas by letting them make their own version of *The Snail* by Matisse.

ASSESSMENT
Note those children who are confident with mixing colours and applying this on paper to extend the idea of combining colours. Organise self-initiated play activities for these children to extend their ideas with paint in other contexts.

LEARNING OUTCOMES
The children will combine colours to create designs using circles. They will consider how they have combined the tints and tones of colours to produce their designs.

FURTHER CREATIVE DEVELOPMENT CHALLENGES
Tones and tints
Divide a large sheet of paper into sections, using either straight or curved lines. Fill each space with tints of the same colour using wax and pencil crayons, pastels, chalk and paint. Invite the children to fill the spaces with solid colour and/or patterns. Challenge some children to make patterns with straight or curved lines only, including the patterns created to fill the spaces.

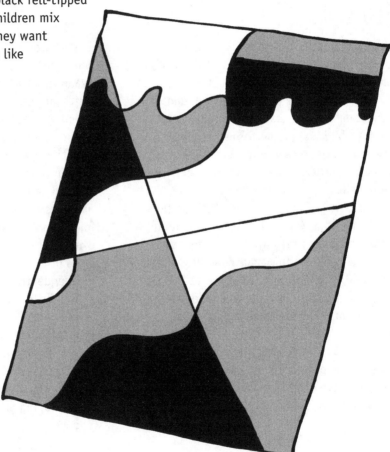

Circles or squares
Cover a page with circles or squares and invite the children to extend the idea by filling in the spaces, using different colours or designs.

EVALUATION SKILLS

INTRODUCTION

The ability to evaluate gives children a useful insight into their own learning and helps them to identify what they need to do next to improve still further. This is a key skill within the national and foundation stage curriculum and one that is often developed well when the children have performed or made something, but not extensively in other aspects of learning. Many teachers already encourage children to say what went well, or what was good about something they have done. However, although the children can say what went well, they often are not given the opportunity to say what it was that made it good. The activities in this chapter address this by giving the children opportunity to say what it is that is useful, of good quality or value when identifying what went well or was good about a particular achievement.

The activities in this chapter are examples of how these skills can be developed and can be adapted to suit other contexts equally well. For example, the activity in which the children evaluate the usefulness of the information on the film box is equally valid when looking at any information. The skill of evaluating the usefulness of something in relation to its purpose is the starting point for identifying which information to collect and which to reject in any research project when they get older. This type of activity will help the children to think about why the information they are analysing is important to the task. The importance of the activity 'What do I need?' is in the self-selection of resources, deciding for themselves which will be useful to the task and which will not. This will give them the necessary skills of organising their own learning needs independently and help them develop initiative.

The evaluation skills are:
- evaluating information
- judging value
- judging usefulness
- judging quality
- suggesting improvements
- developing criteria for judging.

Introducing evaluation skills

Area of learning and ELG, NLS or NNS objective	Activity title	Thinking objective	Activity	Page
Personal, social and emotional development ELG: To select and use resources independently	What do I need?	To evaluate information (judging usefulness)	Selecting resources for a making activity	108
Communication, language and literacy ELG: To explore words and texts NLS objective: To use a variety of cues when reading	What does it tell me?	To evaluate information (judging usefulness)	Evaluating whether text and illustrations provide answers to questions about content	108
Communication, language and literacy ELG: To know that print carries meaning NLS objective: To recognise printed words in a variety of settings	Film cases	To evaluate information (judging usefulness)	Evaluating information on packaging	109
Communication, language and literacy ELG: To use a pencil and hold it effectively to form recognisable letters NLS objectives: To use a comfortable and efficient pencil grip; to write letters using the correct sequence of movements	Letter writing	To evaluate information (judging quality)	Evaluating whether letters are formed correctly	109
Mathematical development ELG: To use language to describe shapes NNS objective: To use a variety of shapes to make models and describe them	Sliding shapes	To evaluate information (judging usefulness)	Investigating 3-D shapes	110
Mathematical development ELG: To use language to compare quantities NNS objective: To use developing mathematical ideas to solve practical problems	Long or short	To evaluate information (judging value)	Looking at the value of different items for measuring	110
Knowledge and understanding of the world ELG: To investigate objects and materials by using all of their senses	Investigating paper	To evaluate information (judging usefulness)	Evaluating which paper is best for different jobs	111
Knowledge and understanding of the world ELG: To find out about and use information and communication technology	Take a picture	To evaluate information (judging quality)	Evaluating the best shot for a photograph	112
Knowledge and understanding of the world ELG: To select the tools and techniques they need to shape, assemble and join materials they are using	Waft and weave	To evaluate information (judging value)	Evaluating the best way to cut and join wood	112
Physical development ELG: To handle tools, objects and construction safely and with increasing control	Marble run	To evaluate information (judging quality); to suggest improvements	Making a marble run to get marbles from one place to another	113
Physical development ELG: To move with confidence, imagination and in safety	Musical movements	To evaluate information (judging value)	Moving in different ways to music	114
Creative development ELG: To sing simple songs from memory	Performing together	To evaluate information (judging usefulness); to suggest improvements	Evaluating how to sing and play different songs to create different moods	114
Creative development ELG: To explore colour, texture, shape, form and space in three dimensions	Flower arranging	To evaluate information (judging quality); to develop criteria for judging	Arranging flowers	115

WHAT DO I NEED?

AREA OF LEARNING: PERSONAL, SOCIAL AND EMOTIONAL DEVELOPMENT. ELG: TO SELECT AND USE RESOURCES INDEPENDENTLY.

LEARNING OBJECTIVE

To select resources needed for making a space rocket.

THINKING OBJECTIVE

To evaluate information (judging usefulness).

THINKING SKILLS

The children will design a class space rocket and identify the resources they will need to make this. They will select and use the resources they need to make the rocket, evaluating as they go along whether the resources are suitable or whether some other resource may be better.

WHAT YOU NEED

Pictures of rockets; a selection of rocket-making resources that are organised in their usual place and where the children can gain access to them independently, such as boxes and empty containers of different shapes and sizes, glue, a hole punch, string, sticky tape, a stapler and staples, paint and felt-tipped pens.

WHAT TO DO

Let the children be inspired by your pictures of rockets and tell them you want them to design their own class rocket. As they work on designing how the rocket will look, get them to identify the resources they are planning to use to make each part of the rocket. Ask, *What are you planning to use to make the rocket? How big will it be? Will it be big enough to sit in or for a model to use in a small world activity? How are you planning to join the top to the rocket? What will you use to add the decoration?*

When the children have finished the design, encourage them to find all the resources they need. This will not be easy as the children will want to come and go during the process of making, finding things as they get to them in the making task. As they go through the making task, help them to evaluate what they are doing, questioning them to see if they have chosen the most appropriate way of joining the boxes and other containers together. Ask, *Is sticky tape the right choice? Is it strong enough for this big box? Is it wide enough? Can you find something else which is more suitable?* Encourage them to explore other ways of joining boxes together, such as using a stapler, or a hole punch and threading string through the holes and tying a knot tightly.

WHAT DOES IT TELL ME?

AREA OF LEARNING: COMMUNICATION, LANGUAGE AND LITERACY. ELG: TO EXPLORE WORDS AND TEXTS. NLS OBJECTIVE: TO USE A VARIETY OF CUES WHEN READING.

LEARNING OBJECTIVES

To use illustrations to help work out what words say; to find answers to questions in text.

THINKING OBJECTIVE

To evaluate information (judging usefulness).

THINKING SKILLS

The children will learn to judge how well illustrations help them work out unfamiliar words or to gain the gist of what is happening on a page of a book. They will also judge whether the text provides them with answers to questions and information about characters, settings and events.

WHAT YOU NEED

Any big book that the children have not read before, containing pictures that give clues to the text (depending on your current focus it could be a fiction or non-fiction book); a set of related questions about the text and illustrations for each page of the book.

WHAT TO DO

As a class, look at the front cover of the big book and discuss what the book may be about. Ask, *How does the picture help us to know what the book might be about? Does it show the characters and one or two things that they may do? Does the title help us to work out what the book might be about?*

Turn to the first page and look at the picture there. Talk about what is happening and who is in it. Focus on the words and ask the children to try to read the text. It does not matter if they are not correct, only that they get the gist of what is written. How did the children know that this is what the text might say if they are not able to read the text accurately? Tell them whether they are close or not by reading what the text actually says, and explain that they were able to make a good guess because the picture helped them. Tell them that is why illustrations are included in books – to help the reader understand what is written.

Turn to the next page and repeat the activity. Continue in this way until you reach the end of the book.

In smaller groups, consider your list of questions and tell the children that you want them to see if the answers to the questions are in the illustrations or written in the text. Turn to the first page of the big book and ask the first question. For example, *Does the illustration or the text tell us if the main character in the book is a giant?* Invite the children to say whether the answer is in the illustration or in the text. Turn to the next page and ask the next question. For example, *Does the illustration or text tell us what the giant says?* Ask the children to point out where it says in the text what the giant says. Read the words together to check. Continue to the end of the book, asking questions the answers for which can and sometimes cannot be found in the illustration or the text.

At the end of the group activity, ask the children to say whether the illustrations and text were useful for answering the questions. Identify those questions for which either the text or the illustrations did not give the answer.

FILM CASES

AREA OF LEARNING: COMMUNICATION, LANGUAGE AND LITERACY. ELG: TO KNOW THAT PRINT CARRIES MEANING. NLS OBJECTIVE: TO RECOGNISE PRINTED WORDS IN A VARIETY OF SETTINGS.

LEARNING OBJECTIVE
To read information.

THINKING OBJECTIVE
To evaluate information (judging usefulness).

THINKING SKILLS
The children will locate the different information on film cartons. They will think carefully about what each piece of information means before evaluating its usefulness to a photographer.

WHAT YOU NEED
Empty camera film cartons, one for each child in your group (ensure that the cartons are from different companies and have some information that is different); sheets of prepared questions (see activity).

WHAT TO DO
In small groups, give each child a film carton and talk about what you can see. After a few minutes, ask a child to select one piece of information from their carton. Ask the others to see if this is on their cartons as well. Why do the children think that this is or is not included? It may be the name of the company, in which case it is an advert. Ask, *Would this information be useful to a buyer?* Someone may suggest that people think this company makes good films; others may think it is not important as most people buy the cheapest film.

Locate other bits of information, making sure you look for whether the film is in colour, and that you find the number of exposures and the type of film it is. This is where the information will be different on each film carton. Ask the children why this information is useful to the buyer. Explain that some cameras need special films and it is useful to know how many photographs the film will allow you to take as this helps you decide how many films you need to buy. For example, you may buy one 36-exposure film rather than two 24-exposure films. Explain what *exposure* means. Talk about why it is important to know when the film gets too old to use, or the expiry date has run out.

Give the following questions to each group. Ask the children to find the information on the film cartons and to say *yes* or *no* about whether the information is useful to know:
⊙ Is it a colour film?
⊙ What is the name of the company?
⊙ How many photographs does the film take?
⊙ When does the film expire or run out?

LETTER WRITING

AREA OF LEARNING: COMMUNICATION, LANGUAGE AND LITERACY. ELG: TO USE A PENCIL AND HOLD IT EFFECTIVELY TO FORM RECOGNISABLE LETTERS, MOST OF WHICH ARE CORRECTLY FORMED. NLS OBJECTIVES: TO USE A COMFORTABLE AND EFFICIENT PENCIL GRIP; TO WRITE LETTERS USING THE CORRECT SEQUENCE OF MOVEMENTS.

LEARNING OBJECTIVE
To learn to form letters correctly.

THINKING OBJECTIVE
To evaluate information (judging quality).

THINKING SKILLS
The children will learn to evaluate for themselves whether they have formed letters correctly by judging the quality of their finished letters. They will compare this with an example of a matching letter which has

been correctly formed, noting whether their letter started and finished in the correct place.

WHAT YOU NEED

A flip chart or board; sheets of paper; pencils; examples of letters written and formed correctly.

WHAT TO DO

Look at a piece of work recently written by each child. Choose a letter that they all have obviously copied correctly, but have not formed correctly. For instance, a letter *b* written like a number *6*, or an *m* and *n* with no first stick, or an *h* with the ascender added afterwards are favourites. Evaluate these with the children and match them to an example that is correctly formed. Ask the children to say what is different between the two. Can they see where the letter started on their example? Have they started in the correct place? How do they know?

Agree a good sitting position with the children before they start to write, as this helps them produce neat handwriting. Choose the letters you want the children to learn. Use your assessment information to match the activity to the children's learning needs. Group the letters together, if the children will be learning new ones, by the way they are formed. For example, *b* and *p*; *h*, *r*, *m* and *n*. Agree where the starting point of the first letter is and form it first on a flip chart or board, letting the children practise this until you are sure they have a secure knowledge of how to form it. Ask, *Does your letter look right? Did you start and finish in the right place?* Link this formation to other letters in the same group. If practising tall and tail letters, ask the children if the tail goes below the line. Are the ascenders tall enough? Praise the children for evaluating the quality of their letter formation and making improvements to their writing.

SLIDING SHAPES

AREA OF LEARNING: MATHEMATICAL DEVELOPMENT. ELG: TO USE LANGUAGE TO DESCRIBE SHAPES. NNS OBJECTIVE: TO USE A VARIETY OF SHAPES TO MAKE MODELS AND DESCRIBE THEM.

LEARNING OBJECTIVE

To learn the properties of 3-D shapes.

THINKING OBJECTIVE

To evaluate information (judging usefulness).

THINKING SKILLS

The children will build a range of models from 3-D shapes, talking about the shapes they have used and why. They will evaluate the shapes to judge the usefulness of each one to build different things.

WHAT YOU NEED

Several sets of 3-D shapes.

WHAT TO DO

Show the children the 3-D shapes and let them explore the shapes to build familiar or imaginary buildings. After a while, go and talk to each individual or pair, depending on how you want the children to work. Ask them to say why they chose particular shapes to build a wall or a tower. Ask questions to prompt discussion, such as *Why didn't you use a pyramid or a cone shape for these? Is it because they have pointed tops? What about a triangular prism? What would that be useful for? Perhaps for a roof?* If necessary, go outside with the children and find a similar shape on a building close by.

Ask all the children to find a shape that would be useful to make a ramp up to the front door of the school (or any door that has steps leading up to it). After a few minutes, ask them why they chose the shape they did and why they think it will be useful for this purpose.

Set up an activity for the children to explore the shapes further. Ask them to find out which ones roll, which ones slide, which will build on top of each other without falling over, which ones only roll in a straight line, which ones roll in a circle. As they work, ask questions, such as *Why do these shapes roll in a circle?* This will develop the children's reasoning as well as them evaluating the usefulness of each shape.

Challenge the children to evaluate the most useful shapes when making models of houses, cars, castles or boats.

LONG OR SHORT

AREA OF LEARNING: MATHEMATICAL DEVELOPMENT. ELG: TO USE LANGUAGE TO COMPARE QUANTITIES. NNS OBJECTIVE: TO USE DEVELOPING MATHEMATICAL IDEAS AND METHODS TO SOLVE PRACTICAL PROBLEMS.

LEARNING OBJECTIVE

To learn to measure by comparison and using non-standard measures.

Thinking objective

To evaluate information (judging value).

Thinking skills

The children will solve real-life problems by evaluating the value of different items for measuring length and space.

What you need

A piece of carpet; home furniture; mirror; pictures; paper cut-out window; two pairs of identical curtains of different sizes and pole; big and small cushions; lengths of string, rulers, metre sticks and other measuring equipment.

What to do

Tell the children that you are going to set up the role-play area to look like a home. Show them the things in your collection, telling them that you are not sure whether they will all fit into the role-play area. Can they think of a way of finding out what will fit where? Suggest they could do this by comparing the size of the space with the size of the furniture.

Look at the piece of carpet and ask the children to think of a way of finding out if it will fit into the space available. If they do not think of anything, tell them that they can measure the space available and the carpet, and then compare the two. Invite the children to say how they could measure the space. Let them use their own ideas for this. Evaluate the things they use and the way they measure. Ask, *What did you use to measure the space? Why didn't you use small cubes?* Agree that the cubes are too small and are not useful as the space is too big. Note the value of using resources such as lengths of string or metre sticks. Agree that footsteps, too, would be fine, so long as they use the same footsteps to measure the space and the carpet. Ask higher attaining children to suggest why.

Repeat the measuring activity with the other things in your collection before putting them into place. Look at your paper cut-out window and decide whereabouts to stick it on the wall. Look at the curtains. Ask, *Which of the two pairs fit the best? Is one pair too big or too small to fit? How do you know?* Hang the curtains that fit best, and add cushions that are not too big for the furniture.

Evaluate the different ways and equipment the children used to measure the spaces available and the things they wanted to put in them. Agree which were the best ways to measure the carpet, the mirror and the curtains.

Investigating paper

AREA OF LEARNING: KNOWLEDGE AND UNDERSTANDING OF THE WORLD. ELG OBJECTIVE: TO INVESTIGATE OBJECTS AND MATERIALS BY USING ALL OF THEIR SENSES AS APPROPRIATE.

Learning objective

To learn that different paper is useful for different jobs.

Thinking objective

To evaluate information (judging usefulness).

Thinking skills

The children will explore a range of papers for different jobs before deciding which is most useful for different jobs. These will include them exploring permeability, how much light each one blocks out, and which is best for wrapping presents. They will evaluate which is best for which job and this will help them to start selecting their own resources for activities such as painting and making things.

What you need

A range of different types of paper, including newspaper, wrapping paper, tissue paper, poster paper, kitchen paper, crêpe paper; sticky tape; scissors; a flip chart or board.

What to do

Display the range of papers you have collected together so that the children can see them. Then present the children with different role-play situations which will make them explore the range of papers. For example, pretend that someone has knocked over a drink on a table and invite the children to think of different papers that might absorb the liquid. Help them to evaluate which paper would be most useful for mopping up spills by carrying out an investigation together as a class.

Organise the children into groups. Explain to one group that you want to make a dark place to watch a film later. Give them the range of papers to see which blocks out the most light. Which papers block out the least light? Let them investigate the range of paper they have. Ask another group to pretend they are going to a party and they need to wrap up a present. Ask them to select from the range of papers to find the one that makes the neatest and strongest wrapping paper. Finally, invite another group to think about painting a picture on the different types of paper. Which do they think the paint would soak into and which would run off? Let them paint pictures on each type of paper to evaluate which is best for this activity.

Together as a class, record the effectiveness of the papers for each job to evaluate which is the most suitable or useful for each one. Look at each of the papers in turn. For each one ask the children to say *yes* or *no* to whether it is good for soaking up liquid, blocking out the light, wrapping a present and painting on. Record their answers as a table displayed on the flip chart. When you have finished evaluating the usefulness of each of the papers for each job, ask the children to decide which paper they would use if they spilt water or if they wanted to paint a picture, by picking out those with *yes* written by the side. Ask the children, *Which paper is best for soaking up spills? Which paper is best to block out the light? Which paper is best for wrapping presents? Which paper is best for painting? How do you know?* Note whether the children have used their evaluation skills to help form their opinions.

TAKE A PICTURE

AREA OF LEARNING: KNOWLEDGE AND UNDERSTANDING OF THE WORLD. ELG: TO FIND OUT ABOUT AND USE INFORMATION AND COMMUNICATION TECHNOLOGY.

LEARNING OBJECTIVE
To use observation skills to find an interesting view.

THINKING OBJECTIVE
To evaluate information (judging quality).

THINKING SKILLS
The children will look for and find a suitable view that they can see from the school grounds. They will evaluate what their shot will look like by looking through a cardboard viewfinder, before using a camera to find the same view and then taking a photograph. They will evaluate the final developed photograph to form an opinion about the quality of this against the original view.

WHAT YOU NEED
Cardboard viewfinders; a camera.

WHAT TO DO
In groups, tell the children that they are going to go outside together to find a view they like for a photograph to include on a map of the school. Tell them that you want them to find something that is interesting to look at, that they like and which they think other children in the school will like.

Before you go outside, show the children the camera, reminding them to handle it carefully. Invite them in turn to look through the viewfinder. Talk about what they can see inside the frame. Explain that when they push the button, that what they can see through the viewfinder is the photograph that will come out. Give the cardboard viewfinders out and tell the children that they can use these to help them find a shot they like.

Go outside with the frames and encourage the children to look for something they like before checking the view through their frame. When they have tried a few different views out, ask them to select one for their shot. Help them to find the same view using the camera viewfinder and to take a photograph. Ask the children why they chose that view. Ask, *What did you like about it? Can you fit it inside the camera viewfinder? Is this the shot you wanted?*

When all the children have taken their photograph, develop these for them. As soon as they are ready, invite the children to find their photograph. Ask, *How do you know this one is yours? Does it match the view you took?* Get the children to evaluate the quality of the photographs against what they saw through their frames. Does it reflect the view they took? Get them to share each other's photographs by passing them around. Invite a few children to say which one they like best and why. Is it the view that they like? Is it the detail that was captured in the photograph? Does it show a particularly attractive plant or geographical feature? Or is it something else?

Repeat the activity as a context for sketching a small view or section of a favourite feature in detail.

WAFT AND WEAVE

AREA OF LEARNING: KNOWLEDGE AND UNDERSTANDING OF THE WORLD. ELG: TO SELECT THE TOOLS AND TECHNIQUES THEY NEED TO SHAPE, ASSEMBLE AND JOIN MATERIALS THEY ARE USING.

LEARNING OBJECTIVE
To learn to cut and join wood.

THINKING OBJECTIVE
To evaluate information (judging value).

THINKING SKILLS

The children will consider how to cut and join wood to make a simple frame. They will learn the method of joining corners with glue and card triangles, thinking about the value of this method to make the structure stronger. The children will join these together to make a class frame for weaving, using card squares or string, evaluating the value of these resources to make the structure strong enough for weaving.

WHAT YOU NEED

Lengths of balsa wood; glue; card triangles and squares; string; coping or hacksaws; jigs to hold the wood in place when sawing; different textured materials for weaving.

WHAT TO DO

Explain to the class that you want to make a giant frame in which to make an interesting weaving pattern to display in the classroom. Tell them that they are all going to contribute to this by making their own small rectangular frame first and then joining everyone's together to make the bigger frame. Ask the children to suggest what they could use to make the frame. After a few moments of discussion, tell them that the best material to make the frame from is wood. Show them the balsa wood and triangular cards. Ask them to suggest how the frame could be put together using these materials. Agree the method with them, explaining how they can join four lengths of balsa wood together by gluing a triangular card over the corners to hold the pieces of wood in place. Evaluate whether the rectangle is strong. Ask, *Why is this? Is it because of the card triangles?* Agree that the triangles are valuable for making the rectangle strong. Explain how the four pieces of wood need to be cut into two pairs the same length so that the two pieces that make the sides of the frame are the same, and the two pieces that will form the top and bottom are the same length. Invite the children to suggest how they should cut the wood. Ask, *How will you hold it still to cut it? What will you use? How will you make sure that the lengths are the same size? Do you think the wood will be strong enough?*

As the children start to make their frame, evaluate with them whether they are using an appropriate method to cut and join the wood.

When the frames are dry, talk about how they could be joined together to make a larger one. Ask, *Can you join the corners in the same way? Will you use triangles or squares of card for this? Will this make the frame strong enough? Would it be better to use string and tie the rectangles together?* Use glue and string to join the sides and card squares to reinforce the corners, creating a larger frame that the children may want. This may not be rectangular. When the frame is dry, weave different textured materials to make a screen.

MARBLE RUN

AREA OF LEARNING: PHYSICAL DEVELOPMENT. ELG: TO HANDLE TOOLS, OBJECTS AND CONSTRUCTION SAFELY AND WITH INCREASING CONTROL.

LEARNING OBJECTIVE

To fit together guttering or commercial construction kits.

THINKING OBJECTIVES

To evaluate information (judging quality); to suggest improvements.

THINKING SKILLS

The children will think about how they can get a marble to run from one place to another, considering the direction they need it to go in, how to get it to start to roll and whether they can make it roll uphill at any point. They will evaluate how effective their marble run is in terms of how smoothly their marble runs, whether it stops at any point and whether it stays inside the channels, before suggesting any improvements to their model. They will then test out their ideas with balls and cars and evaluate the quality of their construction for these objects. If you feel adventurous, you could let them test it out with water.

WHAT YOU NEED

Lengths of guttering and joints; props to hold the joints in place; commercial construction kits; marbles; balls; cars.

WHAT TO DO

Explain to the children what you want them to make a marble run in groups. Explain what this is to them if they are not sure.

Work outside, or in a large space in the classroom, with groups of children to fit together the guttering or pieces from a commercial construction kit to make marble runs. Show them how to do this, guiding their construction ideas where necessary. Let them test the finished model by rolling a marble from one end to the other. Watch it as it rolls and ask them to evaluate the marble run by whether the marble runs smoothly, whether it stops in any places and whether it runs too fast and jumps over the sides of the channel. Note the quality of the model and ask the children to suggest how they can make it better. Let them make the necessary improvements and try rolling the marble down the construction again. Challenge the children to make one part so that the marble has to run uphill for a while, or change direction. What do the children need to do to make sure it has enough, but not too much, speed to do this?

When the children have done this, let them test out their construction with other objects, such as cars, balls or water. Are the children happy with the quality of their construction or can they suggest other improvements they'd like to make?

MUSICAL MOVEMENTS

AREA OF LEARNING: PHYSICAL DEVELOPMENT. ELG: TO MOVE WITH CONFIDENCE, IMAGINATION AND IN SAFETY.

LEARNING OBJECTIVE
To move confidently in different ways, using imagination and considering their own and other's safety.

THINKING OBJECTIVE
To evaluate information (judging value).

THINKING SKILLS
The children will listen to different extracts of music that are very different in style. They will move freely to the music before evaluating which is most valuable for moving to in different ways.

WHAT YOU NEED
A range of musical extracts for the children to move to in different ways, including marching, skipping, trotting, jumping, flowing and crawling (extracts from 'Carnival of the Animals' by Saint-Saëns would be suitable, as well as 'The Typewriter' and 'The Syncopated Clock' by Leroy Anderson, and 'The Flight of the Bumble Bee' by Rimsky-Korsakov).

WHAT TO DO
Play the marching style musical extract and invite the children to respond imaginatively to it. At the end of the extract, ask the children to evaluate the way the music prompted them to move. Ask, *How valuable was it for moving slowly to? Why did it make you feel like moving in a steady way?* Agree that the music is valuable for marching to. Then play a different extract, such as the skipping music. Again, let the children move freely before evaluating the movement it prompted. Agree that this sort of music is valuable for moving in a skipping way to.

Continue like this until you have played all the extracts, making sure you play extracts that are very different in style after one other and that the children have evaluated the value of each extract for certain movements. At the end of the session, play all of the musical extracts through, inviting the children to use their evaluation to move in the way each extract prompts. Afterwards, identify again which extract is most valuable for marching, moving slowly to, quickly to, crawling to, and so on.

PERFORMING TOGETHER

AREA OF LEARNING: CREATIVE DEVELOPMENT. ELG: TO SING SIMPLE SONGS FROM MEMORY.

LEARNING OBJECTIVE
To learn a new song, using dynamics and percussion accompaniment to create the intended mood.

THINKING OBJECTIVES
To evaluate information (judging usefulness); to suggest improvements.

THINKING SKILLS
The children will evaluate the meaning of the words and tune of a song before singing it in quiet and loud voices to create mood and a more dramatic effect. They will then use their imaginations by exploring instruments to add a suitable percussion accompaniment, which will enhance the mood and effect further. This activity develops the children's creative development and the musical skills of performance, composition and listening and their ability to appraise their own work.

WHAT YOU NEED
A copy of 'Snappity, Snappity Crocodile' from the *Multicoloured Music Bus* written by Peter Canwell

(Collins) or a suitable song of your own choice which allows for 'loud' and 'quiet' parts; a picture of a smiling crocodile; a range of percussion instruments, including a guiro, scrapers and sand blocks.

WHAT TO DO

Sing the song to the children, showing them the picture of a smiling crocodile. Ask the children to say what the song is about. Question them to think about what message the song is giving them about what will happen if they go too near a crocodile. (That if you go too close it's sure to snap.) Talk about how this is conveyed in the song's words and in its tune. Ask, *What are the words telling us? Are there parts that we could whisper or sing very loudly?*

Sing the song again and let the children learn it, making sure that they learn from the beginning the parts to sing very loudly – *Snap* – and the bits they should sing quietly – *Take care all the while, Beware of the smile.*

Start to develop the opening phrases by getting the children to gradually sing louder up to the *Snap* part. Evaluate together how the children think this sounds. Ask, *Why does it sound good? What are you doing to make it sound so dramatic? Are you depicting the mood or message of the song?* Talk about how they can add instruments to make a dramatic accompaniment. Ask, *What instruments could you use to improve the performance and add to the mood and effect of the song?* Let the children use a guiro, scrapers and sand blocks, and evaluate together where is the most suitable place in the song to add these. Ask, Which instrument can we use to add drama to the *Snaps*? *Would a cymbal be good for this?* Can the children think of any other suitable instruments to improve their performance of the song?

Perform the song together again, incorporating the children's ideas.

FLOWER ARRANGING

AREA OF LEARNING: CREATIVE DEVELOPMENT. ELG: TO EXPLORE COLOUR, TEXTURE, SHAPE, FORM AND SPACE IN THREE DIMENSIONS.

LEARNING OBJECTIVE

To explore colour, shape and form to create a flower arrangement.

THINKING OBJECTIVES

To evaluate information (judging quality); to develop criteria for judging.

THINKING SKILLS

The children will choose from a range of coloured flowers and greenery to create a flower arrangement. The context for making these arrangements could be a party, a coffee morning for carers and parents or a Christmas lunch, or just to create a display from. The children will evaluate each other's arrangements, considering the way that colour has been combined and shape created in the finished arrangement. This will help them to identify the criteria on which they have based their quality judgement.

WHAT YOU NEED

A flower arrangement; fresh, dried and silk flowers and greenery (you could invite parents to contribute some they are willing to part with, or make some from tissue and crêpe paper); vases, bottles, baskets and containers in different colours and sizes; oasis; water.

WHAT TO DO

As a class, look at the flower arrangement and note the things that the children like. Explore this by questioning the children further so that they are encouraged to talk about the way colours are combined. Ask, *How many different colours have been used? Do the colours balance with the colour of the vase? What do you think of the shape of the arrangement? For example, do you like the different heights and the way it is balanced on both sides (if it is)?*

Show the children the flowers in your collection. In smaller groups, invite the children to create their own arrangement using these flowers. Ask them to think about which flowers they want to choose. Ask, *Why do you like these? Which vase will you use? Which flowers will you put at the back? Which ones will you put here?* Make sure there are enough flowers for them all to have a go.

When the groups have finished their arrangements, ask them to evaluate the quality of each other's work, giving reasons for their opinions.

Unless being used for a specific purpose, arrange the children's work as a display, inviting the children to say where the arrangements should be placed. Consider putting the taller ones at the back or raising some up by standing them on boxes. Ask the children to evaluate the final shape and form of the display, saying why they like it in terms of the colour combinations, the way the shapes are combined and the final overall visual effect.

EXTENDING EVALUATION SKILLS

Area of learning and ELG, NLS or NNS objective	Activity title	Thinking objective	Activity	Page
Personal, social and emotional development ELG: To manage their own personal hygiene	Washing hands	To evaluate information (judging quality)	Evaluating different soaps and towels when washing hands	117
Communication, language and literacy ELG: To use talk to organise, sequence and clarify thinking and ideas	999	To evaluate information (judging quality)	Acting out a scenario of calling an emergency service	118
Communication, language and literacy ELG: To show an understanding of how information can be found in non-fiction texts	Which book?	To evaluate information (judging quality)	Deciding which non-fiction book is most relevant to find out about a topic	119
Communication, language and literacy ELG: To write their own names NLS objective: To write their own names	Labels and captions	To suggest improvements	Designing name labels using a computer and improving their design	120
Mathematical development ELG: To use developing mathematical ideas to solve problems NNS objective: To use language to compare two numbers of quantities	Shopping	To suggest improvements	Deciding which items on a shopping list are not clear enough to be able to buy items in a shopping role-play	121
Mathematical development ELG: To use everyday words to describe position NNS objective: To solve simple problems or puzzles in a practical context	Will it fit?	To evaluate information (judging value)	Completing a jigsaw puzzle, focusing on how to choose pieces to fit into spaces	122
Knowledge and understanding of the world ELG: To investigate materials by using all of their senses	A pillow for a princess	To evaluate information (judging quality)	Judging the quality of materials to make the most comfortable pillow from	123
Knowledge and understanding of the world ELG: To ask questions about why things happen and how things work	Moving parts	To suggest improvements	Joining the limbs of a puppet to make it move	124
Knowledge and understanding of the world ELG: To find out about their environment, and talk about those features they like and dislike	Litter collection	To suggest improvements	Considering ways to improve the local environment by tackling litter	125
Physical development ELG: To show awareness of space, of themselves and of others	Playtime capers	To evaluate information (judging usefulness)	Evaluating which areas outside are best for certain activities	126
Physical development ELG: To travel around, under, over and through balancing and climbing equipment	Moving differently	To evaluate information (judging value)	Exploring a range of PE apparatus to discover which is best to develop particular skills on	127
Creative development ELG: To explore colour in two dimensions	Mounting pictures	To evaluate information; to suggest improvements	Evaluating the colour of paper against paintings to mount their work on	129
Creative development ELG: To express and communicate their ideas, thoughts and feelings by using a widening range of role-play	Pirate Pete	To evaluate information (judging quality); to suggest improvements	Creating costumes for a pirate	130

WASHING HANDS

AREA OF LEARNING: PERSONAL, SOCIAL AND EMOTIONAL DEVELOPMENT. ELG: TO MANAGE THEIR OWN PERSONAL HYGIENE.

LEARNING OBJECTIVE
To learn to take care of personal needs.

THINKING OBJECTIVE
To evaluate information (judging quality).

THINKING SKILLS
The children will use different kinds of soap to wash their hands after a painting activity. They will use their senses to judge the quality of the soap – about the way it feels on their skin and a more objective judgement based on how well it gets their hands clean. They will use different types of towels to judge which is the most efficient for drying them afterwards.

WHAT YOU NEED
Tablets of soap; liquid soap; a water tray; two different ply paper towels; a chart for recording the number of towels used of each ply; resources for the painting activity.

WHAT TO DO
Check for soap allergies before starting the activity. Explain to the children that you want to find out which soap and towels are best for getting their hands clean and dry when washing them. Explain that they are going to experiment by using a tablet of soap today and liquid soap tomorrow. They can also choose whether to use paper towels labelled A or B. Tell them that when they have dried their hands properly, using the least number of towels they can, they should record how many towels they needed to dry them with. You may need an additional adult to supervise the fairness of this part of the activity.

Set up a finger painting or hand printing activity. When the children have finished, invite them to wash their hands using the tablet of soap. As they wash their hands, ask them what they think of the soap. Ask, *Is it soft on your hands? Does it make a good amount of lather? How much soap have you needed to use to get your hands clean? Did you have to wash them more than once?* Get them to dry their hands on their chosen towel, recording on a chart the number of towels they used.

Repeat the activity the next day, using the liquid soap but the same choice of towels. Again, they should record the number of towels used of each type.

At the end of the session or day, whichever is best, ask the children to give their opinion about which soap cleaned their hands best and why. Ask, *Does this help us make a judgement about the quality of the soap?* Wonder with the children whether they think it is the type of soap or the brand of soap that is best. Look at the chart together and decide by looking at the number of towels used to get hands really dry, which is the most efficient towel – A or B? Is there a difference?

DIFFERENTIATION
Give less able children guidance as they wash their hands, describing and identifying for them when they have produced good quality lather. Examine their hands together to make sure they are really clean. Guide them in their choice of towels, making sure that they have used one as efficiently as they can before using another towel, and at the same time making sure that their hands are really dry. Higher attaining children should be encouraged to interpret the results on the chart as a means of judging the quality of the towels. These results can be expressed as a graph for each type of towel, for example the number of times that one, two or three 'A' type towels were used.

WHERE NEXT
Try different brands of soaps, judging the quality by using the children's opinions.

Try different types of towel and add to the chart and graph.

ASSESSMENT
Record whether anyone was able to use data to judge the quality of the towels and those children who had difficulty using their senses to form an opinion about the quality of the soap.

LEARNING OUTCOMES
Most children will be able to use their senses to judge the quality of soap, some will note the quality by expressing an opinion about how well it has cleaned their hands. Some will be able to use data to judge the quality of different types of paper towels.

FURTHER PERSONAL, SOCIAL AND EMOTIONAL DEVELOPMENT CHALLENGES

Bubbles

Challenge the children to say which soap is best for blowing bubbles – a bar of soap or liquid soap. Show them how to lather their hands and to blow through the thumbs and fingers of the clenched hands to blow bubbles. The time to stop is when their hands are all wrinkly!

Bubble sculptures

Get the children to judge the quality of different brands of bubble bath. In the water tray, use different kinds of tear-free bubble bath each day to make bubble sculptures. Time how long the same amount of bubble bath lasts and note the volume of bubbles each one makes.

Bubble mixture

Ask the children to use the different kinds of soap to make bubble mixture. They can test each one out to judge the quality and see which is best for blowing bubbles.

999

AREA OF LEARNING: COMMUNICATION, LANGUAGE AND LITERACY. ELG: TO USE TALK TO ORGANISE, SEQUENCE AND CLARIFY THINKING AND IDEAS.

LEARNING OBJECTIVE

To develop a sequence for asking for help.

THINKING OBJECTIVE

To evaluate information (judging quality).

THINKING SKILLS

The children will act out a scenario of calling one of the emergency services. With adult help, they will record the sequence of information they need to give in a call to the operator. Each group will act out a role-play to the rest of the class who will evaluate the quality of their conversational sequence and whether they gave the correct information.

WHAT YOU NEED

A telephone, sheet of paper and pen.

WHAT TO DO

Talk to the children about what they do if they need to telephone for a fire engine, the police or an ambulance. Agree with the children that they need to call the emergency services by dialling 999. Invite one child to show the others how to dial 999. What do the children think the operator asks on the end of the phone? Write down the question and answer for this:

Q: *What service do you require?*
A: (Let the children decide on a service to ask for.)

Ask the children what should come next in the conversation. Discuss where the children are and ask for a volunteer to give an address. This can be the school address or the children's own address if possible. Encourage parents to teach their child this as a homework activity. Tell the children that the next thing they should do is explain why they want the police, an ambulance or fire engine, by telling the operator what has happened.

In groups, ask the children to practise the conversation in role-play. One child can play the part of the caller, another the operator and ask other members of the group to evaluate each other's performance by thinking about whether the caller gives clear instructions about what has happened and where the service required should go to. The groups could also act out what happens when the services arrive. What do the children think happens first, next and last?

Ask the groups to perform their role-play to the rest of the class, asking the children to say whether each group has included what they should. If they were an operator, would they know where to go and would they know what to expect when they got there? Did the children dial the correct number?

DIFFERENTIATION

Ask less able children questions during their role-play. For example, ask them to say whether the correct number was dialled before they proceed to the next part. Did the operator ask which service? Did they reply correctly? Higher attaining children should be encouraged to work together as a group being given very little direction. When they have finished, ask them to evaluate how good their conversation was and discuss how they know this.

WHERE NEXT

Ask two adults to act out the sequence missing out a crucial part of the conversation, or asking for a service that is not available. Can the children identify what is wrong with the conversation and say what should be said instead?

ASSESSMENT

Note which children are able to evaluate the quality of the conversation by saying it is good because all the things that should be said were said, and all the information that should be exchanged has been achieved.

LEARNING OUTCOMES
Most children will learn to dial 999 and answer questions correctly to ask for help. Some will go further and evaluate for themselves what they need to do without relying on questions as prompts.

FURTHER COMMUNICATION, LANGUAGE AND LITERACY CHALLENGES
Recipe
Follow a recipe to make some biscuits or cakes together. As you make these, check that all the information needed is included. At the end ask the children to evaluate the quality of the recipe, both in terms of whether it has included all the instructions they needed to know, and by tasting the finished cakes or biscuits. Has the recipe too much sugar? Have the cakes or biscuits been cooked for too long? Are they just right?

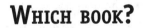

WHICH BOOK?

AREA OF LEARNING: COMMUNICATION, LANGUAGE AND LITERACY. ELG: TO SHOW AN UNDERSTANDING OF HOW INFORMATION CAN BE FOUND IN NON-FICTION TEXTS.

LEARNING OBJECTIVE
To learn that information can be found in non-fiction books.

THINKING OBJECTIVE
To evaluate information (judging usefulness).

THINKING SKILLS
The children will look at a range of non-fiction books and decide which are the most useful for finding out about their chosen topic. They will give reasons for their decisions, such as seeing relevant pictures inside the books or noticing the words in the title on the front of the books.

WHAT YOU NEED
A range of non-fiction books on your chosen topic, some of which will contain relevant information and some that will not; access to the library and the Internet; a flip chart or board.

WHAT TO DO
Introduce the term's new topic to the children. Create a flow chart with them to collect their ideas about the topic and help you find out what they already know. For example, if you intend to do a topic on growing, collect the names of everything that grows. As you record their ideas on the flip chart, separate these into animals and plants. Some children may suggest other things that get bigger or grow, such as people, bread, cakes, balloons and tyres. Discuss these ideas if you like. Explain to the children that to begin with you want to concentrate on natural things that grow, like animals, people and plants.

Show the children the collection of books and explain that they are all non-fiction books. Discuss how they can use non-fiction books to find information about the things they have identified on the flip chart. Take one of the children's suggestions and ask them to find a book from your collection that will tell them something about this. For example, if you choose *daffodil*, ask them to find all the books that will tell them about flowers. Continue like this until you are sure the children are clear about how to find a book that contains the relevant information.

Then start to ask questions about the books, such as *Do some of the books contain information about more than one thing? Are some books only useful for certain bits of information?* Tell the children that you want them to find which books will help them find out about animals, plants or people, if this is your topic. Tell them that you want some of them to find other books from around the school, to look at CD-ROMs and perhaps find useful websites on the Internet.

Organise the children into groups. Let some children work with an additional adult if possible, exploring the non-fiction books and using the pictures to help them ask questions about their topic. Take another group to the library to locate the section for animals, people and plants. Depending on their ability, let them follow the library's coding system to locate the books, especially if it uses colour. Alternatively, ask them to evaluate whether a book is likely to be useful by the design on the front cover. Work with another group, researching the Internet or CD-ROMs to evaluate which ones are most useful to their research.

Gather the groups back together and evaluate which book was most useful for finding out about the body, trees or butterflies, for example. Share with the class the most useful CD-ROMs or website addresses.

DIFFERENTIATION
Teach higher attaining children how to use the contents page and index as a tool to help them

evaluate the usefulness of each book. Give lower attaining children less specific things to research, for example ask them to find all the books which tell them something about people, trees, birds, fish or flowers.

WHERE NEXT
Set up a research topic for the children to evaluate the usefulness of CD-ROMs and websites.

Evaluate the usefulness of video films about your chosen topic in the same way. Have the children learned anything new about animals, plants or people from watching them?

ASSESSMENT
Assess how well the children use pictures, titles and text to evaluate which books are useful to their research. Note those who can locate the books that may be useful by following the library colour-coded system, and those who find the relevant books by looking at the design of the front covers.

LEARNING OUTCOMES
All the children should be able to use pictures to select books that are useful for researching specific things. Most will evaluate the usefulness of the book to specific groups of animals and plants.

FURTHER COMMUNICATION, LANGUAGE AND LITERACY CHALLENGES

Topical research
Give the children a particular animal or plant and ask them to look through the books, first to find the books which are relevant and then to find the one which is the most useful to find information from. Ask them to say why it was the most useful.

Arctic world
Convert your book corner into an Arctic 'icescape'. Cover seats with white sheets or throws, and cushions and beanbags with white covers. Ask the children to find books that would give them useful information about the kind of animals and plants they might find in the Arctic. Ask parents if they can lend any soft toys, posters and pictures to make a display.

LABELS AND CAPTIONS

AREA OF LEARNING: COMMUNICATION, LANGUAGE AND LITERACY. ELG: TO WRITE THEIR OWN NAMES. NLS OBJECTIVE: TO WRITE THEIR OWN NAMES.

LEARNING OBJECTIVE
To write a name label for their drawer or tray.

THINKING OBJECTIVE
To suggest improvements.

THINKING SKILLS
The children will use a computer to design their own name label. They will evaluate its quality and think about how they can make improvements so that it can be easily seen through the use of colour, size and font style. Some may wish to insert a picture or add one later.

WHAT YOU NEED
A computer; appropriate software (see activity); paper; scissors.

WHAT TO DO
As a small group, or if you have the facilities as a class, show the children how they can change the colour, size and style of fonts on a computer. Write your own name and following the children's suggestions, experiment with colour, size and shape until you all agree on the one they like the best. Print and show this to the children.

Evaluate together whether it will fit on a drawer front, considering whether it is too big or too small. Make any adjustments suggested by the children and invite them to say whether they can think of other ways to make it look even better, perhaps by adding a picture or border.

Let the children work individually or in pairs to produce their own name labels. Show them how to insert a picture from a clipart program, making sure that they choose one that will fit, or resizing it for them.

DIFFERENTIATION
Talk to less able children before they start, asking them the colour they would like their labels to be and how big they would like their name to be. Help them to set this up and let them evaluate their label at this stage and decide whether this is what they want. If it is, remind them how to highlight and change the styles. Monitor the children closely to make sure they are making improvements to their finished text. Help them to add a border or picture and show them how to print. Higher attaining children should explore different pictures to insert, researching those that they like and finding ways to reduce them to fit the space available. Let the children explore where they put the pictures on the label, perhaps, at the beginning, the end or above or below their

name. Some children may be able to add a border independently.

WHERE NEXT
Add the labels to the drawers or trays.

ASSESSMENT
Assess how well the children are evaluating their text in terms of whether it is attractive and can be seen easily from a distance. Note how well they use this to judge the quality and suggest improvements.

LEARNING OUTCOMES
Most children will use evaluation skills to note the quality of their name labels during the making process, and use this to suggest and make improvements to them.

FURTHER COMMUNICATION, LANGUAGE AND LITERACY CHALLENGES

Photograph captions
Get the children to make captions for photographs taken during another activity. These can be labels or ideas of what the children or people are thinking or saying to each other. They should make changes to the style of the font before printing their captions out and sticking them underneath the photograph or pictures as labels, or onto thought or speech bubbles. Evaluate the captions and invite the children to suggest improvements they could make, for instance making them clearer, or using more interesting vocabulary.

SHOPPING

AREA OF LEARNING: MATHEMATICAL DEVELOPMENT. ELG: TO USE DEVELOPING MATHEMATICAL IDEAS TO SOLVE PRACTICAL PROBLEMS. NNS OBJECTIVE: TO USE LANGUAGE SUCH AS MORE OR LESS TO COMPARE TWO NUMBERS OR QUANTITIES.

LEARNING OBJECTIVE
To read numbers on product labels to select the one they want to buy.

THINKING OBJECTIVE
To suggest improvements.

THINKING SKILLS
The children will look at a shopping list and look for the items they want from a supermarket role-play area. Some items on the shopping list will be specific and some will not so that it is not always clear which carton the children need to buy. The children will then improve the shopping lists so that they will know precisely which things they need to buy when they go back to the 'supermarket'.

WHAT YOU NEED
A range of bottles, cartons and containers with matching products, but different sizes and flavours; shopping lists (that aren't particularly clear) for example, *A bottle of coke, a packet of biscuits, a tin of fruit*; baskets.

WHAT TO DO
Set up the role-play area to look like a supermarket, or create shelves from where the children can locate and select the products. Give pairs of children a shopping list and ask them to read it together. Help them if necessary, and when the children are comfortable with what is on the list, ask them to go to the shelves to find the things they need. Tell them that if they are in doubt they should take all the products with the same name. For example, the shopping list says *a bottle of cola, a packet of biscuits, a tin of fruit* and on the shelf are two bottles of coke, but one is a litre bottle and the other a 2-litre bottle, there are chocolate and plain biscuits and tins containing pineapple and peaches.

When they return, check that they have bought the things on their list by taking the things out of their basket one at a time and ticking them off on the list. Which things have they more than one of? Why did they bring more than one of this item? Ask, *Was the list not precise enough? How can we make the list more precise? What should we add? Do we need to write the size and type of biscuits more clearly so that the shopper knows precisely what we want them to buy?* Add the extra information needed that will make the list more precise. Then return the items to the shelves and repeat the activity with the children's new lists. Are the lists clearer now?

DIFFERENTIATION
Work alongside less able children, asking them questions to find the precise things the shopping

list states. Limit the evaluation of the list to size only. For example, for a bottle of coke, ask them which of the two bottles they need to buy. Ask direct questions, such as *Does the shopping list tell you which size to buy?* And then, *What do we need to add to the shopping list to make it clearer?* Make the additions to the list as you go along, using language such as *big* and *small* only to compare the two sizes. Higher attaining children should be challenged to note the differences in flavour or additions to some products. For example, the list could say *Two litres of cola* but have a choice from diet, caffeine-free or cola with lemon. The children should add which type of cola precisely the list should say.

WHERE NEXT

Repeat as an independent activity with the children acting out different supermarket role-play activities.

ASSESSMENT

Note the children who not only identify that the list is not precise enough but also how to make improvements to make it better.

LEARNING OUTCOMES

Most children will be able to judge the quality of the lists and say whether they are precise enough. Some may be able to suggest how they can be improved so that they are precise enough to make sure that the exact items are bought.

FURTHER MATHEMATICAL DEVELOPMENT CHALLENGES

Shopping list

Give the children a set of empty cartons and containers and challenge them to write a list, which gives precise instructions about the things to buy. Return the items to the shelves, give the list to another child, and ask them to evaluate the quality of the list by finding the things listed. Check to see if the correct things have been 'bought' and if not make suggestions on how to improve the shopping list.

Label facts

Use the same shopping list but blank out some of the detail on the labels. Ask the children to evaluate what is missing and what needs to be included to make sure they buy the right items.

WILL IT FIT?

AREA OF LEARNING: MATHEMATICAL DEVELOPMENT. ELG: TO USE EVERYDAY WORDS TO DESCRIBE POSITION. NNS OBJECTIVE: TO SOLVE SIMPLE PROBLEMS OR PUZZLES IN A PRACTICAL CONTEXT, AND RESPOND TO 'WHAT COULD WE TRY NEXT?'

LEARNING OBJECTIVE

To learn to orientate a shape to make it fit into a space.

THINKING OBJECTIVE

To evaluate information (judging value).

THINKING SKILLS

The children will complete a simple jigsaw puzzle, thinking about the shape of the pieces and whether they help to establish where these will go in terms of pattern or space. They will talk about how they know in terms of a piece's size, shape and orientation. They may also refer to the colours and detail of the picture. As they talk about the pieces, the children will be evaluating the value of the shape, size, orientation and colour in helping them to complete the jigsaw.

WHAT YOU NEED

A floor jigsaw puzzle; several jigsaw puzzles.

WHAT TO DO

Sit the class in a circle around the spread-out pieces from a large floor jigsaw. Choose one that the children have not done before, either by buying a new one or borrowing one from a different class or school. Show the children the picture on the box and talk about what the jigsaw is about. Can the children see any parts of the picture on the jigsaw pieces? Invite them to pick up a piece and match it to the picture. Ask, *Where does this piece go in relation to the picture? Is it in the middle, at the top, at the bottom or to one side? Is it a corner piece?*

Talk about the shape of the picture. What can the children tell you about the shape of the picture? Agree that the puzzle is a rectangle and has four corners and four straight sides. Ask, *How valuable is this knowledge in helping us to fit the puzzle together? Does it tell us that there are four pieces that have to make a corner?* Ask the children to find the four corner pieces, to look at the picture and find their place. Next, note with the children the value of knowing that the puzzle has straight sides. Ask, *How does this information help?* Ask them to find all the pieces with straight sides and, using the picture to help if necessary, fit the outside frame of the puzzle together.

Then let the children start to fit the inside pieces together, asking the children to look carefully at the shapes of any spaces that are left. Tell them to look at the pieces that are left and note which ones could fit the spaces and which ones could not. Ask, *How do we know which way around this piece goes? Do we need to turn it? How valuable are the design, size and shape of the puzzle pieces in helping us decide this?* Continue until the puzzle is complete.

Work with the children in smaller groups to fit together other puzzles, noting how well they evaluate the shape of the puzzle to fit together the outside and then the shapes of the spaces to find the missing pieces.

DIFFERENTIATION

Set up some half-completed puzzles for less able children to complete. Work with them, talking about the shape of the spaces and agreeing how valuable this is to helping them to find the missing pieces. Ask questions, such as *Is the missing piece the same size, shape and colour as the space?* Give those who find puzzles easy circular ones and other odd-shaped puzzles to complete. Help them to evaluate how the shapes of the pieces and the spaces help them to fit the correct piece in place.

WHERE NEXT

Set up puzzles for the children to complete as an independent activity.

Organise shape-posting activities for the children to complete, where they should evaluate how their knowledge of the properties helps them post the correct shape through the correct hole.

ASSESSMENT

Note the children who are beginning to evaluate the value of their knowledge and understanding of shape to help fit puzzles together. Note those who still try to do the puzzles through trial and error and are not using the information to help them.

LEARNING OUTCOMES

Most children will start to evaluate the value of their knowledge and understanding of the properties of shape to help them fit together puzzles with which they are unfamiliar. Some will be able to extend this to puzzles with unusual shapes.

FURTHER MATHEMATICAL DEVELOPMENT CHALLENGES

Puzzle challenge

Mix up two puzzles that are very different and ask

the children to sort them into the correct puzzles by fitting them together. They should evaluate the pieces by their shape and size, and use this information to help them fit the right pieces into the right puzzle.

3-D city

Set up a model of a building where one side is finished but the other side is not. Challenge the children to evaluate the shapes on one side and use this information to make the other side the same or symmetrical. Challenge them to make a similar model for their friends to finish.

A PILLOW FOR A PRINCESS

AREA OF LEARNING: KNOWLEDGE AND UNDERSTANDING OF THE WORLD. ELG: TO INVESTIGATE MATERIALS BY USING ALL OF THEIR SENSES AS APPROPRIATE.

LEARNING OBJECTIVE

To investigate different materials to make a pillow or cushion for a princess.

THINKING OBJECTIVE

To evaluate information (judging quality).

THINKING SKILLS

The children will explore different materials and, judging the quality of each in terms of its comfort, will choose the one that is best to make a pillow or cushion for a princess.

WHAT YOU NEED

A range of materials with different textures and properties, including cotton wool, fir cones, bricks, stones, wood, fabric, sponge, upholstery stuffing; empty cushion covers and pillowcases; a copy of the traditional story 'The Princess and the Pea'.

WHAT TO DO

In small groups, let the children explore the properties of the different materials. Ask the children to say which material would be the best for a pillow or cushion for a princess. Go around the groups asking them questions as they discuss this, such as *Why do you think this one is best? Is it because it is more comfortable? Why do you think this one is most comfortable?* Use this context to identify some of the properties of the materials, putting those that are soft together and those that are not to one side.

Test out the children's hypotheses. Invite the children to stuff empty pillowcases or cushion covers with those materials from your collection that they think will be comfortable to sit or lie on. Let the children individually make a decision about the comfort of each one by sitting and lying on them in turn, agreeing in their groups on the material that they think is most suitable. Discuss with the children how they went about evaluating the quality of the materials they used to stuff the pillowcase or cushion cover.

Read the story 'The Princess and the Pea' and evaluate whether their pillows and cushions will be acceptable to this princess.

DIFFERENTIATION
Let less able children investigate each material carefully if necessary, including the bricks and fir cones. This will help them understand what hard and soft means before using this to help them evaluate the quality in terms of comfort.

WHERE NEXT
Let the children evaluate the quality of other materials by investigating their properties and use.

ASSESSMENT
Note the children who use the property of comfort to evaluate the quality of the pillow or cushion they have made.

LEARNING OUTCOMES
Most children will evaluate the quality of their cushion or pillow in terms of comfort by testing this out using their senses.

FURTHER KNOWLEDGE AND UNDERSTANDING OF THE WORLD CHALLENGES

Umbrellas and boots
Invite the children to evaluate the quality of a range of materials for keeping our heads and feet dry. Outside, open out an umbrella and pour water from a watering can over it, asking the children to note the amount of water collected in a container directly underneath. Ask them if they think this method of testing can be used to evaluate the quality of other materials in keeping people dry. Challenge the children to find a way of evaluating the quality of footwear for keeping their feet dry. Model this by stuffing a pair of socks inside wellingtons and standing them in a tray of water. Ask the children to note whether the wellingtons let in water and the socks get wet.

Warm hands
Let the children evaluate the quality of gloves and mittens made from different materials for keeping hands warm. They can carry out tests to see whether they can feel the cold of a cube of ice when held in the hand.

MOVING PARTS

AREA OF LEARNING: KNOWLEDGE AND UNDERSTANDING OF THE WORLD. ELG: TO ASK QUESTIONS ABOUT WHY THINGS HAPPEN AND HOW THINGS WORK.

LEARNING OBJECTIVE
To learn to fit together things so that they move.

THINKING OBJECTIVE
To suggest improvements.

THINKING SKILLS
The children will work in small groups to try to make moving puppets by joining the limbs as they wish in the first instance. They will evaluate how well these move before thinking about using a joining method that will allow more movement.

WHAT YOU NEED
Card, cut into a torso and limbs to make a puppet of a human (enough for each child in the class to make a complete 'human'); scissors; sticky tape, glue, stapler and staples, paper fasteners.

WHAT TO DO
On a tabletop, loosely place the cardboard shapes into the shape of a person. Ask the children to suggest how they can fit these pieces together so that the legs, arms and head will move. Some will suggest sticky tape, others staples and glue. If they have used paper fasteners before, someone may suggest these. If they have not, let them work in small groups to join their puppets together how they want to.

Afterwards, evaluate together whether the head, arms and legs move, and if not, why not. Show the children the paper fasteners and how to join two parts together with them. Show them how these help make the limbs move. Make another puppet, but this time show them how to join the limbs with pins. Join the head to the body and show the children how it can move from side to side.

Give this started puppet to one child and let the others start from scratch. Some children may need some help with using the paper fasteners. If they do, use a sharp pencil and Plasticine to make the hole in the card first before pushing the paper fastener through. Help them to pull the fastener open if necessary before they push the sides down tightly onto the card. Compare the first puppet they made with the second puppet and identify together how the children have made improvements. Ask questions such as, *Does the second puppet move? Is it more interesting to look at? Why?*

DIFFERENTIATION
Let those who are more able improve their puppets further by making elbows and knees move.

WHERE NEXT
Ask the children to suggest other things that they could make using paper fasteners. Let them make their own models which have moving parts.

ASSESSMENT
Note the children who understand how they have made improvements to their puppets by using paper fasteners to make the limbs move. Let these children also work independently on a follow-up task and work with those who are not clear on another focused making task.

LEARNING OUTCOMES
Most children will learn how they can make improvements to a basic card puppet design. Some will make suggestions on how this way of joining can be used to make other things to make them more interesting.

FURTHER KNOWLEDGE AND UNDERSTANDING OF THE WORLD CHALLENGES

Windmills
Look together at other things that move and talk about how they work. These could include scissors, windmills, vehicles with wheels and whisks. Note with them how the parts are joined so that they are free to move. Let the children make models of cars from construction kits, or windmills from plastic or card. Evaluate where they could make improvements to their finished models.

Moving designs
Design a class model that has parts that move. Let the children think of ideas to make themselves first. If they get stuck, suggest car wheels, clock hands and pendulums, rabbit or elephant ears, and the legs on Little Miss Muffet's spider.

LITTER COLLECTION

AREA OF LEARNING: KNOWLEDGE AND UNDERSTANDING OF THE WORLD. ELG: TO FIND OUT ABOUT THEIR ENVIRONMENT, AND TALK ABOUT THOSE FEATURES THEY LIKE AND DISLIKE.

LEARNING OBJECTIVE
To identify how they can improve the parts of the environment they dislike.

THINKING OBJECTIVE
To suggest improvements.

THINKING SKILLS
The children will think about how litter spoils the way the local environment looks. They will consider how they can improve this and suggest ways to do so. This will be by placing litterbins at appropriate places.

WHAT YOU NEED
Photographs of litter left lying on the ground; small world toys of small buildings or labels of buildings; empty yoghurt pots; a flip chart or board.

WHAT TO DO
Look at the photographs as a class and ask the children to say whether they think it makes the area look nice. Ask them to suggest how they could improve the way it looks. Note their suggestions on the flip chart.

Depending on the policy in your school or setting you may need to adapt the next part of the activity. Either refer the children to the playground and the bins you may already have. Ask the children to think about what they do with the rubbish when they have a snack outside. Do they put it in the bins? Where are these located? Are they in the best place? Can the children think of a better place to put them? If you have a new bin to place somewhere, even better. Ask the children to think where a good place for this bin would be so that all the rubbish would be put away.

Alternatively (or additionally), set up a model with the small world toys to include shops, a playground with picnic spot and a takeaway restaurant. Talk about the activities that go on in these places and together identify all those places that are likely to generate litter. Ask, *Where would you place litterbins if you had the chance?* Use empty yoghurt pots as litter bins and invite the children to put these in the places they think are most suitable.

DIFFERENTIATION
Ask higher attaining children to consider how big the bins should be. Ask, *If a small bin were put outside*

a takeaway restaurant, how long would it be before it was full? How often would a small bin need emptying and would it be better to have a bigger bin there? With lower attaining children, concentrate on a place they can visit or the school grounds, thus keeping the activity within their personal experience.

WHERE NEXT
Use posters and pictures of different environments, asking the children to note those that would definitely need litterbins and those where people should take their litter home.

ASSESSMENT
Assess how well the children evaluate where the bins should go. Are they basing this on the likelihood of there being more litter there?

LEARNING OUTCOMES
Most children will express an opinion about their likes and dislikes of litter and use this to evaluate where to place litterbins.

FURTHER KNOWLEDGE AND UNDERSTANDING OF THE WORLD CHALLENGES
Take your rubbish home with you
Get the children to make signs to remind people to take their rubbish home with them. Where might they want to put such signs?
Class assembly
Lead an assembly about how to dispose of rubbish. Get the children to make up a play with someone dropping rubbish on the floor because there is no bin to put it in. Invite the children to say how they can make this better, perhaps by providing a bin or asking someone to take the rubbish home. Use the assembly to plan a campaign to keep the school tidy and make the school environment really attractive.

PLAYTIME CAPERS

AREA OF LEARNING: PHYSICAL DEVELOPMENT. ELG: TO SHOW AWARENESS OF SPACE, OF THEMSELVES AND OF OTHERS.

LEARNING OBJECTIVE
To learn to use a range of toys in a small space.

THINKING OBJECTIVE
To evaluate information (judging usefulness).

THINKING SKILLS
The children will think about the space outside before evaluating which are the best areas to do different activities in, from dressing up to reading. They will decide themselves where to organise these activities before evaluating the usefulness of each space in terms of its size and position (whether it is sheltered enough if it needs to be).

WHAT YOU NEED
Small games equipment; large wheeled toys; climbing equipment; paper; pens, crayons and paint; books.

WHAT TO DO
On different days, organise activities outside that take up a lot of space. For example, on one day plan to use the large wheeled toys with the children, on another day use the games equipment and organise a drive-through take-away role-play activity. After several days, ask the children to evaluate how much room they needed to enjoy the equipment and toys to the full. Ask, *How well did the space available support the activities? Was there enough space? Was there any room left for other activities? Would there be room for the large wheeled toys and the games equipment to be used at the same time?*

Ask the children to think about some of the other things they like to do outside. This will depend on the children, but try to encourage some activities that take up a lot of room, such as dressing up, pretending to be science detectives, hopscotch, organising an obstacle course, and some that take up a small amount of room, such as drawing, jigsaws, painting, looking at books. Evaluate how much space each activity would need and the best place to organise it.

Plan the next day's activities to take place outside, including either the games or large wheeled toys and a number of the activities the children thought of, including activities that will take up a large and a small amount of space. Monitor this the next day and during each activity ask the children if they think they have enough room for each of the activities and whether they are in a suitable place. Ask, *How well is the space being used? Do you have enough room? Are you in a suitable place? For example, is the drawing in a place that is sheltered from the wind so that the paper does not blow away?* Reorganise the space if necessary, taking into account the children's evaluations.

At the end of the week, decide with the children where the best place for certain activities is. Where should the children play with the wheeled toys? Where is the safest place to put easels or sand trays so that those children running around will not bump into them? Follow the children's lead with the suggestions, making sure that what they suggest is safe.

DIFFERENTIATION

Limit the activities that less able children consider. For example, identify four activities on one day for this group of children to consider. Higher attaining children can plot where the best place for the different activities to take place should be on a plan of the school grounds, with an adult writing an evaluation of why they have placed them where they have.

WHERE NEXT

Organise the classroom into activity areas, taking into account the children's suggestions for suitable areas.

ASSESSMENT

Note the children who understand that certain activities need more room, some need certain places due to the type of activity and the need to keep equipment out of harm's way.

LEARNING OUTCOMES

Most children will be able to think about how useful particular parts of the outdoors are in relation to certain activities. Some will be able to relate this to safety issues. Most will evaluate the usefulness in terms of the amount of space or room available to meet the needs of particular activities.

FURTHER PHYSICAL DEVELOPMENT CHALLENGES

Team games

Tell the children you want them to organise a space for a range of team games, for example transferring balls from one place to another, a role-play road safety activity or an obstacle course. Ask them to evaluate how much room the chosen activity will need and the space most useful to support it.

Climbing frame

Evaluate together which is the most suitable place to install a climbing frame. This will need to be somewhere that will not interfere with the range of other activities that the children take part in. Assess why the children think it should be put where they have suggested. Have they considered the amount of space it needs? Is it away from the areas designated for more active games and where it does not encroach on an area that is only suitable for another activity, for example planting and caring for the garden?

MOVING DIFFERENTLY

AREA OF LEARNING: PHYSICAL DEVELOPMENT. ELG: TO TRAVEL AROUND, UNDER, OVER AND THROUGH BALANCING AND CLIMBING EQUIPMENT.

LEARNING OBJECTIVE

To recognise and identify which pieces of apparatus support their skill development.

THINKING OBJECTIVE

To evaluate information (judging value).

THINKING SKILLS

The children will explore a range of PE apparatus and suggest which can be used to best develop different skills. They will evaluate the value of each piece of apparatus for balancing and climbing and note those that lend themselves to moving over, under, through, around and along. They will evaluate and plan how each piece can be set up to challenge and extend their skills.

WHAT YOU NEED
A range of PE equipment, such as benches, tables, planks, ladders, climbing frames and mats.

WHAT TO DO
Put out the apparatus and let the children explore each one. Moving from apparatus to apparatus, let them identify the range of movements they can perform on each one. Ask questions to help them try out different movements, such as *Which ones can you use to climb and which ones to balance on? Can you climb onto the tables? Can you balance along a ladder?* Ask someone to demonstrate these two latter ideas and then let all the children consolidate this evaluation through further exploration.

After a few minutes, ask the children to say how they can make their climbing movements more challenging, perhaps by introducing wall bars, or by attaching two ladders at an angle. Repeat this for balancing movements, perhaps turning over a bench, placing a ladder on the floor or by attaching a plank between two tables at a low height for the children to develop their balancing skills. Again, let the children explore their climbing and balancing skills on the new set of apparatus.

Next, talk about which pieces of apparatus the children can travel through, then over, then along and finally under. Ask the children to explore the range of directions that they can move in on each piece of apparatus by directing the mode of travel. For example, say *under* and expect the children to find a piece of apparatus and travel under it, and so on. Finally, talk about the pieces that the children can move around. This will include most pieces of apparatus, except perhaps the wall bars.

Finish by evaluating which pieces of apparatus the children liked best for climbing and which the least. Which pieces were best for travelling under, and so on? Which was the piece of apparatus that lent itself to developing both climbing and balancing skills?

DIFFERENTIATION
Be specific and give more direction to lower attaining children, asking them to find something they can climb over, then balance along. Ask them why they chose the piece that they did. Can they find another piece? Challenge higher attaining children to evaluate the best piece for climbing through, balancing along and crawling through. Which are the most and least difficult pieces of apparatus to perform these actions on and why?

WHERE NEXT
Set up the apparatus in different ways for the children to explore and evaluate in terms of which is

the best to develop climbing skills and the best for balancing skills. Can the children think of a different way to join the different pieces of apparatus to extend their skills further?

Help the children to develop other skills, such as rolling and jumping in the same way.

ASSESSMENT
Note the children who understand that certain pieces of apparatus are best for climbing rather than balancing, and vice versa, and can evaluate which pieces of apparatus they can travel in different ways on. Note the children who understand that some apparatus are good for developing both climbing and balancing skills.

LEARNING OUTCOMES
Most children will learn to evaluate which pieces of apparatus are good for developing the specific skills of climbing and balancing. Some will begin to use this evaluation to suggest ways of organising and joining different pieces of apparatus to extend these skills further.

FURTHER PHYSICAL DEVELOPMENT CHALLENGES
Magical mats
Get the children to explore mats and evaluate which skills they can most usefully develop on them. Can the children travel under or through them? How many different ways can they find to travel over them? Introduce a table. Can the children develop other skills now? What are they? Agree with the children that they can now travel under and through these, and can climb as well as balance on them.
Ladders and tables
Set up different organisations of tables and ladders, some joined and some not. Challenge the children to evaluate these in terms of which ones they can climb, which they can balance on and which ones they can do both on. Which is the most useful combination to develop both skills? Next, ask the children to evaluate the most useful way of setting up tables and ladders for developing travelling under, over,

around, along and through and then the most useful combination to develop all of these modes of travel.

MOUNTING PICTURES

AREA OF LEARNING: CREATIVE DEVELOPMENT. ELG: TO EXPLORE COLOUR IN TWO DIMENSIONS.

LEARNING OBJECTIVE
To combine colour to make a contrast.

THINKING OBJECTIVES
To evaluate information; to suggest improvements.

THINKING SKILLS

The children will evaluate different coloured paper to mount their paintings or other work on. They will evaluate whether the colour of their mounted paintings works against the colour of a display board and make a double mount, if necessary.

WHAT YOU NEED
A display board; a range of different coloured papers to cover a display board and on which to mount paintings; a staple gun and staples; glue.

WHAT TO DO
After a painting activity, and when the children's work is dry, explain that you want to display all the pictures on a display board. Look at the colours the children have used in their painting and talk about the different colours of backing paper they can use to show their work off best. Try these out by putting their paintings on top of each colour of backing paper until the children have decided on the colour they want to use. Ask an adult to cut the paper to size before asking the children to glue their painting to their chosen backing paper.

When the children have finished, look at the range of colours of backing paper they have chosen. Decide together from your selection which colour will show

off all the mounted paintings best. Later that day, or the next day, depending on when you have had time to cover the board, Blu-Tack or pin each painting against the board. Ask the children, *Do they all stand out?* Get them to evaluate those that do and staple them into place. Identify those that don't and ask the children to suggest how you can make them stand out better. Some may suggest backing the paintings on another colour. Ask the children how you can do this, but still keep the current backing colour because this is a good contrasting colour. Agree to mount it again onto another colour to make a double backing frame. Ask those children whose pictures have been chosen to be double mounted to evaluate the colour of backing paper already attached and to choose a backing they think will contrast well with the display backing paper. Choose this paper and decide if it also contrasts well and sets off their painting. Glue this second frame into place before stapling the finished mounted picture to the board. Add a border to finish off the display.

DIFFERENTIATION
Limit the range of colours for lower attaining children to choose from, but include some that are very different or almost the same so that they get the idea of contrast into their evaluations. Higher attaining children should be encouraged to think of a colour before trying to find a close match in the range available. Why did they choose the one that they did? Suggest that they try their painting against other colours just in case they decide there is a better alternative.

WHERE NEXT
Encourage the children to mount their own work as an independent activity. Make sure that the backing papers are cut to size so that they do not have to cut them themselves.

Choose a colour for a display board first and ask the children to evaluate the colours to use in a painting with this in mind. Ask them to find a backing paper for their painting in a colour that will contrast with both their picture and the colour of the display board.

ASSESSMENT
Assess the children who evaluate the colour carefully and try out different combinations before making their final choice of backing paper. This will show that they are continually looking for a better and improved effect.

LEARNING OUTCOMES
Most children will be able to evaluate how well their colours contrast and use this information to make

improvements to their work. They will decide for themselves the best colours to use to contrast with their own work and the colour of the display board.

FURTHER CREATIVE DEVELOPMENT CHALLENGES

Black and white, blue and red
Choose two colours to use for backing paper and picture mounts and use these to make a chequer board effect. The children should suggest where to staple their picture to make sure that it is on the contrasting colour.

Textured displays
Extend the ideas in the main activity by asking the children to make textured pictures and to mount these on fabric or paper materials with similar or different textures. Let them evaluate a range of different materials before choosing those they will use.

PIRATE PETE

AREA OF LEARNING: CREATIVE DEVELOPMENT. ELG: TO EXPRESS AND COMMUNICATE THEIR IDEAS, THOUGHTS AND FEELINGS BY USING A WIDENING RANGE OF ROLE-PLAY.

LEARNING OBJECTIVE
To create a design for a pirate costume.

THINKING OBJECTIVES
To evaluate information (judging quality); to suggest improvements.

THINKING SKILLS
The children will think about what a costume for a pirate might look like. They will suggest improvements to an existing costume and then make different props that help to make a pirate costume more realistic.

WHAT YOU NEED
Dressing-up clothes; a pre-made sword, hat and eye patch; card; glue; paint; paper; elastic.

WHAT TO DO
Using the dressing-up clothes, invite a child to dress up as a pirate. What do the other children think he

or she looks like? Ask, *Does he or she look like a real pirate? Why? Is there anything that we could add to make him or her look even more like a pirate?*

Encourage the children to think about some of the things a pirate might wear. Prompt them to think about the sort of hat a pirate might wear, an eye patch, a sword. Produce each one of these from your collection and ask the child who has dressed up to put them on. Get the rest of the class to evaluate the costume again. Ask, *Does it look better now? Have the props helped? Does he or she look like a pirate now?*

In small groups, ask the children to make a hat, an eye patch and a sword and to dress up a member of their group to look like a pirate.

DIFFERENTIATION
Look at pictures of pirates with lower attaining children to help them think of ideas on how to improve the costume. Higher attaining children should be encouraged to add a suitable design to their hat, such as a skull and crossbones or a parrot.

WHERE NEXT
On a designated day, hold a pirate's tea party so that the children can dress up as pirates.

ASSESSMENT
Assess how well the children evaluate the quality of the costume, as well as expressing their likes and how the costume can be improved. Note those who need extra support to suggest improvements.

LEARNING OUTCOMES
Most children will make suggestions about how a costume can be improved, based on their initial evaluations of the costume.

FURTHER CREATIVE DEVELOPMENT CHALLENGES

Storybook character
Let the children search through the dressing-up box to find items to make different costumes for storybook characters. Let some of the children dress up in these and get others to evaluate them and identify further improvements that can be made.

CROSS-CURRICULAR PROJECTS

INTRODUCTION

This chapter draws together the full range of thinking skills into activities which can be taught as complete projects. There are two themed projects – 'The cinema' and 'Sing a Song of Sixpence' – within which all the areas of learning are taught. The themes in this chapter incorporate the five thinking skills and show how these can often be linked in activities. There are some activities, for example, that show how information is processed to help the children to reason, enquire or evaluate what is happening, and this helps them to hypothesise or think creatively.

The purpose of this chapter is to highlight the thinking skills, and it is the questioning and organisation of learning which carries most importance. Due to the flexibility of the activities, each activity can address several learning objectives. As the purpose is to show how to organise lessons to address the children's development of thinking skills, you may wish to focus on a different learning objective in some lessons.

THE CINEMA

The first project is based around the theme of the cinema, through role-play. It aims to help the children to learn through first-hand experience and helps them to understand new learning in a real context.

Through the cinema role-play, the children will develop their personal, social and emotional skills through thinking about and developing an understanding of healthy snacks. Speaking skills and vocabulary will develop through the acting out of stories and talking about things they notice. They will use their maths skills to deduce and learn about time, number and solve money problems. The knowledge and understanding activities will encourage them to ask and answer questions about what is happening and how things work.

SING A SONG OF SIXPENCE

The second project is based within a nursery rhyme context, in this case 'Sing a Song of Sixpence'. It demonstrates how thinking skills can be developed through favourite rhymes and stories with a little imaginative thinking. Any rhyme or story lends itself in the same way for similar treatment with a little imagination. You may wish to adapt the context to suit the children in your class or setting.

Prepare three role-play areas in the classroom or setting:

Area 1: Parlour
Make this comfortable and fit for a queen with luxurious soft furnishings and lots of colour. Include a sofa, table, various pot plants and ornaments, books, cushions, pictures and a mirror on the wall, a tea set and a plate of honey sandwiches.

Area 2: The King's counting house
Make this practical, decorated by money pictures, posters and huge pound signs. Include practical resources for counting out money, such as a calculator, abacus, moneybags and boxes and coins. Place a table and chair for the King to carry out the counting of the money and a clipboard for him or a helper to record the amounts.

Area 3: The garden
Create an attractive place to walk around and sit in, but also a practical area for the maid to hang out the washing. Take care to hang the washing line where the children cannot walk into it but where it is within their reach to carry out the activities. If creating the area inside, paint pictures of trees, grass and plants on the walls surrounding the area. As well as the washing line, include resources such as pegs, plastic and silk flowers and plants, flowerpots, wheelbarrow, watering cans, grow bags with real flowers for borders, fake grass, garden chairs and a parasol. Place pictures of blackbirds in the trees and plants. The children will think of other ways to make the garden beautiful in the activity 'Garden competition'.

THE CINEMA

Area of learning and ELG, NLS or NNS objective	Activity title	Thinking objective	Activity	Page
Personal, social and emotional development ELG: To consider the consequences of their words and actions	Code of conduct	To make judgements	Deciding rules of behaviour in the cinema and the impact their actions have on others	133
Communication, language and literacy ELGs: To read a range of familiar and common words independently; to write their own names NLS objectives: To recognise printed and handwritten words; to read on sight a range of familiar words; to read and write their own name	Multi-screen	To make decisions; to deduce	Deciding which film to watch and when	134
Communication, language and literacy ELG: To use language to recreate roles and experiences	Ticket booth	To sequence	Role-playing buying and selling cinema tickets	135
Communication, language and literacy ELG: To use talk to organise, sequence and clarify thinking and ideas NLS objective: To understand that writing can be used for a range of purposes	Films and adverts	To create ideas; to form opinions; to give reasons	Making posters for their favourite films	136
Mathematical development ELG: To use developing mathematical ideas to solve problems NNS objective: To begin to read o'clock time	Starting time	To locate; to analyse	Analysing the position of hands on a clock to understand what time films in a programme start	137
Mathematical development ELG: To say and use number names in order in familiar contexts NNS objective: To recognise numerals 1 to 9, then 0 and 10, then beyond 10	Seating plan	To deduce	Finding the seat written on their cinema ticket	138
Knowledge and understanding of the world ELGs: To find out about past and present events in the lives of their families; to find out about the uses of everyday technology	Bill and Ben	To plan research	Comparing old and modern versions of the same television programme	139
Knowledge and understanding of the world ELG: To investigate materials by using all of their senses	Blackout	To infer; to deduce	Making a dark place for a role-play cinema	140
Knowledge and understanding of the world ELG: To use ICT to support their learning	Ice creams	To collect, sort, analyse and interpret information	Making a graph of favourite ice cream flavours	141
Knowledge and understanding of the world ELG: To look closely at similarities, differences, patterns and change	Popcorn	To ask questions	Watching the changes in popcorn during the heating process	142
Physical development ELG: To recognise the importance of keeping healthy and those things which contribute to this	Suitable snacks	To plan research; to evaluate information	Evaluating which snacks are healthier than others	143
Physical development ELG: To show awareness of space	Car parking	To think laterally	Designing a car park considering the best use of the space available	144
Creative development ELG: To express and communicate their ideas using a range of materials	Actors unite	To think imaginatively	Acting out a story, finding their own props and costumes	145
Creative development ELG: To express and communicate their thoughts and feelings about a variety of songs	Musical interlude	To evaluate information (judging quality and usefulness)	Choosing music suitable to play before and after a film	145

CODE OF CONDUCT

AREA OF LEARNING: PERSONAL, SOCIAL AND EMOTIONAL DEVELOPMENT. ELG: TO CONSIDER THE CONSEQUENCES OF THEIR WORDS AND ACTIONS FOR THEMSELVES AND OTHERS.

LEARNING OBJECTIVE
To develop rules for the cinema role-play area.

THINKING OBJECTIVE
To make judgements.

THINKING SKILLS
The children will think about how they behave in cinemas and the importance of behaving in certain ways. They will consider the impact of their actions on others and the importance of considering respect for others. They will use their judgements to write a code of conduct for how they should behave in the cinema area.

WHAT YOU NEED
A flip chart or board.

WHAT TO DO
Sit the children in a circle and ask a volunteer to recall a visit to the cinema. Ask the class, *Do you enjoy the films you see? What do you like about visits to the cinema?* Then ask them to think about the things they do not like. What helps them to enjoy the films? Is it because everyone in the cinema is quiet and considers other people's enjoyment?

Ask the children a series of *What if...* questions to focus their thinking on behaviour. Talk over a few scenarios about people behaving in different ways:

Ask, *What if someone is careless and keeps dropping popcorn on the floor, or spills their drink? Do you think this is nice for people sitting next to them? Why? Will they feel uncomfortable? Will they be worried that they may get drink spilled on them?*

Or, *What if the person sitting in front of you keeps jumping up and down? How will this behaviour stop you from enjoying the film? How should the person in front behave? Should they try to sit still?*

Going through these scenarios will help the children link cause with effect and use this to make judgements about the way people should behave. For instance, empathise with the children about how they would feel if the person in front of them kept jumping up and down so that they could not see properly, so that they learn that this sort of behaviour has a negative impact on other people.

Ask, *What if someone keeps wanting to leave their seat and moving about the cinema when the film is playing? How would this interrupt the film?* Explain that sometimes it is necessary for people to leave their seats, for example to go to the toilet. Talk about if they need to leave their seat to go to the toilet. What would they say to the person sitting next to them? Emphasise the use of *Excuse me*, *Please* and *Thank you* in the conversations.

For each of the scenarios you present to the children, get them to think about how this behaviour can be prevented. Ask, *What should we do to consider the feelings and enjoyment of others? How should we behave?* Together, use the discussions to write a list of rules for how the children think they should behave in the cinema and put these rules in the cinema role-play area.

DIFFERENTIATION
Establish links with lower attaining children with the actual things that they are likely to do with the way they should do them. For example, moving around the cinema links with walking sensibly, therefore the rule is to walk sensibly; watching the film links with considering the enjoyment of themselves and others, so the rule is to watch the film quietly so as not to disturb the enjoyment of others. Expect higher attaining children to write their own rules and to explain why they have chosen the ones they have. Question them to make sure they are basing their rules on regulating their behaviour to consider others' feelings and enjoyment.

WHERE NEXT
Make rules for other events, areas and activities in the classroom.

ASSESSMENT
Note the children who make judgements about the activities that go on in a cinema and the way they should behave when doing them. This will be reflected in their rules and the reasons they give for choosing these.

LEARNING OUTCOMES
Most children will make judgements about the way they should behave and give reasons for this in terms of considering the needs and feelings of others.

THINKING SKILLS: AGES 4–5

FURTHER PERSONAL, SOCIAL AND EMOTIONAL DEVELOPMENT CHALLENGES

Eating popcorn

Talk about ways in which the children can eat and drink quietly when in the cinema. How can they remove crisps and sweets from their paper wrappers without making too much noise? How can they eat crunchy popcorn without disturbing the people around them? How can they make sure they do not make a noise when sucking their drinks through the straw? Practise some of these skills in the cinema role-play area and make judgements about the way they are carried out.

Acting out

Set up situations for the children to act out needing to go out of the cinema while the film is being shown. Talk about what they will say, how they will move and how carefully they will leave their seat so as not to block the views of others around them. Write rules for this that reflect the children's judgements.

MULTI-SCREEN

AREA OF LEARNING: COMMUNICATION, LANGUAGE AND LITERACY. ELGS: TO READ A RANGE OF FAMILIAR AND COMMON WORDS INDEPENDENTLY; TO WRITE THEIR OWN NAMES. NLS OBJECTIVES: TO RECOGNISE PRINTED AND HANDWRITTEN WORDS; TO READ ON SIGHT A RANGE OF FAMILIAR WORDS; TO READ AND WRITE THEIR OWN NAME.

LEARNING OBJECTIVES

To read simple titles and times; to write their names independently.

THINKING OBJECTIVES

To make decisions; to deduce.

THINKING SKILLS

The children will look at the details and times of different films, and decide which film they want to watch. They will also need to deduce what time it starts and whether there are enough seats left in the cinema for them to see the film.

WHAT YOU NEED

Posters displaying the films you will show in the cinema that day, and times that each film will be shown; a list of numbers to accompany each poster which relate to the number of seats available (some taken); pens.

WHAT TO DO

Before the lesson, put the posters advertising the different films up around the cinema role-play area. Put up a list next to each, making sure these are displayed at a height where the children can reach them.

When the children come into the role-play area, look together at each of the posters in turn and locate the information on them. Read the names of the films and ask the children what they think they will be about. Ask the children, *What time is this film showing?*

Help the children to decide which films they want to watch. When they have decided, ask them to look at the list next to the poster. Ask, *Are there any seats left?* Ask the children to deduce whether there are and to write their name on the list to indicate the film they want to see and to book themselves a seat. If there are no seats left, tell them they will have to make a second choice, and help them to repeat the process.

DIFFERENTIATION

Lead the children to their deductions by asking them to say whether there are any empty spaces next to the numbers on the lists. If there are, ask them to say where they should write their name. Together, write their name on the next empty space. Ask higher attaining children to look at the lists and deduce which films have empty spaces and which ones are sold out.

WHERE NEXT

Set up the activity for the children to do independently as part of their start-of-the-day routines.

ASSESSMENT

Note the children who can work out for themselves where to write their names. Do they deduce that each space means there is a seat left? Did they find it easy to make a decision about which film to watch?

LEARNING OUTCOMES

Most children will be able to decide which film they want to watch. They should also be able to locate a space to write their names independently. Most will realise that each space relates to a seat in the cinema, which enables them to choose that particular film to watch or not.

Further communication, language and literacy challenges

Seating plan

Give the children a seating plan of a cinema. Ask them to colour, or put a cross on, the seats that are sold. Ask them to deduce how many seats there are still available and where these are in the cinema. Set up a sales pitch in the role-play area for the children to sell the empty seats.

Tickets

Help the children to make tickets for each of the films advertised in the role-play area. Suggest they make each ticket a different colour depending on the film. They should write the title of the film and the seat number on each ticket. They should deduce whether they have enough tickets for all the seats and whether the films have the correct matching colour to the tickets.

TICKET BOOTH

AREA OF LEARNING: COMMUNICATION, LANGUAGE AND LITERACY. ELG: TO USE LANGUAGE TO RECREATE ROLES AND EXPERIENCES.

LEARNING OBJECTIVE
To learn how to ask for something.

THINKING OBJECTIVE
To sequence.

THINKING SKILLS
The children will take part in a role-play, deciding what questions they need to ask and the order in which actions take place when selling and buying a ticket for a film. One child will play the part of the ticket seller and their partner will be buying a ticket, going through the sequence of questions and answers they decided upon and recorded previously.

WHAT YOU NEED
Strips of card small enough for the children to hold, divided into four sections; pencils, crayons or felt-tipped pens.

WHAT TO DO
Tell the children they are going to act out a role-play where they will be buying tickets to watch a film at the cinema, but that you want to decide with them how to do this first. Give them each a strip of card and explain that this is where you want them to record the stages of buying a ticket. Divide the class in two, telling one half they will be buyers, the other half they will be sellers.

Talk to the children about what they do when they go to the cinema. When they arrive what is the first thing they need to do? Decide together that they need to visit the ticket booth in order to buy a ticket. Ask the children to draw a picture of this in the first section of their card and to label it with the number 1.

Then talk about what the ticket seller will say first. For example, *Can I help you?* What answer do they think the buyer will give? For example, *I would like to buy a ticket to see the film please.* Talk about how many tickets they could ask for. Relate this to the size of the group that is going to the cinema. For example, if you are going to the cinema alone, you only want one ticket, but if you have several people in your group you will need to ask for the corresponding number. Ask the children to note either the greeting in the next section of their card if they are sellers, or the response if they are buyers.

Continue with your sequence covering what the children will need to say to each other. Questions to ask could include, *Where do you want to sit? Are there any seats left? How much are they? How many seats do you want?* Make sure the children record their part of the conversation on the cards. Let them all draw a picture in the last section of both cards that shows the children paying for the tickets.

Ask the sellers and buyers to form pairs and, relying upon their cards, help them act out the role-play until you are sure that they know the sequence independently.

DIFFERENTIATION
Ask an adult to partner lower attaining children for each of the roles until they know the sequence of the role-play. Help them to think of when to use *Please* and *Thank you*. Higher attaining children can be asked to develop the sequence further by adding extra things to ask for, such as where to buy popcorn and drinks to take in to the show.

WHERE NEXT
Set up the activity as a self-initiated play activity. Let the children buy and sell tickets on their own for the actual films that day.

ASSESSMENT
Note the children who can sequence a conversation independently, those who use the card for support and those who need an adult to help them buy tickets.

LEARNING OUTCOMES

Most children will be able to act out buying and selling tickets, recalling the sequence of requests and actions required. Some will do this independently and others will need help.

FURTHER COMMUNICATION, LANGUAGE AND LITERACY CHALLENGES

Full up

Pretend the cinema for the children's favourite film is full up and that there are no tickets left for the show. Set up role-plays that require the children to sequence conversations for this. The conversations will start the same, but the ticket seller's first response will be different. They may say: *I'm sorry, there are no tickets left for this film* or *That film is sold out.* Help the children to think of a set of possible questions that might come next in the sequence, for example:

- What else is available to watch?
- When does the next film start?
- What time is it now?
- Will I have time to get popcorn?
- What film is showing next?
- Can I have (3) tickets please?

Model answers for each of these questions to help the children to set up the conversation sequence.

Which film?

Sequence a number of films in order of start time and ask the children to use this information to decide which one they want to watch. Set up a conversation sequence for pairs of children to act out that involves asking the ticket seller for a ticket to watch a film:

A: When does the next film start?

B: In five minutes.

A: Is it *Shrek*?

B: Yes.

A: Can I have a ticket please?

B: That will be £1.50 please

A: Thank you.

The sellers should then sell tickets for the show. Work with the children in small groups so that each child has a turn to buy their own ticket for a show, following the sequence each time, and does not have to wait too long. Ask lower attaining children to have their turn in the middle of the groups so that they can listen to the others before trying out the conversation for themselves.

Sweet kiosk

Set up a conversation sequence for the children to buy their pretend sweets, popcorn and drinks from the kiosk before the show starts. You may wish to buy and sell the usual snacks at this time as part of the conversation sequence. Note the sequence on cards to act as prompts for the children to remember what

to say and when, and remind them to say please and thank you.

FILMS AND ADVERTS

AREA OF LEARNING: COMMUNICATION, LANGUAGE AND LITERACY. ELG: TO USE TALK TO ORGANISE, SEQUENCE AND CLARIFY THINKING AND IDEAS. NLS OBJECTIVE: TO UNDERSTAND THAT WRITING CAN BE USED FOR A RANGE OF PURPOSES.

LEARNING OBJECTIVE

To talk about familiar characters, settings and events in films.

THINKING OBJECTIVES

To create ideas; to form opinions; to give reasons.

THINKING SKILLS

The children will use their reasoning skills of forming opinions and giving reasons by talking about the content of their favourite films, and saying why they like them. They will use this information to create a poster, using their imagination to attract others to watch a certain film.

WHAT YOU NEED

Posters, pictures or video cases of the children's favourite films, or a collection of films they will recognise; photocopies of these; large sheets of paper; glue; scissors.

WHAT TO DO

Prior to the lesson, talk about the children's favourite films. Ask them to say which they like and why. Talk about the characters and settings of the films and some of the events that happen. Relate these details to how they feel about the films.

Try and get hold of either pictures, posters or video cases of some of these films for the lesson, otherwise use a selection of well-known films. Read the title of the films together and talk about the pictures. Discuss how the person who produced these used colour and chose the size of the pictures and lettering to attract people to watch the film.

Choose one of the films and ask the children to say what they would include on a poster to advertise it. Collect their ideas on a large piece of paper by drawing the pictures they suggest and writing the words, talking about the colour and size they want for each. When you have finished, cut around these and decide with the children where they would put them on the poster to attract a reader. Ask, *Would you put the writing at the top, middle or bottom?* Decide where to put the pictures in the same way by questioning the children.

Now tell the children they are going to make individual posters for a film of their choice. Let the children choose one of the film posters or video cases from your collection to use as a guide. Provide them with pictures and words and let them decide where to stick them on their piece of paper. Some children may wish to draw their own pictures. They should be encouraged to use their imagination to colour and place the things on the paper in a way that they think would attract people to watch the film.

DIFFERENTIATION
Higher attaining children should be encouraged to write a short blurb about the film to add to their posters to attract watchers.

WHERE NEXT
Every week, introduce different films to the 'cinema' and ask the children to make posters to advertise these.

ASSESSMENT
Note the children who give reasons for their likes and dislikes and use these to form opinions about the position of title and pictures on their posters. Look at the finished posters to see which children have presented the information imaginatively.

LEARNING OUTCOMES
Most children will form opinions about what to include on their posters and where to position these. Some will do this independently while others will need some direction through questioning. They will use this to create imaginative posters to advertise their favourite films.

FURTHER COMMUNICATION, LANGUAGE AND LITERACY CHALLENGES
Films
Make posters with the children for some of the films. They can use these to read the title and details about a film before they watch it. Discuss with the children how they should arrange the information in an imaginative way to make people want to watch the film. Get the children to add labels of the characters' names and to write short sentences to describe some of the action that will take place in the films. Read these before the film starts so that the children can look out for different characters and events as they watch.

Adverts
Look in the local newspaper for adverts for the cinema. Show these to the children and get them to use the information to help them write adverts for the films showing in the role-play cinema. Put these around the room for the children to read, or in a class book of stories.

STARTING TIME

AREA OF LEARNING: MATHEMATICAL DEVELOPMENT.
ELG: TO USE DEVELOPING MATHEMATICAL IDEAS TO SOLVE PROBLEMS. NNS OBJECTIVE: TO BEGIN TO READ O'CLOCK TIME.

LEARNING OBJECTIVE
To read o'clock time.

THINKING OBJECTIVES
To locate; to analyse.

THINKING SKILLS
The children will learn to understand what time *o'clock* means by locating the time of the film they want to watch on the poster and making sure that the time matches the one on their ticket. Draw the children's attention to the hands on the clock and help them to analyse the position of these and how this tells us the time. The children will analyse the position of the hands and say whether this shows o'clock, or in some cases half past the hour. The children's attention should be drawn to the actual time on the classroom or setting clock as they enter the cinema for their chosen showing to make sure that it is the correct time.

WHAT YOU NEED
A display board with the list of films you intend to show that week or day, the screen number written by the side, the cost of different seats in the cinema, an analogue clock face by the side of each show time, using the times with which the children are familiar (these will usually be o'clock only); tickets with matching screen number, price, time of show and seat number on.

WHAT TO DO
In groups, look with the children at the different films showing in the role-play cinema during the day or the week. Ask the children to say what they are. If they do not know, tell them what each one says.

Ask the children to choose which film they would like to watch. Ask them what time it starts, which screen it is showing at and how much it costs for the different seats. Locate the clock face and analyse the information together, noting the position of the clock's hands and how this tells us the time the film will start. Give them the tickets for their chosen show and ask them to make sure that the time, screen number, seat and cost are correct.

When it is time for the first film to start, invite those children with tickets to enter the cinema. Draw their attention to the classroom clock and analyse the position of the hands and whether it is showing the matching time on their tickets. Check the tickets and let the children try to find the correct seat by themselves, helping those who are having difficulty after a short time.

Play the film and complete the planned work associated with this. This could be watching a favourite film as a story time activity.

DIFFERENTIATION

Have some films starting at half-past the hour for higher attaining children to analyse and find on the clock. This will mean repeating the activity on another day especially for this group and telling lower attaining children when the film starts. Lower attaining children need to be constantly reminded to look at the clock, especially every time that it shows o'clock in order to realise that their film is showing.

WHERE NEXT

Set up clocks around the room that show different times. Ask the children to analyse these and find those that show o'clock only.

Give the children clocks and ask them to match the times that are on your clock.

ASSESSMENT

Note the children who can read the times on the clock and relate this to a starting time on a film or poster. Note those who read o'clock and those that can read half-past the hour.

LEARNING OUTCOMES

Most children will be able to understand the time that their chosen film starts and to understand when the real time shows this.

FURTHER MATHEMATICAL DEVELOPMENT CHALLENGES

What time does it start?
Look in television magazines with the children and ask them to find all the times that start at o'clock. Stick a clock showing the correct time next to these.
O'clock
Ask the children to draw several clock faces and to draw a different o'clock time onto each of them. Let them use a clock to draw from if appropriate.

SEATING PLAN

AREA OF LEARNING: MATHEMATICAL DEVELOPMENT. ELG: TO SAY AND USE NUMBER NAMES IN ORDER IN FAMILIAR CONTEXTS. NNS OBJECTIVE: TO RECOGNISE NUMERALS 1 TO 9, THEN 0 AND 10, THEN BEYOND 10.

LEARNING OBJECTIVE

To recognise and find numbers 1 to 20.

THINKING OBJECTIVE

To deduce.

THINKING SKILLS

The children will read the number on their ticket and analyse the way the seats are organised in the cinema. They will use this information to deduce which is the matching seat.

WHAT YOU NEED

Twenty chairs organised into four rows of five; number labels for each chair; tickets numbered 1 to 20.

WHAT TO DO

Organise the cinema seating plan into four rows of five, numbered from 1 to 20 on one day and from 20 to 1 on the second. Sell the children tickets and ask them to read the number on the ticket. Look together at the way that the seats are organised and ask them whereabouts they think their seat is. Ask, *Will it be near the front or the back? Will it be in the middle? Will it be at the end of a row or nearer the middle?* Ask them to use this information to find their correct seat. When the numbers are swapped around on the second day, go through the questioning process again.

DIFFERENTIATION

Give less able children lower numbers to find. Get them to match the number to the ones that you want them to learn, however, to add challenge. For example, if they are learning the number 6, give this number to children in turn for them to find. Organise the cinema into two sides with even and odd numbers for higher attaining children to deduce which side of the cinema they should sit on.

WHERE NEXT

Organise the cinema seats into different organisations for the children to find their seats.

Assessment
Note the children who can locate their seat quickly by deducing the order and arrangement of the seats in the cinema.

Learning outcomes
Most children will learn to use their knowledge and understanding of the order of numbers to deduce where their seat number comes in relation to the way the seats are arranged.

Further mathematical development challenges
Find a seat
Organise the seating plan into rows labelled A, B, C and D, each with 2, 3, 4, 5, 6, 7, 8, 9 or 10 seats, depending on the ability of the children. Challenge the children to deduce which is the corresponding seat to the one on their ticket, and to find their own seat ready to watch the show.

Chart the seats
Give the children a seating plan with the same sized squares as the ticket sizes. Ask the children to match the correct ticket to the plan by placing a ticket onto a space. Differentiate this activity by giving higher attaining children a coordinated seating plan as in the challenge above, and less able children a plan with numbers ordered from 1 to 10.

BILL AND BEN

AREA OF LEARNING: KNOWLEDGE AND UNDERSTANDING OF THE WORLD. ELGS: TO FIND OUT ABOUT PAST AND PRESENT EVENTS IN THE LIVES OF THEIR FAMILIES AND OTHER PEOPLE THEY KNOW; TO FIND OUT ABOUT AND IDENTIFY THE USES OF EVERYDAY TECHNOLOGY.

Learning objective
To identify things that are different and the same between TV films today and in the past.

Thinking objective
To plan research.

Thinking skills
The children will watch *Bill and Ben* programmes from today and in the past, and learn that when they are finding out about things that are the same and things that are different they are carrying out research.

What you need
Videos of *Bill and Ben*, both modern and from the original series (both available from BBC videos); a TV and video player; large sheets of paper and crayons.

What to do
During one lesson watch the modern version of *Bill and Ben*. Make sure all the children watch this at some time. Recall the significant parts of the video together, focusing on the characters, events and dialogue.

The next day, watch the older version together. As the children watch, stop the video occasionally to talk about the things that are different. At the end, retell the story together, recalling what happened and who is involved. Ask, *How does the programme start, and how does it finish? How do Bill, Ben and Little Weed talk?*

In smaller groups, encourage the children to talk about all the things that are different between the two versions of the programme. Ask them to draw large pictures of Bill, Ben and Little Weed as they look in the modern version and as they look in the older version. Note the differences between the colour and the black and white pictures. Ask the children to draw speech bubbles for each character and help them to write in them the dialogue the characters usually say. Underneath each picture, help the children to write a few sentences about what happened in the story. Note how each programme ends and note whether this is the same in each.

Explain to the children that when they are finding out what is the same and different about things, they are researching. Finding similarities and differences is a good way to start learning how to carry out research.

Use this activity to develop the children's awareness of the use of everyday technology by letting them take it in turns to operate the remote control on the video player.

Differentiation
With higher attaining children write two lists together, one of things that are different between the two programmes and one detailing things that are the same. Lower attaining children should be encouraged to look at pictures of each programme and notice things about how the characters look, noting only the things that are different.

Where next
Plan other research for the children to find similarities and differences. This can be through looking at photographs, watching other films or looking at identical objects used today and in the

past. Ask the children to say what they found out from their research.

ASSESSMENT
Most children will identify things that are different from their research. A few will begin to identify similarities.

LEARNING OUTCOMES
The children will start to understand that one way to plan research is to look for things that are different and the same.

FURTHER KNOWLEDGE AND UNDERSTANDING OF THE WORLD CHALLENGES

Which is Bill and which is Ben?
Look carefully at Bill and Ben and ask the children to distinguish who is who. List the things that are different between them that can help the children tell which is Ben and which is Bill.

Who is the gardener?
Plan class research to find out who the gardener is in the programme. Identify questions with the children that they want to find out from their research about the gardener, such as where he lives and how long he spends eating his dinner.

BLACKOUT

AREA OF LEARNING: KNOWLEDGE AND UNDERSTANDING OF THE WORLD. ELG: TO INVESTIGATE MATERIALS BY USING ALL OF THEIR SENSES AS APPROPRIATE.

LEARNING OBJECTIVE
To think of things that can be used to make the cinema role-play area darker.

THINKING OBJECTIVES
To infer; to deduce.

THINKING SKILLS
The children will think about which area in the classroom, or school, is most suitable to make a cinema in. They will base their suggestions on their inference that a particular area is dark. They will then consider different ways of making the area darker, to deduce how to make the best blackout.

WHAT YOU NEED
An area in the classroom or immediately outside suitable for a cinema role-play area; screens; fabric suitable for blackout curtains; a pole or similar to hang these from which can be attached to the ceiling or walls.

WHAT TO DO
Talk with the children about the cinema role-play area that you have made in the classroom. Talk about what a cinema is like. Ask, *What about the room where the films are played? What is this like? Are there seats, lights and music to listen to? Is this place dark when the films are shown? How do they make the cinema dark?* List the children's suggestions about how a cinema is made dark, for example there are no windows, doors are closed and lights are turned off. From the list, help the children to understand that no light is let into the room.

Use this knowledge to develop the children's inference skills. Identify with them an area of the classroom, or one immediately outside, which fits the criteria for making an area dark. If they can suggest one, ask *Is it dark enough?* Talk to the children about how they can make it darker. Write their suggestions down and use them to make the area as dark as you can after the lesson (you could use blackout curtains and screens if their suggestions do not make the space dark enough).

Next day, sit together in the darkened area and talk about how you have made the area darker. Show the children how it gets even darker when the lights are turned off.

DIFFERENTIATION
This is a whole class activity and the differentiation is outlined below in the 'Where next' extension activity.

WHERE NEXT
Let the children make their own dark place in small groups. Let higher attaining children do this independently and assess how they use their inference skills to deduce where to make their place and that they need to get rid of as much light as possible. Ask an additional adult to work with lower attaining children to question and prompt them as they make their dark place, to develop their inference skills of finding a dark place first and then deducing which fabrics to use to keep out the most light.

ASSESSMENT
Assess the children's use of previous experience to infer where the best place is to make the cinema. Assess how well they deduce which materials will make good blackouts.

LEARNING OUTCOMES

Most children will use inference skills to deduce where to build their dark place. Some will need support with this while others will work independently.

FURTHER KNOWLEDGE AND UNDERSTANDING OF THE WORLD CHALLENGES

Glow in the dark

Hang glow-in-the-dark stars in the cinema and show the children what happens when the lights are turned off. Show them glow-in-the-dark creatures made from the same material and ask them to infer what will happen when the lights are turned off. Note those who correctly infer that they will also glow in the dark.

In a dark, dark street

Draw a picture of a street in daylight. Include cars, streetlights, a sky (with no sun) and houses with curtains open. Ask the children to use their inference and deduction skills to turn the picture into a night-time scene.

ICE CREAMS

AREA OF LEARNING: KNOWLEDGE AND UNDERSTANDING OF THE WORLD. ELG: TO USE ICT TO SUPPORT THEIR LEARNING.

LEARNING OBJECTIVE

To represent information as a pictogram or block graph.

THINKING OBJECTIVES

To collect, sort, analyse and interpret information.

THINKING SKILLS

The children will think about their favourite ice creams and collect the information together, sorting the information to represent this on a graph. They will analyse and interpret the information to find out which is the class's favourite ice cream flavour.

WHAT YOU NEED

Paper and drawing materials; a flip chart or board and writing materials; a computer and printer.

WHAT TO DO

Ask the children about the sort of snacks they might eat when they go to the cinema. Move them towards talking about ice cream and discuss the children's favourite ice creams. Ask each child to draw a picture of his or her favourite ice cream and collect these in.

As a class sort the children's pictures into sets. These could be sets of the same type or flavour. Organise the pictures into columns of ice creams, sticking them onto a sheet of paper to make a pictogram. Write numbers 1 to 10 (or more if there are more than ten ice creams in one column) by the side of each ice cream in a column. Explain to the children that they have collected the information and made a pictogram.

Interpret the information together by talking about what it tells us about our favourite ice creams and use this to think of some questions to ask. For example, *How many children like strawberry ice cream best? Which is the class's favourite flavour? Which flavour is the least favourite? Does the information tell us how many children like mint-chocolate-chip ice cream?* (Choose a flavour for this question that is not represented on the pictogram.) List the questions on a flip chart and write the children's answers underneath each one. Talk about what you have found out about the class's favourite and least favourite ice creams.

Use the computer to put in information about the children's favourite ice creams. Show the children how to sort and organise these as a block graph. Print out copies for the children to display in the cinema role-play area. Talk about how the information is sorted quickly using a computer – a matter of minutes in comparison to sorting and sticking pictures to paper manually. Note how clearly the information is presented and how this helps us find what we are looking for easily and quickly.

DIFFERENTIATION

Lower attaining children should use the class pictures only to make a pictogram. Higher attaining children can start to represent the information as a bar chart and read the vertical axis to say how many of each variety of ice cream the children in the class like.

WHERE NEXT

Sort and present information about other cinema snacks with the children, such as who likes their popcorn with salt or honey, which flavour of crisps they like and which drinks are their favourite.

ASSESSMENT

Most children will understand that computers help to collect, sort and present information clearly, and consequently help us to interpret what the information is telling us more easily.

LEARNING OUTCOMES

The children will learn that information can be sorted and presented quickly and clearly using computers, and that the way the information is presented helps them interpret it to find answers to questions.

FURTHER KNOWLEDGE AND UNDERSTANDING OF THE WORLD CHALLENGES

How many?

Give the children a graph produced on the computer showing the number of different snacks available to buy at the cinema in the role-play area and how many of each there are in stock. Ask the children to say how many of each snack there is. Are there any snacks that need to be ordered before the cinema opens the next day?

POPCORN

AREA OF LEARNING: KNOWLEDGE AND UNDERSTANDING OF THE WORLD. ELG: TO LOOK CLOSELY AT SIMILARITIES, DIFFERENCES, PATTERNS AND CHANGE.

LEARNING OBJECTIVE

To learn to look closely at how things change when they are heated.

THINKING OBJECTIVE

To ask questions.

THINKING SKILLS

The children will learn to ask questions that will help them notice similarities and differences in popcorn before and after it has been heated. They will answer their own questions and this will help them notice change.

WHAT YOU NEED

A microwave; basin and plate to cover it; uncooked popcorn; a flip chart or board.

WHAT TO DO

Open a packet of popcorn and look with the children at its uncooked state. Ask them questions about the popcorn. For example, *What does it feel like? What does it look like? What colour is it? Are the pieces big or small? What shape is it?* Think with them what popcorn that they have eaten in the past was like. Ask, *Was it hard when eaten? Was it yellow? Were the pieces small?*

On the flip chart, list questions that will help the children think about the changes that occur to popcorn when it is cooked. For example, *Will the popcorn look different when it is cooked? How will it be different? What colour will it be? Will its shape and size change?* Help the children try to answer the questions at this stage and think of additional questions that will help identify the changes.

Cook the popcorn and note together the changes that have taken place by answering the questions the children identified in relation to its uncooked and cooked states. Draw conclusions from the answered questions about whether it looks and feels different. Agree together how the questions helped them do this.

DIFFERENTIATION

List what the children notice about the popcorn before it is cooked and phrase these as simple questions about what they see and feel with lower attaining children. For example, *What does it look like? What colour is it? What does it feel like?* When the popcorn is cooked, help them to answer the same set of questions. Note how the answers to the questions are different to help them identify the changes. Expect higher attaining children to ask their own questions about the popcorn after it is cooked, using the first set as prompts.

WHERE NEXT

Repeat the investigation with other things that change when cooked, getting the children to identify questions about shape, colour, size and texture.

ASSESSMENT

Assess the children who know what a question is and can think of some independently. Can they ask relevant questions which help them to find out about what things look like, feel like and the changes that occur when heated or cooked?

LEARNING OUTCOMES

Most children will learn to ask questions as a means of identifying features of objects and materials, and use the information they get from the answers to identify changes.

FURTHER KNOWLEDGE AND UNDERSTANDING OF THE WORLD CHALLENGES

Biscuits for sale

Bake biscuits with the children. At each stage of the process, encourage them to think of questions to ask about what the ingredients, mixture and finished biscuits look, feel and taste like. Answer the questions at each stage to identify how the ingredients and mixture change. Finally, eat the biscuits, asking the questions again to bring out the final changes that have taken place.

SUITABLE SNACKS

AREA OF LEARNING: PHYSICAL DEVELOPMENT. ELG: TO RECOGNISE THE IMPORTANCE OF KEEPING HEALTHY AND THOSE THINGS WHICH CONTRIBUTE TO THIS.

LEARNING OBJECTIVE

To learn to look after their own health and needs.

THINKING OBJECTIVES

To plan research with the teacher; to evaluate information.

THINKING SKILLS

The children will plan research with the teacher into the amount of sugar different snacks contain by looking carefully at the information on food packets, especially at pictures. They will use the information to evaluate which snacks are healthier than others and decide which ones to include in the role-play cinema's snack shop. They will consider the effects of sugar on their teeth.

WHAT YOU NEED

Full or empty packets of sweets, raisins, popcorn, ice cream, crisps and other favourite snacks; a flip chart or board and coloured pens.

WHAT TO DO

Explain to the children that you want to find out which snacks are healthier options for us to eat and which help protect our teeth. Tell them that you are going to plan some research together to find the answer to this question. Ask them how they think they can find out this information. How can they set up some research? Some children may suggest that they should look at what different snacks contain and use the information to reach their decisions. Note with the children what they need to know before they can make a decision and plan the research together. Note things such as deciding what we should not eat, what is not good for our teeth and finding out which snacks contain sugars. List the stages of the research plan to focus the children's attention as they carry out their research. This might look like:

- Find out what is harmful to our teeth.
- Find out which snacks contain sugar.
- Find out which snacks contain the most or least sugar.

Focus the children's attention on looking for sugary things on the packets you have in your collection. Pass empty packets of snacks around for the children to look at the pictures. Use the pictures to help the children to decide what each snack contained. Then ask the children, or read to them, the ingredients on the packets and ask them, *Which snacks contain sugar? Which don't?*

On the flip chart, draw each of the snacks and next to them draw the main ingredients to remind the children of what each contains. Look carefully at how much sugar each one contains and decide together which can be most harmful to their teeth. Put a ring round the snack each time sugar is mentioned and note the figure by the side. Use the information to evaluate which snack contains the most sugar. Give each snack marks out of ten, where 1 has the most sugar and 10 has the least.

Ask the children to find out which of the snacks can be bought at the cinema. If they do not know, tell them which ones can. Decide together which ones to include in the cinema role-play shop. Ask the children to explain why they have chosen the ones they have.

DIFFERENTIATION

Find snack cartons which have pictures of the ingredients on for lower attaining children to research. Tell them which ones have sugar in, drawing pictures and writing labels in small groups. Higher attaining children can work out which snacks have the most sugar by comparing the sizes of the numbers and using the information to evaluate which has more or less sugar.

WHERE NEXT

Make graphs of the children's favourite snacks.

Make charts to show which snacks have sugar and which ones do not.

Talk about the importance of cleaning teeth after eating.

ASSESSMENT

Note the children who understand they need to plan research to find out which snacks contain sugar to evaluate which are healthy.

LEARNING OUTCOMES

The children will learn to research what different snacks contain before evaluating which are most healthy for them to eat.

FURTHER PHYSICAL DEVELOPMENT CHALLENGES

Snack challenge

Photocopy empty packets of snacks, or give the children actual empty cartons. Challenge them to highlight the names, flavours and ingredients. Ask the children to say what the packaging tells us about the snacks. How do we know? Make a decision about whether it is healthy to eat a lot, or only some, of each snack.

Sugar attack

Evaluate together the best times to eat sugary snacks. Talk about whether these times are when they can clean their teeth easily afterwards, or when they are eating other food which contains sugar at the same time (to get all the sugar over in one go and then brush their teeth). Is it a good thing to eat sugary snacks during a visit to the cinema?

CAR PARKING

AREA OF LEARNING: PHYSICAL DEVELOPMENT. ELG: TO SHOW AWARENESS OF SPACE.

LEARNING OBJECTIVE

To organise a space to park cars in.

THINKING OBJECTIVE

To think laterally.

THINKING SKILLS

The children will identify the space available within a given area to think about the different ways that they can park cars in it. They will decide which is the best organisation to park the cars in before drawing parking bays on the ground.

WHAT YOU NEED

A space in the playground; playground chalk; toy cars.

WHAT TO DO

Look at the space outside and decide together how many cars the children think would be able to park on it. Think about the position these should park in. Ask, *Which way should they face? How much space should we leave between each one? Should they park them in a line?*

Give groups of children a number of toy cars and let them explore the different ways to park the cars in the space outside in the playground. When they have had enough time exploring the space available, gather the children together and talk about what they found out. Ask, *Which was the best way to park the cars? How many could you fit into the space by parking the cars in different ways? Did you park the cars in a line, in a square, around the outside or in the middle of the space? Did other cars block in any cars?* If necessary, let the children explore the suggestions that come from the questioning session.

Afterwards, decide together how the children want to design the car park. Use playground chalk to draw the parking bays within a set area. Give each bay a number. Set up a ticket machine so that the children can buy a ticket to display before they park the cars to go to the cinema.

DIFFERENTIATION

Give higher attaining children more cars to park in a bigger space. Do they apply the same principles and think laterally to design the space? Give lower attaining children fewer cars to park.

WHERE NEXT

Organise the car park bays in different ways each day of the week for the children to role-play parking games.

ASSESSMENT

Assess whether the children try different ways to park the cars. Note the children who think laterally and try to park the cars at different angles in an attempt to park more cars in the space.

LEARNING OUTCOMES

The children will think laterally to find different ways to park cars to use the space available. They will think how to park the greatest number of cars in the space available.

FURTHER PHYSICAL DEVELOPMENT CHALLENGES

Seat arrangements

Get the children to reorganise the cinema seats to try to fit more of them into the space. Can they think of different ways to organise them to make use of the available space more efficiently?

Toy car park

Make a tabletop car park for small world cars with the class. Set up a pretend trip to the cinema and ask the children to leave home and park their cars.

ACTORS UNITE

AREA OF LEARNING: CREATIVE DEVELOPMENT. ELG: TO EXPRESS AND COMMUNICATE THEIR IDEAS USING A WIDENING RANGE OF MATERIALS AND ROLE-PLAY. NLS OBJECTIVE: TO USE KNOWLEDGE OF FAMILIAR TEXTS TO RE-ENACT OR RE-TELL THE MAIN POINTS IN THE CORRECT SEQUENCE.

LEARNING OBJECTIVE

To act out a familiar story.

THINKING OBJECTIVE

To think imaginatively.

THINKING SKILLS

The children will identify a story they want to act out and use their imagination to find props and costumes to support their performance.

WHAT YOU NEED

Props; costumes; a space for the children to perform a play in.

WHAT TO DO

Put the children into groups and tell them you want them to work together to plan a play to perform to the rest of the class at story time. Invite them to choose a familiar story around which to base their play. This can be a traditional or modern tale – give them the freedom to decide.

Help the children in each group to plan what they will need to support them in their play. Prompt their ideas by asking, *What props will you need? Will you need costumes or will hats or scarves be enough? What about sound effects?* Work out together where they will enter the stage from, where they will stand and what they will say and when. Encourage them to think about any other factors, such as what they will use to produce sound effects if they decide these are needed. How will the children know when to perform the sound effects? Who will perform them?

Let the children rehearse their plays before they start to act it out in front of the class. You could play the part of narrator to move the action along.

DIFFERENTIATION

Encourage lower attaining children to mime a story while you read it. Give very direct stage directions so that the children are clear about what they have to use, where they have to go and what they have to do. Higher attaining children should be expected to plan their play as independently as possible.

WHERE NEXT

Encourage the children to act out other stories and rhymes as part of live theatre week.

ASSESSMENT

Note the children who act out the story in an imaginative way, thinking about where they go on stage and what they use to support their re-enactment of the story.

LEARNING OUTCOMES

Most children will use their imagination to re-enact a familiar story, either using language or mime.

FURTHER CREATIVE DEVELOPMENT CHALLENGES

Sound effects

Tell the children a familiar story, asking them to add sound effects. Ask the children to identify where and what these will be. Make cards together that show what sound effect to play to act as prompts for the different parts of the story. Encourage the children to use their imagination to choose instruments and everyday objects with which to make the sound effects.

MUSICAL INTERLUDE

AREA OF LEARNING: CREATIVE DEVELOPMENT. ELG: TO EXPRESS AND COMMUNICATE THEIR THOUGHTS AND FEELINGS ABOUT A VARIETY OF SONGS.

LEARNING OBJECTIVE

To listen and respond to a variety of songs and music.

THINKING OBJECTIVE

To evaluate information (judging quality and usefulness).

THINKING SKILLS

The children will listen to several pieces of music and decide which ones are most suitable to play before a film starts. They will decide the criteria for judging the quality and suitability before applying this to their choice.

WHAT YOU NEED

Several pieces of music that are different (include lively pop songs, quiet instrumental pieces and extracts from different cultures); a player to play the music on; a flip chart or board.

WHAT TO DO

With small groups (around six children per group), play a range of music to them and talk about how each piece makes them feel. Ask the children questions to focus their thinking, such as *Does the music make you feel calm? Does it make you feel like dancing? Which piece makes you really listen? Which pieces do you like?*

Then go on to ask the children, *Which pieces do you think will settle an audience to watch and listen quietly to a film when it starts?* Ask them whether they think they should choose calm or lively music for this purpose. Encourage them to decide whether they think the music should be for people to listen to or to move to, and any other criteria they think is important. Make a list of these on the flip chart. Then play each piece again and ask, *Which of these pieces of music fits our criteria?* Invite the group to decide on one piece.

Share each group's choice of music with the rest of the class. Note any pieces of music that more than one group have chosen. Play the most popular piece at the beginning of a film in the cinema role-play area. Ask the children if they like the choice of music.

DIFFERENTIATION

Listen to extracts from one type of music only with lower attaining children, inviting them to choose their favourite piece from this limited selection.

Expect them to give reasons for their choices. Play a wider range of music for higher attaining children to consider and evaluate.

WHERE NEXT

Ask the children to evaluate and choose music to play during other activities, such as music to tidy up to, music for getting changed to before and after PE, music to listen to as they enjoy books in the book area.

ASSESSMENT

Assess the children's ability to evaluate what each piece of music is like and whether they can give reasons why it would make a good choice to play before their film starts. Note whether they consider the feelings and moods that each piece of music creates.

LEARNING OUTCOMES

The children will be able to choose pieces of music to play in the cinema prior to the film starting. Some will evaluate the music carefully in terms of the atmosphere it creates for the audience.

FURTHER CREATIVE DEVELOPMENT CHALLENGES

Music to act to

Identify a story and decide which pieces of music reflect the mood of the story. Play this piece of music before reading the story to the children to prepare them for listening.

SING A SONG OF SIXPENCE

Area of learning and ELG, NLS or NNS objective	Activity title	Thinking objective	Activity	Page
Personal, social and emotional development ELG: To have a developing awareness of their own needs, views and feelings and be sensitive to the needs, views and feelings of others	Taking care of the maid	To hypothesise	Considering the maid's feelings in the rhyme and how they could help her	148
Communication, language and literacy ELG: To hear and say initial and final sounds in words NLS objectives: To hear and identify initial sounds in words; to discriminate 'onsets' from 'rimes' in speech and spelling	Can you hear the rhyme?	To find pattern and relationship	Listening for rhyming pairs and identifying onset and rime in words	149
Communication, language and literacy ELG: To use language to imagine and recreate roles and experiences	Ambulance please	To sequence	Calling an ambulance and role-playing what to say to an operator	150
Communication, language and literacy ELG: To link sounds to letters, naming and sounding the letters of the alphabet NLS objective: To sound and name each letter of the alphabet in lower and upper case	Alphabet line	To sequence; to match	Hanging clothes on the washing line in alphabetical order	150
Mathematical development ELG: To begin to relate addition to combining two groups of objects NNS objective: To begin to relate addition to combining two groups of objects	How many pegs?	To deduce	Working out how many pegs will be needed to hang out washing	151
Mathematical development ELG: To use developing mathematical ideas and methods to solve practical problems NNS objective: To sort coins	How much money?	To sort and classify	Sorting money into groups to help count it	152
Mathematical development ELG: In practical activities and discussion begin to use the vocabulary involved in adding NNS objective: To being to use the vocabulary involved in adding	How many blackbirds?	To deduce; to explain	Listening to numbers and adding totals	153
Knowledge and understanding of the world ELG: To build and construct with a wide range of objects and adapting their work	Scarecrows	To create ideas	Making scarecrows by joining sticks and creatively adding features	154
Knowledge and understanding of the world ELG: To find out about their environment and talk about features they like and dislike	Garden competition	To evaluate information (judging quality); to suggest improvements	Evaluating the qualities of gardens in the local environment and expressing likes and dislikes	155
Knowledge and understanding of the world ELG: To investigate materials by using all of their senses	Honey with or without	To evaluate information; to suggest improvements	Evaluating different types of ingredients to combine with honey to make sandwiches	156
Physical development ELG: To use a range of small and large equipment	Peg boards	To analyse	Working out how things work with a peg action	157
Physical development ELG: To handle objects with increasing control	The King's moneybags	To sequence moves	Stitching two edges together neatly by learning a sequence of sewing moves	158
Creative development ELG: To recognise how sounds can be changed	Sounds right	To create ideas; to suggest improvements	Adding sound effects to the rhyme	159
Creative development ELG: To express and communicate their ideas, thoughts and feelings by using role-play	The King and Queen's house	To create ideas; to extend ideas	Making role-play areas and choosing resources to act out parts of the rhyme	160

Sing a song of sixpence
A pocketful of rye
Four and twenty blackbirds
Baked in a pie
When the pie was opened
The birds began to sing
'Wasn't that a tasty dish
To set before the King?'

The King was in his counting house
Counting out his money
The Queen was in the parlour
Eating bread and honey
The maid was in the garden
Hanging out the clothes
When down came a blackbird
And pecked off her nose.

148 TAKING CARE OF THE MAID

AREA OF LEARNING: PERSONAL, SOCIAL AND EMOTIONAL DEVELOPMENT. ELG: TO HAVE A DEVELOPING AWARENESS OF THEIR OWN NEEDS, VIEWS AND FEELINGS AND BE SENSITIVE TO THE NEEDS, VIEWS AND FEELINGS OF OTHERS.

LEARNING OBJECTIVE
To develop a growing awareness of the feelings of others.

THINKING OBJECTIVE
To hypothesise.

THINKING SKILLS
The children will consider the needs and feelings of the maid in the rhyme and think about how they could help her in this situation. They will hypothesise about how they could stop the bird's attack from happening in the first place. They will think about situations in their own experience and decide what they can do to consider their own and others' feelings and needs.

WHAT YOU NEED
A space for the children to talk to each other in a small group or in a class group.

WHAT TO DO
Focus on the last part of the rhyme together, repeating the last four lines. Hypothesise with the children about what could happen afterwards. Ask them questions to help them think about this, such as *What could you do to help the maid? How would you make her feel better? Who would you fetch to help?*

Would you get the King or Queen? Would you call the doctor for help? Would you take her to the hospital?

Ask the children to hypothesise how they could prevent the blackbird from pecking off the maid's nose. Talk about how they could warn her, or stop it happening in the first place by perhaps scaring the blackbird away before it reaches the maid.

Relate this to the things that the children do in the playground. Talk about how they should play with the toys and other equipment and perhaps prevent things from happening. For example, perhaps they see someone riding towards a person on a bike. How can they stop a collision from happening? What can they do to prevent this? If a ball accidentally hits someone, what should we say to that person and the person who did it? Was it an accident?

DIFFERENTIATION
Talk with lower attaining children about how they would help the maid, while expecting higher attaining children to think about prevention.

WHERE NEXT
Set up a role-play for taking someone to hospital, or for calling the doctor. Let the children develop acts of kindness towards dolls and each other in these situations. They could act out the situation in assembly for other children to consider.

ASSESSMENT
Assess what the children say against their ability to hypothesise what they should do in certain situations. Use their responses to set up similar situations to develop this skill.

LEARNING OUTCOMES
Most children will begin to hypothesise about what could happen and how this information can help to prevent things from happening in the first place.

FURTHER PERSONAL, SOCIAL AND EMOTIONAL DEVELOPMENT CHALLENGES
Helping each other
Hypothesise with the children what would happen if no one were there to help the maid. Ask, *What should*

she do? Should she call for help? Should she sit still and wait? Who should she call first? Encourage the children to help the maid by giving her advice as to what she should do. Afterwards, let them play the part of a helpful neighbour who sees her predicament and help them to act out different scenarios where the neighbour helps her.

Please can we have the maid's nose back?
Plan with the children how they would go about getting the maid's nose back. What would they say to the blackbird? Ask someone to play the part of the blackbird and invite the rest of the class to persuade them to give the maid her nose back. Hypothesise together the kind of things the children could say when trying to persuade someone to do something. What other situations can the children think of where they might need to persuade someone to do something good?

CAN YOU HEAR THE RHYME?

AREA OF LEARNING: COMMUNICATION, LANGUAGE AND LITERACY. ELG: TO HEAR AND SAY INITIAL AND FINAL SOUNDS IN WORDS. NLS OBJECTIVES: TO HEAR AND IDENTIFY INITIAL SOUNDS IN WORDS; TO DISCRIMINATE 'ONSETS' FROM 'RIMES' IN SPEECH AND SPELLING.

LEARNING OBJECTIVE
To hear and say initial sounds, and to identify onset and rime in written words.

THINKING OBJECTIVE
To find pattern and relationship.

THINKING SKILLS
The children will listen for rhyming pairs or words in the rhyme before looking at the way the words are spelt and identifying how they look the same, and how they look different. They will use this knowledge of pattern and relationship to identify onset and rimes in other words they come across. They will notice that sometimes rimes look the same and sometimes they look different.

WHAT YOU NEED
A copy of the rhyme; a flip chart or board; a highlighter pen.

WHAT TO DO
Recite the rhyme and ask the children to put their hands up when they hear a rhyming pair of words. Write each pair of words down, one under the other, on the flip chart. Continue in this way until you get to the end of the rhyme.

Say the rhyme again and ask the children to evaluate whether you have collected all the rhyming words in it. When they are sure all the rhyming pairs have been collected, ask the children to listen and note that the words sound the same except for the first or initial sound. Highlight the part of the words that rhyme with a highlighter pen. What do the children notice about the letters? Do they look the same? What about the beginnings of the words? Are they always different?

Continue by asking the children to think of other words that rhyme with *King*. Show them how the ends of the words are often the same and the beginning is different. Use the correct language when describing this. Explain that they are looking at the pattern and relationship between the rimes, and how sometimes they look the same at the end and sometimes they don't, and how the onsets are different.

DIFFERENTIATION
Choose CVC words with lower attaining children for them to hear and note the rimes. Extend the activity for higher attaining children by noting that sometimes the rime looks different but sounds the same, such as *rye* and *pie*.

WHERE NEXT
Look at other poems with the children and listen and find the rhymes in the rhyming words.

ASSESSMENT
Note the children who can hear the pattern in rhyming words and recognise that they sound the same except for the first sound.

LEARNING OUTCOMES
Most children will learn to hear the pattern in rhyming words and realise that these sound the same except for the first or initial sound.

FURTHER COMMUNICATION, LANGUAGE AND LITERACY CHALLENGES
Onset and rime
Choose a different nursery rhyme that has rhyming pairs where the rimes look the same. For example, 'Three Blind Mice' and 'Jack and Jill'. In each rhyming pair, highlight the onset with one colour and the rime with another. What do the children notice about the beginning of the words? What about the ends?

Small word search
Set up an independent activity for the children to look at the rhyme 'Sing a Song of Sixpence' and highlight all the little words inside the large ones. Repeat this with other nursery rhymes.

AMBULANCE PLEASE

AREA OF LEARNING: COMMUNICATION, LANGUAGE AND LITERACY. ELG: TO USE LANGUAGE TO IMAGINE AND RECREATE ROLES AND EXPERIENCES.

LEARNING OBJECTIVE
To act out the process of calling for an ambulance.

THINKING OBJECTIVE
To sequence.

THINKING SKILLS
The children will think about what they need to do to ring an ambulance in an emergency. They will consider the order of the conversation and the information they need to have to answer the operator's questions. You will take the role of the operator and in this way help them to sequence the conversation correctly.

WHAT YOU NEED
A telephone.

WHAT TO DO
Talk about the injured maid in the rhyme. Ask the children to decide whether she needs an ambulance. Look at the telephone together and ask the children what number they have to dial to call an ambulance. Agree that this is 999. Locate the number on the phone and ask a volunteer to press it three times.

Play the part of the operator, acting out how the phone is answered. Ask the children, *Which service do you require?* Invite them to say whether they want the police, a fire engine or an ambulance. Agree that they should ask for an ambulance and ask the operator for one together. Ask the children, *Where are you calling from?* Agree with the children where they are calling from and together explain this to the operator. Ask, *What has happened?* Encourage the children to describe the maid's injuries to the operator. Explain to the children that the ambulance is on its way. Invite the children to say *Thank you.*

DIFFERENTIATION
Work with lower attaining children individually and take them through the conversation a few times until you are sure they know the sequence. Ask higher attaining children to record the sequence in pictures

and text for others to follow. They may need some help with the writing, depending on their skills.

WHERE NEXT
Set up conversations for the children to practise getting help from other emergency services.

ASSESSMENT
Note the children who understand that some conversations have a sequence and can use this to support their role-play.

LEARNING OUTCOMES
Most children will be able to follow a sequence to hold a conversation with a pretend operator.

FURTHER COMMUNICATION, LANGUAGE AND LITERACY CHALLENGES
The ambulance arrives
Ask the children what happens when the ambulance crew arrive. What do they do first, next, finally? Record the sequence as pictures with the children.
Catch the blackbird and rescue the nose
Plan with the children how they would go about catching the blackbird. What will they do first? What equipment will they need? How will they go about catching the bird? What will they do with it when they catch it? Record their sequence in pictures on a flip chart or board.

ALPHABET LINE

AREA OF LEARNING: COMMUNICATION, LANGUAGE AND LITERACY. ELG: TO LINK SOUNDS TO LETTERS, NAMING AND SOUNDING THE LETTERS OF THE ALPHABET. NLS OBJECTIVE: TO SOUND AND NAME EACH LETTER OF THE ALPHABET IN LOWER AND UPPER CASE.

LEARNING OBJECTIVES
To learn to link sounds to letters, and to recognise and say letters of the alphabet.

THINKING OBJECTIVES
To sequence; to match.

THINKING SKILLS
The children will identify the sounds that each item

of clothing starts with before matching it to its corresponding letter name. They will decide which item matches with the letter in the sequence of the alphabet.

What you need
Items of clothing which start with as many different letters of the alphabet as possible (include socks or a skirt, gloves or a gymslip, mittens, trousers, a hat, a cardigan or a coat, a jumper, a waistcoat, a blouse, a dress, a vest, pants or a petticoat or pyjamas, knickers or a kilt, nightdress, dressing gown and leotard); large letter squares with each letter of the alphabet represented; a washing line that you can put up in the classroom; 26 pegs.

What to do
Remind the children of how the maid was hanging out the clothes in the rhyme. Show them the items of clothing in your collection and tell the children that you intend to hang out the washing, like the maid, but that you are going to hang the clothes out in alphabetical order. If necessary, remind the children of the order of the alphabet by saying or singing it together. Think together about the sound with which each item of clothing starts. Ask the children to say each of the sounds and its matching letter. Then ask the children to think about the first letter in the alphabet. Get them to look again at the items of clothing and find any that begin with A. If there is an item, ask them to hang it on the line at one end and to peg the letter on top of it. If there is no item, ask someone to peg the letter to the line. Continue until all the items are hanging on the line in alphabetical order.

Finish by saying the letter names together, pointing at the items and letters as you say each letter.

Differentiation
Use items that match with letters at the beginning of the alphabet with lower attaining children. With some, you may wish to have several items that start with the same letter. Some higher attaining children may cope with sequencing items that start with the same letter where they need to look at the alphabetical order of the second letter to make their decisions.

Where next
Get the children to order other items in alphabetical order. Try to keep these within the same groups, for example pictures of animals, fruit or vegetables.

Assessment
Note the children who are unable to sequence the items correctly and set up additional activities for this group of children.

Learning outcomes
Most children will realise how they can sequence things using the alphabet as an order.

Further communication, language and literacy challenges
Missing socks
Hang out socks on the line in pairs with some missing. Ask the children to use this information to establish which socks are missing. Repeat the activity with gloves and mittens.
Colour coordinated line
Hang out the clothes with matching coloured pegs, grouping clothes of the same colour together. Get the children to sequence the colours by agreed criteria. This could be by the order of the colours in the rainbow, or which colours mix together to make each other. For example, red, purple, blue; green, yellow, orange; red, white, pink; black, white, grey.

How many pegs?

Area of learning: Mathematical development. ELG: To begin to relate addition to combining two groups of objects. NNS objective: To begin to relate addition to combining two groups of objects.

Learning objective
To learn to add by counting how many altogether.

Thinking objective
To deduce.

Thinking skills
The children will consider whether they need one or two pegs to hang out each item of clothing on the washing line before deducing how many pegs they need altogether. Most children will do this by counting and some may do this by adding. The children will explain the strategies they used to work out the total number.

What you need
Pegs; items of clothing; a washing line.

WHAT TO DO

Look together at the items of clothing and ask the children to decide whether they will need one or two pegs to hang each item on the washing line. See if the children can find different ways of deducing how many pegs they will need altogether to hang all the items on the line. One way is to put all those items that need one peg into one group and all those that need two pegs into a second group.

Ask the children to match the correct number of pegs to the amount they have deduced they will want. Get them to count these one at a time, or to count some in twos and then in ones. Ask, Do *you reach the same answer when working it out in both ways?* Let the children explain how the total is found each time. Can they think of a different way to work out how many pegs they will need?

DIFFERENTIATION

With lower attaining children restrict the number of items so that there are fewer than 10 pegs needed. To begin with, use items that only need one peg which requires them to count in ones. Extend the activity for higher attaining children by asking them to decide whether they have enough pegs to hang out the items they have before starting to peg them on the line.

WHERE NEXT

Include items that need three pegs to hang them out, for example towels, sheets, cardigans and jackets.

ASSESSMENT

Note the children who count the pegs one at a time and those that deduce that they can find the total by adding one or two on each time.

LEARNING OUTCOMES

Most children will be able to deduce the number of pegs by counting, some will add and some will be able to use these skills by deducing whether they have enough pegs before they start.

FURTHER MATHEMATICAL DEVELOPMENT CHALLENGES

Gloves and mittens

Get the children to deduce how many pegs are needed to hang out gloves by their fingers, and mittens by the base. Can they deduce how many pegs they will need for two, three, four and five pairs of gloves and mittens? Which will need more pegs? Which will need the least?

Are there enough pegs?

Look at the clothes and the number of pegs and decide whether there are enough to peg them all on the line. Organise several sets of clothing and pegs for the children to deduce whether there are enough pegs. Check their predictions by hanging the items on the line and deducing whether there are enough pegs. Organise some problems where there are not enough pegs unless two items are joined together with one peg. Deduce the least number of pegs needed to hang out each set of clothing.

HOW MUCH MONEY?

AREA OF LEARNING: MATHEMATICAL DEVELOPMENT. ELG: TO USE DEVELOPING MATHEMATICAL IDEAS AND METHODS TO SOLVE PRACTICAL PROBLEMS. NNS OBJECTIVE: TO SORT COINS, INCLUDING £1 AND £2 COINS.

LEARNING OBJECTIVE

To learn the values of coins.

THINKING OBJECTIVE

To sort and classify.

THINKING SKILLS

The children will look carefully at the values of the coins and sort these according to their colour. They will use the information and process to identify which coins are pence and which are pounds.

WHAT YOU NEED

A collection of different coins, including some coppers, some silver coins and £1 and £2 coins; a moneybag; labels.

WHAT TO DO

Show the children the moneybag and empty the coins from it. Ask if they think this is what the King's moneybag looked like in the rhyme. Talk about the colours, shape and size of the coins. Relate these features to the values of each. Ask the children if the coins are all the same? Are some different?

Sort the coins into sets of colour. Look at the copper coins and ask, *How are they the same? How are they different?* Point out that the values of the coins are different, as well as their size. Do the same with the silver coins. Talk about how they are the same and how they are different. Use the features to help the children remember the value of each coin. Are there any coins left? What colour are these? (Gold.) Note together that the copper and silver coins are pence while the others are pound coins. Put the £1 coins together and the £2 coins together and help the children to label the sets.

Finish by counting up how much money there is altogether in the King's moneybag.

DIFFERENTIATION

Sort the coins only with lower attaining children. Use the process of sorting to recognise the copper and silver coins. Expect higher attaining children to count up how much each set of coins makes. Use totals that make less than 20p, except for the 20p and 50p coins.

WHERE NEXT

Put other totals in the King's moneybag and repeat this as an independent activity. On some days, forget to put some coins in the bag and challenge the children to say which ones are missing.

ASSESSMENT

Assess the children's ability to sort the coins and use the process to help them recognise the value of each.

LEARNING OUTCOMES

Most children will use sorting to recognise that coins have some things in common, such as their colour, but are different because of their shape and size

FURTHER MATHEMATICAL DEVELOPMENT CHALLENGES

Copper and silver

Help the children sort the copper coins into pairs and count in twos to count how much money there is altogether. Do the same with the silver coins and count in tens or fives. Explain to the children how the sorting of the coins can help them to count how much money there is altogether.

Making pounds

Get the children to make totals of £1 from the same kind of coins. Which pile has the least number of coins? Which has the most?

HOW MANY BLACKBIRDS?

AREA OF LEARNING: MATHEMATICAL DEVELOPMENT. ELG: IN PRACTICAL ACTIVITIES AND DISCUSSION BEGIN TO USE THE VOCABULARY INVOLVED IN ADDING. NNS OBJECTIVE: TO BEGIN TO USE THE VOCABULARY INVOLVED IN ADDING.

LEARNING OBJECTIVE

To learn that some numbers are made of tens and units.

THINKING OBJECTIVES

To deduce; to explain.

THINKING SKILLS

The children will listen to the numbers you read out and deduce how many blackbirds there are altogether each time. They will explain why they have reached the total they have.

WHAT YOU NEED

A list of addition sums to sing to the children, according to their abilities; a flip chart or board.

WHAT TO DO

Ask the children to listen carefully to the rhyme and then work out together how many blackbirds there are in the pie. Show the children on the flip chart how $4 + 20 = 24$. Invite them to explain how this makes 24. How did they work this out? Did they think of the 20 first and then the 4? How does this help them work out the total?

Say the rhyme again and this time substitute another number for *Four and twenty blackbirds*, for example *Five and twenty*, *Four and ten blackbirds*, *Three and thirty blackbirds* where the children use whole tens and units to work out the answer. Each time, deduce with the children how many blackbirds there are in the pie and encourage them to explain how they worked out the total, writing the sum on the flip chart if necessary. Get the children to think about the pattern of the numbers and use this to help them deduce how many. Invite the children to make up a rhyme for the rest of the class to deduce and explain.

DIFFERENTIATION

Make smaller totals for lower attaining children. For example, *Three and four blackbirds*. Ask higher attaining children to think about how the tens and units are put together to make the larger number, choosing a number between 10 and 20 to begin with. Ask them to explain their thinking.

WHERE NEXT

Group numbers of items together in tens and units

for the children to deduce how many there are by counting tens and units rather than units.

ASSESSMENT

Assess the children's ability to explain how they deduce the total number of blackbirds.

LEARNING OUTCOMES

Some children will begin to see a pattern in numbers greater than 10 and will use this information to deduce how many blackbirds are in the pie. All children will learn to explain how they reached their answer, some in terms of adding the units to the 10 each time.

FURTHER MATHEMATICAL DEVELOPMENT CHALLENGES

How many eyes?

Ask the children to deduce how many eyes there are in total if there are two, three or four blackbirds in the pie. (Choose numbers of blackbirds that make totals only up to 20.) Ask the children to explain their thinking. Did they count in ones or twos? Repeat the activity, but this time ask how many wings or feet there will be in the pie. Do the children relate the strategies they used to deduce how many eyes to these new problems?

How many blackbirds?

Ask the children to deduce how many blackbirds there are if they can see two eyes, four eyes, and so on. Ask the children to choose a number of eyes for others to deduce the number of blackbirds. Do they always choose even numbers?

SCARECROWS

AREA OF LEARNING: KNOWLEDGE AND UNDERSTANDING OF THE WORLD. ELG: TO BUILD AND CONSTRUCT WITH A WIDE RANGE OF OBJECTS, SELECTING APPROPRIATE RESOURCES, AND ADAPTING THEIR WORK WHERE NECESSARY.

LEARNING OBJECTIVE

To join dowelling strips in different ways.

THINKING OBJECTIVE

To create ideas.

THINKING SKILLS

The children will learn to think for themselves how to join two sticks to make a cross shape to use as a basis to make a scarecrow. They will make a basic tunic before adding their own creative ideas to make the hands and head. They will decide what to use and whether to add hair and a hat and features on the faces.

WHAT YOU NEED

A picture of a scarecrow; lengths of wooden dowelling, sticky tape, string, fabric, sewing thread and needle, flowerpots and sand; straw, raffia, wool, card and a selection of empty cartons to make the features, hat, head and hair.

WHAT TO DO

Tell the children that you want them to make scarecrows to scare away the blackbirds to stop them coming down into the garden to peck off the maid's nose. Show them the picture of a scarecrow and talk about whether they think it is scary enough to scare away the blackbirds. Ask, *What is it about the scarecrow that makes it scary?* Muse with the children why it is called a scarecrow – to scare away the crows! Look at the things in your collection and think about how they can be used to make the scarecrow look scary.

Show the children how to make a frame for the scarecrow by making a cross from wooden dowelling. Let the children decide whether to tie or tape the wooden dowelling into a cross shape. Show the children how to cut a hole in the middle of the fabric and stitch up the sides of the fabric with a simple running stitch. Put this tunic over the top of the wooden cross.

Invite the children to create their own ideas by choosing from the range of materials to add a head, hair features and hands. Let the children add other items if they wish, for example a ribbon round the neck, or designs on the tunics. Talk to them about how they are making their scarecrows scary. Let them use their own ideas to create their finished scarecrows. Stand the scarecrows in the ground or in flowerpots filled with sand to display them in the garden and to frighten away the crows.

DIFFERENTIATION

Look at pictures of scarecrows with those children who have difficulty thinking of ideas themselves to help them create their decorations. Invite higher attaining pupils to add designs to their tunics with stitchwork or shapes cut from felt. They can stitch or glue these into place.

WHERE NEXT

Put the scarecrows outside in the garden during the day to scare the birds away from your plants.

Look at scarecrows in garden centres and in

gardens near to your setting. Alternatively, take photographs of some to show the children.

ASSESSMENT
Note the children who needed additional help creating their ideas and organise additional activities for them to create and decorate items.

LEARNING OUTCOMES
Most children will use their imagination to create ideas for decorating their scarecrows to make them individual.

FURTHER KNOWLEDGE AND UNDERSTANDING OF THE WORLD CHALLENGES

Bird scarers
Make bird scarers with the children. Decide which materials will be suitable for making a noise before attaching them to a simple cross frame. Include silver foil, tin cans and lengths of metal piping, which bang together when moved.

A giant scarecrow
Make a life-sized scarecrow by stuffing clothes with newspaper. Stuff straw into the ends of the trousers and jumpers tying it into place with string. Use a simple wooden cross frame pushed through the arms and trousers to make the scarecrow stand up. Use a deflated ball for a head. Add features together to create a scary scarecrow.

GARDEN COMPETITION

AREA OF LEARNING: KNOWLEDGE AND UNDERSTANDING OF THE WORLD. ELG: TO FIND OUT ABOUT THEIR ENVIRONMENT AND TALK ABOUT THOSE FEATURES THEY LIKE AND DISLIKE.

LEARNING OBJECTIVE
To identify things they like and dislike about gardens.

THINKING OBJECTIVES
To evaluate information (judging quality); to suggest improvements.

THINKING SKILLS
The children will think about the qualities of the gardens they see in the local environment or in pictures and talk about what they like and dislike about them. They will use this knowledge to make

their own gardens for a specific person, and after judging the quality of each other's gardens, will look at how to make improvements.

WHAT YOU NEED
Large sheets of paper; crayons and pencils; large trays or rectangular planters (enough for each group to have one); soil; stones; shells; greenery; flower heads, both real and silk; materials for making garden sculptures.

WHAT TO DO
Take the children for a walk around the local area and look at the different gardens you pass on the way. If there are none in the immediate locality, look at videos, pictures or paintings of gardens. Discuss with the children which aspects they like and which they do not like.

Divide the class into groups and tell them you want them to design their own garden. Let them decide whether they want to make a garden for the King or the Queen in the rhyme. Read the rhyme together so that the children can identify the things they will need for the garden they have chosen. Let them plan what they will need by drawing pictures and labelling what they have included.

When they have finished their designs, let them select the resources they will need to create their garden. They may wish to involve their parents and find things from home. Give them time to make the gardens and afterwards look at them together to judge the quality of each one. Let the class evaluate each group's garden together and decide what is good about each one. Ask questions to prompt their evaluation, such as *Is it welcoming because of the colours used? Is there somewhere to relax? Does it have sculptures to make it more interesting? Are there any other interesting features? How does it relate to the rhyme?* Give each strength that the children come up with a point and then add up the points to decide which would win a garden competition.

Let the children improve their gardens, addressing some of the things that were not identified as being particularly good. Hold the competition again so that another group has the chance to win after making their improvements.

DIFFERENTIATION
Organise the children into mixed ability groups, observing their cooperation and making sure no one is excluded.

WHERE NEXT
Look with the class at paintings of famous gardens, or visit one locally for a picnic.

Show the children how to grow flowers in an area outside, adding features to make it look prettier.

ASSESSMENT

Assess the children's ability to evaluate the gardens in terms of the variety of items used, the colours and whether they are practical for their purpose and the person they were designed for. How good are they at improving their gardens?

LEARNING OUTCOMES

The children will learn to evaluate their own and others' work in terms of the qualities that make it look pretty or interesting, and suggest improvements to make their work better.

FURTHER KNOWLEDGE AND UNDERSTANDING OF THE WORLD CHALLENGES

Vegetable paradise

Design and grow vegetables in a variety of pots and garden areas with the class. Include some plants that have different smells and textures. Ask the children to evaluate what the garden looks and smells like when the vegetables have grown. Do the same with flowers, getting the children to evaluate the quality of colour, shape, size and scent.

HONEY WITH OR WITHOUT

AREA OF LEARNING: KNOWLEDGE AND UNDERSTANDING OF THE WORLD. ELG: TO INVESTIGATE MATERIALS BY USING ALL OF THEIR SENSES AS APPROPRIATE.

LEARNING OBJECTIVE

To use their sense of taste to evaluate sandwiches and make improvements.

THINKING OBJECTIVES

To evaluate information; to suggest improvements.

THINKING SKILLS

The children will experience what bread and honey tastes like with and without butter. They will evaluate the way the two different sandwiches taste and use this evaluation to make improvements to the sandwiches, trying out different ingredients to combine with honey until they find the sandwich that they like best.

WHAT YOU NEED

Bread; butter; a knife for spreading; plates; honey; bananas and strawberries (or whatever choices the children make for possible fillings); a flip chart or board.

WHAT TO DO

Check for food allergies amongst the class before starting the activity and do not let any children with nut allergies choose anything that contains nuts or nut-based products.

Read the rhyme to the children and ask them to tell you what the Queen was eating in the parlour. Tell the children you are going to make honey sandwiches together to taste. Organise the children into groups and help them to make some sandwiches with butter and some without. Ask the children to say which sandwich they prefer. Talk about other things that would go well with honey and write these as a list of suggestions on the flip chart (things to try could include bananas and strawberries, and also white and brown bread as possible choices). Create these sandwiches with the children over the next few days for snacks and let the children taste a different one each day. Let them decide which sandwiches they like and which they do not. You could also make the honey sandwiches every day with and without butter so that the children always have something they like.

At the end of the week, let the children taste all the sandwiches and decide which combination is the class's favourite.

DIFFERENTIATION

o begin with, organise lower attaining children in pairs to make and try the sandwiches. This will give them chance to say which ones they like best and why. Ask higher attaining children to think of other things that could be combined with honey to make sandwiches. Perhaps they can suggest alternatives to bread, too.

WHERE NEXT

Make other things for the Queen to try in the parlour which have honey in them, for example honey biscuits and honey-covered cakes. Ask the children to evaluate these and to improve them to make them even nicer for the Queen to eat with her tea.

ASSESSMENT

Record the children's suggestions for improvements and note whether they understand how these build on their earlier evaluations. Assess the children who do not understand how to evaluate which is the class's favourite and repeat the same type of activity in another context.

LEARNING OUTCOMES

The children should all be able to express a preference for their favourite sandwich. Some will create new combinations based on their evaluations. Others may be happy to suggest items with which they have experience.

FURTHER KNOWLEDGE AND UNDERSTANDING OF THE WORLD CHALLENGES

Marmite sandwiches

Make Marmite and Bovril sandwiches and let the children decide which they like best. Create other sandwich fillings for the children to try and evaluate.

Colour sandwiches

Make sandwiches with a different coloured filling on each day of the week. Let the children decide which ones they like best and to make improvements to these. For example, on red day you could make tomato, jam, apple or tomato sauce sandwiches, adding salt and pepper, salad cream or red cheese to some of the fillings.

PEG BOARDS

AREA OF LEARNING: PHYSICAL DEVELOPMENT. ELG: TO USE A RANGE OF SMALL AND LARGE EQUIPMENT.

LEARNING OBJECTIVE

To learn to manipulate pegs.

THINKING OBJECTIVE

To analyse.

THINKING SKILLS

The children will look at how a peg works and analyse how to operate it. They will analyse other things that work in the same way, looking at some everyday objects in the process. They will make their own clipboards using cards and pegs and use these to attach paper to draw pictures and write messages.

WHAT YOU NEED

Pegs, bulldog clips, badges, freezer bag clips and clamps; items that attach in different ways to pegs such as paper clips, glue sticks, safety pins and zips; paper attached to a painting easel; pieces of card, pegs and paper for the children.

WHAT TO DO

Look at the pegs with the children and decide how they work. Talk about how they open and shut as you squeeze the ends together and release them. Then look at the other things in your collection that work in the same way, such as the bulldog clips. Show the children how paper is attached to the painting easel and talk about how the mechanism works in the same way as the pegs. Look at those that do not work in the same way as the pegs, such as the paper clips. Help the children organise the items into two sets, according to whether they work like a peg or not.

Give the children pegs and card and ask them to make models of clipboards to attach paper to for drawing and writing activities. Glue the pegs to the front top of the card as clips for the children to attach paper to. They can use the clipboards to record how much money the King has counted today.

DIFFERENTIATION

Ask higher attaining children to decide for themselves what they will use to attach their paper to their clipboards. Challenge them to use something that works in the same way that has the same mechanism as a peg, for example a small bulldog clip. Work with lower attaining children to point out how the peg can be used to attach the paper to their board when they have finished. Revisit some of the analysis with them at this point.

WHERE NEXT

Find different things that can be attached to the washing line with pegs, and let the children play with these every day. For example, they could peg their name onto a picture of a play activity during a self-initiated play session, or peg a painting on the line to dry.

Let the children make labels with their names on. They can attach these to the washing line with a peg as a self-registration activity.

ASSESSMENT

Note the children who analyse how a peg works and use this to attach things to their clipboard.

LEARNING OUTCOMES

The children will analyse how a peg works and use a similar mechanism to create a clipboard.

FURTHER PHYSICAL DEVELOPMENT CHALLENGES

Name badges

Make name badges with the children using rectangles of card and small clips. Glue one side of the clip to the card, leaving the other side to clip onto a lapel or neck of a jumper.

THE KING'S MONEYBAGS

AREA OF LEARNING: PHYSICAL DEVELOPMENT. ELG: TO HANDLE OBJECTS WITH INCREASING CONTROL.

LEARNING OBJECTIVE

To learn to join fabric by sewing.

THINKING OBJECTIVE

To sequence moves when sewing.

THINKING SKILLS

The children will consider how two edges can be joined when sewing them together. They will learn to stitch the two edges by following a sequence of two moves together rather than doing them one at a time, which often leads to tangles and messy stitchwork!

WHAT YOU NEED

Pieces of rectangular fabric with the two narrower edges hemmed to thread a lace through to make a drawstring bag (crêpe paper will do if you cannot find suitable fabric); sewing needles with large eyes; thread; laces; blunt, long needles.

WHAT TO DO

Prepare your fabric rectangles before the activity.

Tell the children that they are going to make some moneybags to put in the King's counting house for him to keep his money in. In small groups, show the children how to fold a piece of fabric in half to make a bag shape. The hemmed edges should meet together to make the open top. Note with them how the two sides match. Explain that you are going to work out together the sequence for stitching the two sides together with thread.

Invite the children to tell you where to start and with them watching in their group, ask, *In which direction do I need to go next to form a running stitch? Do I need to go over or under the fabric?* Show the children what happens if you go from the bottom up rather than the top down. Get them to think about the sequence of moves by asking them questions, such as *Do I go under or over next? Do I go through from the top or up from underneath?* Complete a series of running stitches showing the children how you go

through from the top and up from the bottom before pulling the thread through. This understanding of the sequence of moves should stop them getting the thread tangled.

Give each child a piece of fabric and work with them, monitoring to make sure that they are following the sequence correctly, to sew both sides of the fabric together. Finish off the top of each one to make sure that there is a gap for the needle to thread through with the lace.

When the sides are sewn together, show the children how to thread through a lace at the top to make a drawstring with which to close the bag.

DIFFERENTIATION

Higher attaining children can think about the sequence of an overstitch to make the joins stronger. Work out together how to go over the fabric edge each time to sew from the bottom through to the top. Draw dots along the edge of the fabric for lower attaining children to follow. Put a symbol on the front of the bag so that the children know they should only pull the thread through when they can see this symbol.

WHERE NEXT

Get the children to make bags of different sizes using the same sequence of stitches.

Let the children decorate the bags with cut-out pictures of coins stuck to the front of the finished bags with glue.

ASSESSMENT

Assess the children who follow the sequence correctly to join the edges together using a running stitch.

LEARNING OUTCOMES

Most children will understand the sequence of moves for making a running stitch and will successfully join two edges together without getting in a tangle. Some will learn a sequence for joining the edges together with an overstitch.

FURTHER PHYSICAL DEVELOPMENT CHALLENGES

Money symbols and coins

Draw simple monetary designs on the front of some of the bags before they are joined for the children to embroider with running stitches. Any designs with straight lines will be suitable, including squares around coin pictures, rectangles around recorded totals, the two straight lines on a pound sign and the vertical line of a pence 'p'. More able sewers can try to embroider the complete pound sign.

SOUNDS RIGHT

AREA OF LEARNING: CREATIVE DEVELOPMENT. ELG: TO RECOGNISE HOW SOUNDS CAN BE CHANGED.

LEARNING OBJECTIVE
To add sounds effects to the nursery rhyme.

THINKING OBJECTIVES
To create ideas; to suggest improvements.

THINKING SKILLS
The children will think about the sounds they could hear in the rhyme before considering which sounds they can make on the instruments and everyday items to match these. They will suggest changes to sounds to improve on their collective ideas.

WHAT YOU NEED
Pitched and non-pitched percussion instruments; everyday items that chink; the rhyme written on a flip chart or board with enough gaps above and below each line to add possible sound effects and how these will be made.

WHAT TO DO
Read the rhyme on the flip chart through with the children. Invite the children to suggest where it is possible to put sound effects in. Mark these places with a pen. Let the children explore the range of instruments to think of possible sound effects they could make. Ask them to share their ideas. Ask, *Which sound effect have you thought of? Why have you chosen that particular instrument/item? How have you produced the sound? Where in the rhyme do you want to make this sound?* If they are having difficulty thinking of ideas, help them by suggesting some sounds they could create. For example, the sound of the coins, a song which the blackbirds sing, the sounds in the parlour or the garden. Read the rhyme again, letting the children add their sound effects to the different parts. Choose some of the best sounds

and draw symbols or pictures of the accompanying instruments next to the relevant places in the rhyme.

Let half the class at a time perform the rhyme with the sound effects, following the symbols drawn into the rhyme on the flip chart. Let the other half of the class talk about how the sound effects sounded. Ask, *Which sounds do you like? Are there any you want to change, improve upon or keep the same? How can you make the part when the blackbird pecks off the maid's nose more dramatic?* Make any improvements the children suggest and perform the rhyme again, agreeing when they are happy with the finished effects.

DIFFERENTIATION
Give lower attaining children the easier parts of the rhyme to add effects to, where they will be able to hear the sounds, such as *The birds began to sing*. Suggest types of sounds they could make for example, louder, quieter, faster, slower, and let the children explore these. Higher attaining children should be given less tangible effects to think about, for example the sun shining, thus depicting a calm quiet day before disaster strikes in the form of the blackbird.

WHERE NEXT
Let the children add effects to other familiar and favourite rhymes as an independent focused activity.

ASSESSMENT
Note the children who require lots of support and those who go further when creating their ideas. Which children are able to consider changes in sound and musical elements to improve and extend their ideas?

LEARNING OUTCOMES
All children will create suitable effects to accompany different parts of the rhyme, either with or without support. Some will go beyond this and consider the changes in sound to extend their ideas.

FURTHER CREATIVE DEVELOPMENT CHALLENGES
Blackbird chorus
Write a class tune to depict what the blackbirds sing when the pie was opened. Write how the children think the blackbirds are feeling and use these as words for each verse. Then ask them to think of a tune to sing each line to. They could choose one they know or write one that goes down or up in steps. For example, they could use the tune of 'Oh dear, what can the matter be?', singing their own line to the tune, which might be *We're going to be eaten, oh*

what can we do about it? repeated over again to the end. Let the children extend their ideas by writing additional verses to the tune.

THE KING AND QUEEN'S HOUSE

AREA OF LEARNING: CREATIVE DEVELOPMENT. ELG: TO EXPRESS AND COMMUNICATE THEIR IDEAS, THOUGHTS AND FEELINGS BY USING ROLE-PLAY.

LEARNING OBJECTIVE
To act out different parts of the rhyme.

THINKING OBJECTIVES
To create ideas; to extend ideas.

THINKING SKILLS
The children will plan how to create the three different role-play areas from the rhyme. They will decide what resources they need before putting these together to use for acting out the different parts of the rhyme in a short play. They will extend their ideas by refining their role-play areas and taking on board any feedback from their classmates after performing their plays.

WHAT YOU NEED
Three areas in the classroom; large sheets of paper and pencils; resources identified on the children's plans and that correspond to the three areas of the rhyme.

WHAT TO DO
Ask the children to think about the settings in the nursery rhyme and to think together how they can create these in the classroom. Encourage all the children to share their thoughts on how they could create the parlour, the counting house and the garden.

Divide the class into three groups and let each group plan what one of the areas will look like. Tell them that you want them to perform a play in their area so they should also think about the things they will need to have there and the kind of things they will want to do in their area.

With each group, record on a large sheet of paper their design and layout, the resources they want and the plays they will make up to perform in their area. Discuss whether they have included everything they want. Ask, Is there anything else you want to add? Let them extend any ideas at this point.

Let the children gather the resources they have included in their plan and create their role-play area. Then suggest they play in their role-play area to decide for themselves if there is anything missing.

Let them extend their ideas by solving any problems they come up with, such as making flowers stand up, or erecting the washing line in the garden. They might also want to plan additional things to have in the parlour, for instance, such as a telephone, magazines for the Queen to look at while she is eating her bread and honey or a radio for the King to listen to while he is counting his money.

Finish by giving the children time to create a short play and to practise and perform this to the rest of the class. Can the other children think of any improvements to the role-play areas that could be made?

DIFFERENTIATION
Let lower attaining children design the parlour as this will be closer to their experience of the home corners with which they are probably more familiar. Higher attaining children should be encouraged to plan and make the counting house as this won't be familiar to them.

WHERE NEXT
Read the rhyme to the class. As you get to each different setting, invite each group to perform their role-play scene.

ASSESSMENT
Make a note of the children who do not play a full part in the planning stage of the activity and organise further opportunities for them to develop other role-play areas.

LEARNING OUTCOMES
Most children will enjoy using their imagination to create their role-play area. Some will extend their ideas by making suggestions for additions.

FURTHER CREATIVE DEVELOPMENT CHALLENGES

The kitchen area
Challenge the children to design and create a kitchen area to add to the rhyme. Ask them questions to help them to plan their ideas, such as What will you need in the kitchen? Where will you make this? What will the people be doing in the kitchen? How can we write them into the rhyme?

Washing the clothes
Ask the children where they think the King and Queen's clothes are washed. Ask them to design and create an area where this activity can take place. Convert the water tray for the activity and let the children wash the doll's clothes, hanging them either outside or on the washing line to dry.